Some Opinions of the Press.

"This work is designed to enlighten the general realm on the subject of government, as it obtains in this country, and is a production that cannot fail to be perused with profit by any citizen."—*Noah's Sunday Despatch.*

"This book is devoted to the great municipal interests of society, and altogether a hit in the right direction, and as such we recommend it to the attention of every intelligent voter, and, above all, to that immaculate class, our city fathers."—*Hunt's Merchants' Magazine.*

"We wish to see the MUNICIPALIST in the hands of all farmers, of all our citizens who take a sincere interest in the management of our public affairs, in Congress, States, counties, towns, cities, and villages. The parallel drawn between Washington's 'Farewell Address' and Macchiavelli's 'Prince,' is alone worth the price of the book."—*Country Gentleman.*

"People who wish to be better governed, must study the art of organizing society politically. The MUNICIPALIST starts from the opinion, supported by St. Paul, that government should be restricted to the realization of justice, showing conclusively that the Federal Constitution followed up this plan. It is in favor of an appointed Judiciary, of the family suffrage, and contains not only an explanation of the Federal Constitution, and that of the State of New-York—recommending its alteration and amendment—but also other important documents, with useful remarks."—*N. Y. Journal of Commerce.*

"We recommend a careful perusal of the MUNICIPALIST to our readers, and we think that they will be pleased with its general tone and spirit. It contains a portrait of Washington, and will be an acceptable companion to all who take an intelligent interest in political affairs and constitutional questions."—*The News.*

"This work contains many excellent suggestions, and well-considered comments on the history of the working of American institutions."—*Philadelphia North American.*

"We desire to commend this truly instructive and comprehensive manual to the favorable consideration of all our readers. The attention of the ladies is invited to the work. It is written in the form of familiar letters, and, with many wise and philosophic reflections, contains a vast amount of information in regard to the structure and operations of our National and State Constitutions and governments."—*Godey's Lady's Book.*

"We should judge that the MUNICIPALIST would be found a very useful book for politicians, and, indeed, for all who take an interest in the welfare of our common country."—*Hartford Christian Secretary.*

"This work is devoted to the municipal interests of society, and treats, with much candor, a variety of subjects, interesting to such as would understand the theory of our government, the position of parties, and the prejudices of sections."—*Providence Post.*

"This is a work of great research, thought, and labor, in which the whole subject of internal government, in a republic, is investigated. It is written with special reference to the Constitution of New-York, but the same principles apply as well to all the States. It is a convenient book for politicians, young or old, whether engaged in public life, or having only the interest that every citizen has in public welfare."—*Daily Spy,* Worcester, Mass.

"We should think it a useful work."—*Providence* (R. I.) *Journal.*

"This book contains highly valuable suggestions, opening a wide field for thought and action, to citizens and statesmen. Farmers and mechanics, forming the majority of the people—and may therefore be called the conservators of liberty, order, and justice—should notice it. The book is not only embellished with a likeness of the great Virginia farmer, but is also a real monument to this great man."—*Prairie Farmer,* Chicago, Ill.

"The object of this work is a very important one. It is well written, and calculated to be highly useful."—*Christian Family Baptist,* Chicago, Ill.

"The MUNICIPALIST is intended for familiar elucidation of the Constitution, and to familiarize its provisions to the youth of the country."—*Daily Richmond Inquirer.*

"This work is an appeal to renewed exertions for the creation of a dignified American Judiciary."—*San Francisco Bulletin.*

G. Washington

INTERNAL RELATIONS

OF THE

CITIES, TOWNS, VILLAGES, COUNTIES,

AND

STATES OF THE UNION;

OR,

THE MUNICIPALIST:

A

HIGHLY USEFUL BOOK

FOR

Voters, Tax-Payers, Statesmen, Politicians and Families.

Motto:

"*L'Etat c'est Moi.*"—Louis XIV.—Napoleon I.
"*L'Etat c'est la Raison.*"—Frederick the Great.
"*L'Etat c'est la Justice.*"—Constitution of the United States.

SECOND EDITION.

NEW-YORK:
ROSS & TOUSEY, DEXTER & BROTHER,
AND
WM. RADDE, 300 BROADWAY.
1859

TO

HIS CHILDREN

AND

THE RISING GENERATION

THE FOLLOWING LETTERS

Are Inscribed

BY THE AUTHOR.

PREFACE

TO THE SECOND EDITION.

It is due to the practical aid of a number of gentlemen—Governor Morgan, Mayor Tiemann, Peter Cooper—and many lawyers, merchants, and others, as well as to the favorable opinion of the press, that the first edition of the Municipalist has made, under an amended title, room for the second edition. In preparing it, we express our sincere thanks to all the friends of this book for their support, and wish that this "timely, useful, and popular book, which places the political sciences upon the firm rock of Holy Writ," may enjoy the patronage of all friends —at home and abroad—of our system of government, as it has been inaugurated by our Federal Constitution.

The vote of the people of the State of New-York on the Constitutional Convention, in November, 1858, was but small, viz., 155,120 against a Convention, and 139,748 in favor of it. But, in the main, the result is like that of the vote in Maryland, on the same subject, (see Letter XXII., Part II.,) viz., that the majority of the voters in the cities of New-York and Brooklyn, like those in Baltimore, were for a Convention, and those in the rural towns against it: a fact which, under prevalent circumstances, shows that the inhabitants of those cities are decidedly against an elective Judiciary, while the farming population think differently about it; and further, that, in regard to realizing justice, there exists a necessity to organize large cities entirely different from rural towns. It will be interesting to watch the result of the proposed voting on the amending of the Constitution in Ohio—where the Judiciary is also elective—in regard to Cincinnati. The oversight of this fact must, in the length, naturally lead to State separations, in consequence of the immense interests which, in large cities, come in question, and are not always appreciated elsewhere. While, however, the Constitution ordains that in 1866—unless anticipated by the Legislature—a similar vote shall be taken, this book loses nothing of its bearing upon this act, rather gains time for general circulation, and a more thorough, quiet investigation of this important subject.

One of our critics remarks, that this book is a monument (perhaps the sincerest of all) to the memory of Washington and his co-workers in the arduous task of forming our Union. They founded an empire of peace. Still, we had our wars, and even a show of civil war—the worst species of this kind of political business—in the Territories of Kansas and Utah: the latter mainly occupied by the Mormon sect, who call it, in their official documents, the State of Deseret.

But this Mormon war seems to be a mere mystification. This settlement is so remote from profitable intercourse with the rest of society, that people there would suffer or starve, if not supported by the gold of the United States Treasury. To get as much as possible of it, they boldly defied the authority of the Territorial Federal officers, who fled, and were, of course, replaced by an army, spending much money there, while, since the baffling of the federal authorities in the exercise of their functions, according to their statement, continues as ever. Meanwhile, the leaders of the sect use the political powers of its members as town and county officers, jurors, legislators, &c., for the promotion of their peculiar Church, incorporated by the so-called "State of Deseret," and possessed of almost all the best land within the Territory, according to its act of incorporation and trustworthy reports.

Thus, by a faulty political districting, and organization of society, of which this book treats especially, our Federal Government indirectly fosters Mormon arrogance, the Mormon Church and harems of their priests, and—a Mormon empire in embryo.

We point out this instance here, because the military expedition against the Mormons, and the pardon granted them, do not seem to have altered their rebellious disposition, which, obviously, cannot be cured by any measure short of the entire abolition of the territorial organization of Utah, and its annexation to adjacent states or territories where this sect are not in the ascendency.

Another recent instance of the paramount necessity of strictly organizing the public business, in conformity with the principles explained in this book, is the Post-Office Department. Its recent report shows a deficit of four millions, while, in all European states, this branch produces a net income. We insert here the following extract from an article in the New-York *Journal of Commerce:*

"The mail business, obviously, is emphatically a retail or detail business, requiring, accordingly, a set of men particularly trained for it, working under a steady direction of men who understand the business thoroughly, and an organization which renders it entirely independent of law-doctors, who do not know anything about it. We humbly venture the following plan:

"Divide the United States into a certain number of United States mail districts; form in each district a United States mail company or agency (not to be consolidated); let these do all the mail business, inland and foreign, accruing to their districts, according to their own tariffs; make them responsible for all losses, and let each give a security for the faithful performance of their duties. The effect or advantage of such an organization would be:

"1. The training of proper men for the business.

"2. Security of the public.

"3. Experienced direction.

"4. Competition, and, consequently, constant improvement and cheapness.

"5. Cessation of all claims on the Treasury, for post-sites, houses, offices, &c.

"6. The establishing of a general exchange business, for a certain class of remittances.

"7. Daily mails, almost everywhere.

"8. The termination of the franking privilege.

"9. The management of the whole in a true business manner.

"10. The cessation of party-influence and patronage."

To this article, written with reference to the MUNICIPALIST, a correspondent to the same journal later added: "That the execution of this plan would result in a penny-postage for letters within each district, and, consequently, in the whole United States." This arrangement, moreover, would create at once an excellent American ocean mail-service.

The MUNICIPALIST often dwells upon the dangers of undue centralization. It is the main cause of the failure of the present mail business in the Union.

Several religious papers have noticed this book very favorably, and we hope that it ever will be welcome to the thinking Christian citizen, for being, from the preface to the last page, based upon the precepts of our religion, a rare instance in juridical commentaries, and political works in general.

PREFACE.

It is customary to say that republics can not exist without public virtue. There is much truth in this saying, which, also, is applicable to monarchies; but, by a careful study of the history of both, it will be perceived that the causes of the downfall of republics in particular, are principally owing to their imperfect organization in regard to three entirely *material*, and constantly varying subjects, namely: *Population*, *Size of State*, and its subdivisions, and *Public Business*, and not exactly to a too great deficiency of public virtue alone, because men, on an average, are the same, at the time when they set up republics, and when they suffer them to become monarchized. The difference is that, at the first epoch, population, size, and business, were adequate to the republican, and at the latter period to the monarchical form of government. It is, however, true and obvious, from all we see and read, that public virtue is, with us, at a low ebb. Why is this? We have schools for all, innumerable churches, religious meetings and publications, colleges and academies in all towns and cities, books in all houses, and newspapers showering upon us in clouds; pushed on by a noble zeal for improvement, we organize universities, scientific associations, tract societies, reading-rooms, libraries, one after another; still, the inestimable principles and durable advantages of honesty and justice to communities, and individuals composing them, seem to be lost sight of, and hence, public corruption is constantly increasing. Why, we ask again, is this? It is further true, that a state institution is either the most powerful social agent, to promote the sense of honesty and justice, the mother of public virtue, or the most effective machinery to sow the seed of vice, from which spring up public corruption, broadcast over the land. History tells of bad and good states, of their bad and good influences upon the public morals, characters, and inclinations of men. A close observer may discern, in this regard, a great difference even between our own states, although all are republics. Now, when we can not deny that our society, although in the full possession of the most abundant moral and intellectual means for the general improvement of which ever an age could boast, from day to day is degenerating, we must necessarily come to the conclusion that our political institutions, generally speaking, are working in the wrong direction, and therefore need reforming.

This conclusion has been virtually admitted by the legislature of the largest state in the Union, that of New York, when resolving, without a dissenting vote, to take the sense of the people on the amending of the constitution at the next November election. The press has been teeming with loud complaints of public corruption, and a deficient administration of justice, in fact, a failure of the state institution itself. This resolve of the legislature should, therefore, have not taken it, or the citizens, by surprise. A glance at the commercial crisis, the effects of which are still felt all over the world, and the role which the banks and judiciary of the empire state played in it — at the legislative encroachments upon the simplest, clearest, and most sacred municipal rights of towns — at the defective management of the public works — at the overpowering influence of the lobbies on the legislature — at the increase of public debt, taxes, crime, and mobism — at the delay, confusion, and corruption, in the judicial procedures — at the abuse of the executive pardoning power — at the defective workings of the jury — at the insecurity of life and property; a mere glance, we say, at these crying evils, comprised by the words "public corruption," necessarily more acutely felt by the legislators themselves than others, because more directly evident to them, was sufficient to determine them at once, without waiting for renewed newspaper discussions, to resort to the revision of the constitution, perhaps involving an overhauling of the whole state machinery.

The voting upon the amending of the constitution, at this period of our state history, is, therefore, a most important act of the people, because it depends upon it to restore the sullied honor of our noble form of government, and to check, in a large measure, the onward course of public corruption. We will succeed if we go earnestly to work, with a thorough knowledge of the causes of the evil and the way to remove them.

To afford, now, to each voter, to each family, an easy opportunity to inform themselves thoroughly of those causes and remedies, and the paramount necessity of amending their present constitution, is the aim of this book.

This, so we thought, could not be done better than by a comprehensive explanation and critical discussion of the American system of governing, as it originally is, that is, of the federal constitution, the ruling guide for the management of the national public business, and of the state constitution, *under revision*, serving as a guide for the management of the municipal public business, with regard to the prevalent practice in both Congress and state.

Almost simultaneously with the legislature of New York, that of Maryland resolved to take the sense of the people upon the amending their constitution of 1851. The vote, soon after cast, was against a change. Both have introduced an *elective* judiciary; from both states come loud complaints of a defective administration of justice! These are significant signs on the political horizon. If we have exposed and explained them frankly as we find them, we did not intend to reflect upon any man; no, but merely to show what defects, especially, in the municipal social organization, have been instrumental to produce the complained-of results. We hope, therefore, that this book, written as it is from mere patriotic motives, will meet a patriotic welcome, and recommend itself to the candid and generous notice of the press.

Besides a critical examination of these constitutions, the reader will find in this book general instructive remarks on the nature and organization of the public business, and some important public documents, partly in connection with our political fabric and that of Europe: among others, "Washington's Farewell Address," contrasted with Macchiavelli's celebrated book, "The Prince."

By the "crisis," the publication of this book has been delayed, which will account for some remarks on the last congressional election and other political events of the time, when the letters in the first part were written. It is hoped that it will find favor with the readers of all parties, impossible as it is to please all men, even when aiming at nothing but truth, *i. e.*, the exposition of great principles and "sound doctrine." The words "sound doctrine" taken from Paul's first letter to Timothy, induce us to respectfully solicit the particular attention of all Christian ministers to this book. Its leading idea that the state is set up exclusively for the realization of justice (the main source of public virtue), has been clearly enunciated by Paul, the great propagator of Christianity, and real founder of our Christian institutions. Moreover this idea has been strictly followed up by the framers of our federal constitution, as shown in the book; it has been further recognised and carried out by those who achieved the separation of the state and church; but it has been, in the course of time, lost sight of by Congress and states, and thus become the cause of most of the public corruption and decline of public virtue complained of. This to prove, in order to show how to stem the dangerous current, is one of the main objects of the book. But here it will meet opposition, and even condemnation, from many sides. But time will prove that Paul and the framers of the federal constitution, and those who achieved the separation of church and state, were right.

The members of the judiciary, who are in the habit of drawing wisdom from the classical fountains, will remember the line of Virgil:—

"Discite justitiam moniti, et non temnere Divos!"

We wish they may please consider this book as an humble common-sense appeal to renewed exertions for the creation of a dignified, independent, American judiciary, based upon an indigenous American common law, emanating from and in harmony with the grėat principle of self-government, and therefore in many respects different from the law ideas commonly prevalent in subject society.

To the rising generation the book has been dedicated, and therefore written in familiar letter style, because those who are just entering into actual citizen life will have to finish the work of a great political reform, which stern necessity is forcing upon us.

This book is, as its title indicates, particularly devoted to the great municipal interest of society. It appears before the public under similar circumstances which called forth the Federalist, then working for the abrogation of the unsatisfactory articles of confederation and the adoption of the present excellent federal constitution.

The municipalist advocates the alteration of the present constitution of the state of New York, and its replacement by one more suitable to the urgency of the times.

Before we conclude these prefacial lines we owe *to the ladies* a few words of apology, for having so often in our letters invited them to listen to our political discussions. We belong to those who are convinced that the career of a republic is of a doubtful duration if the whole population is not penetrated with a sufficient knowledge of its public affairs, to prevent them from coming under the exclusive possession of a favored few or control of mere party politicians. In regard to the importance of this knowledge there is no difference between the sexes, for women have, if not more, as much interest in the well-being of families, promoted by good government, as men.

We possess excellent constitutional commentaries for students and professionists, but none, to our knowledge, which is calculated to promote an easy understanding of that what is called all over the world public or political business. Our book, certainly, is no novel, no flashy literary product, but a novelty, as the reader, acquainted with this kind of literature, will find out. It spreads notions and light over that material upon which the security and happiness of home and society everywhere are built. Such a book would not answer its purpose if it should not meet the favor of mothers and daughters as well as of fathers and sons.

We hope, therefore, not to be considered intruding, if we desire for it a place among the select books of every household.

BROOKLYN, *September*, 1858.

INDEX TO SUBJECTS.

PART I.

PART II.

CONTENTS.

PART. I.—THE NATIONAL GOVERNMENT.

LETTER I.

LETTER II.

LETTER III.

LETTER IV.

LETTER V.

LETTER VI.

LETTER VII.

LETTER VIII.

LETTER IX.

LETTER XVI.

LETTER XVII.

LETTER XVIII.

LETTER XIX.

LETTER XX.

LETTER XXI.

LETTER XXII.

LETTER XXIII.

LETTER XXXI.

LETTER XXXII.

LETTER XXXIII.

LETTER XXXIV.

LETTER XL.

LETTER XLI.

LETTER XLII.

LETTER XLIII.

PART. II.—MUNICIPAL GOVERNMENT.

LETTER XX.

LETTER XXI.

LETTER XXII.

LETTER XXIII.

PART FIRST.

THE NATIONAL GOVERNMENT.

LETTER I.

Introduction. — Causes of the Letters. — Little Appreciation of the Federal Constitution. — The Church a Comforter, but no Governor. — Restoration of the Authority of Law. — Influence of Woman. — Resistance against the Execution of Laws. — Vigilance Committees. — Ten-Thousand-Dollar Subscription for Rebellion in Kansas. — Ancient Rome. — Dangers to the Constitution and Union. — Articles of Confederation of 1777. — New Constitution for a Society of European Descendants, Africans, and Indians. — The Object, Union and an independent, powerful National Government, excluding all Municipal Affairs, Bond Labor included. — The Contents in Seven Articles.

My Dear Children: I have often thought of writing for you, and perhaps others too, a kind of common-sense commentary on the federal constitution; and why? Because I have too many proofs that this organic law is not so well known and appreciated as it deserves. In a conversation I once had with one of our most patriotic men and writers, on the state of our turbulent, growing public affairs, he said, "Nothing can save us but the church." I have often inquired, in houses stocked with books, for a copy of the federal constitution, but in vain; there was none. This justifies what I said. If the church is our help, why set up a constitution at all? Why organize a state or Congress? Is not the church older than our Union? Why has the church never checked political corruption? What society is losing by the bad administration of the laws, and excesses of parties and factions, no church, Christian or not, can restore, unless the church turns state. Religion can *comfort* men when suffering from anarchy; a Christian preacher may exhort rioters and rebels to keep the peace; church organizations may charitably lessen misery in civil commotions and war, but the church can not do more. It can not re-establish justice or rule, without becoming state or government. An earnest and strong sense of justice, strict fidelity to our constitutions, and a faithful, manly execution of the laws — in one word, the restoration of the sunken *authority* of the laws alone — can save our commonwealth. We still have, for this purpose, patriotism, virtue, and honesty enough, in the country. It only wants to be brought into activity.

I wish, besides, to make the powerful social influence of woman available. When this influence upon society in general is regulating, moderating, pacifying, and ennobling, why should woman not exert a similar influence upon the public social affairs? This is impossible without a clear understanding of the objects, principles, and provisions, of our supreme law of the land, the federal constitution. To make it as plain as household words is the aim of these letters — which, however, have been written with due regard to the constructions of the various departments of the government, and the academical and juridical commentaries. I have consulted the best, and even maintained their own words in some instances; so you may be assured that I give you the constitution and nothing but the constitution. Its general, thorough understanding, in our time, where it is so often misrepresented, and even openly opposed by men of talents and learning, is most desirable. All public affairs directly concern families, and hence the private interests of families must necessarily suffer from bad governing.

Look out what course the ship of state is taking! In the East, men of parts are outraging, by their public speeches and behavior, all sense of justice and propriety, and openly give their support to resistance against the officers of the United States, so that the troops have been ordered for their protection. This is the beginning of the end of civil government. In the West, vigilance committees act as courts. Wealthy men subscribe ten thousand dollars for rebellion, and associations furnish partisan voters and fighters for newly-settled territories. Powerful ancient Rome fell when single citizens were rich enough to keep armies of their own, to fight out their ambitious schemes. Our ten-thousand-dollar men and associations are in the same manner undermining the stability of our republic.

That this happens is not the fault of our institutions, or of the federal constitution, but the effect of error and ignorance about it. This constitution is the work of the best men America has produced; it is the true native glory of our country, unsurpassed by any products of indigenous art and skill, however useful and excellent in their way. This constitution has created our Union, the parent of our immense commerce and gigantic industrial and social progress. Our existence as a nation may be jeoparded by a few errors about the meaning of our constitution, if taken hold of by fanatics, parties, and factions. I shall dwell upon such errors, and try to make them harmless by exposing the plain truth, and shall therefore be as practical as possible.

The convention elected by the thirteen states, in 1787, for the purpose of projecting a new constitution for the United States, existing as such under the celebrated articles of confederation of November, 1777, had, for its material, a most peculiar society, composed of European descendants, Africans, and American Indians. The first were the ruling race, open to increase by immigration; the second were domesticated as slaves, a few of whom were then manumitted, open to increase by birth and slave importation; the third were living in tribes, with chiefs, under the surveillance and jurisdiction of the first, open to increase by territorial acquisition. The convention had no power to alter this material or the elements of society. Its only duty was to set up an organic law by which the whole would form a more compact union, represented by a more independent and powerful central government than that established by the just-mentioned articles of confederation.

This body, therefore, had no power to make provisions for general reforms, municipal affairs, civil and criminal or police laws, bills of rights, voting, religious, educational, scientific subjects, etc. It had nothing to do with domestic affairs, concerning labor and service for time or life. Those who say that the federal constitution, the product of this convention, has established bond labor or slavery, or is maintaining it, mistake it entirely, as will become more evident later.

The great fundamental law is exceedingly simple, plain, and short, and contains seven articles, with the following heads:—

ARTICLE I.—*Of the Legislature.*

ARTICLE II.—*Of the Executive.*

ARTICLE III.—*Of the Judiciary.*

ARTICLE IV.—*Miscellaneous* (relating to the validity of public acts and records, the equal rights of citizenship, the treatment of fugitives from justice and service, admission of new states, administration of the territory, the guaranty of a republican form of government).

ARTICLE V.—*Of Amendments.*

ARTICLE VI.—*Miscellaneous* (relating to public faith and justice in regard to the war-debts, etc.; declaring the constitution the supreme law of the land; to the general oath or affirmation of all public officers, and members of Congress and legislatures; the abolishing of the religious test).

ARTICLE VII.—*Of the Ratification.*

Of which more in my following letters.

LETTER II.

The Constitution.—Its Reading.—Preamble.—Short History of the Country.—The Revolution.—Necessity of a National Government.—Greeks, Romans, Germans, Italians.—United States of America.—Family, Tribe.—Constitution of the People, and not of the States.—Object of the Constitution.—National, municipal, free, non-political or private Affairs.—Justice.—St. Paul's First Letter to Timothy.—Common Defence.—Insubjection.—Licentiousness.

IN the following letters I shall converse with you on the federal constitution, section by section. Please imagine that you are attending some lectures on this all-important subject. I hope it will not be a tiresome labor for you to make, in this manner, the closer acquaintance of a written work, which millions of free and happy men are considering as a sacred legacy of George Washington and his illustrious compatriots.

CONSTITUTION OF THE UNITED STATES.

"*Preamble.* — We, the people of the United States, in order to form a more perfect union, establish justice, insure domestic tranquillity, provide for the common defence, promote the general welfare, and secure the blessings of liberty to ourselves and our posterity, do ordain and establish this Constitution for the United States of America."

Preambles and prefaces are generally considered unprofitable reading, especially by ladies; but you must make an exception with this preface. It closes the epoch in the history of our country from 1643 to 1787, which may be termed the time of incubation of our present Union.

After the colonists had opened the path for European culture through the primitive American forests, erected towns where before stood wigwams, subdued powerful Indian tribes, and had in those struggles for life and independence acquired the skill of self-government, so easily lost in luxury and affluence, they felt the necessity of a government of their own, and a union of their colonial forces. Many attempts were made for this purpose, during the period I have indicated, as you know from the history of the United States. When the right time came to strike the blow, the right men were at the head of the public affairs to secure success.

As the colonists always managed their municipal affairs themselves, under English governors, the question after the liberation was to give a proper form and place to that part of the public affairs which belong to a nation, and which were, with the usual haughty, lordly spirit of a monarch, withheld by the English crown.

If you throw a glance at the history of the world, you will discover that it is this kind of public business which has caused the great revolutions and struggles for freedom. The ancient Greeks managed their municipal affairs as well as we ours; but they never succeeded, although repeatedly trying it, in organizing the national business well. They deserved, on this account, hardly the name of a nation, and became therefore an easy prey to their monarchical adversaries. The success of the Romans, on the other hand, resulted from the strong consolidation of the national affairs in Rome, similar to that of France in Paris. To set this business right, the Germans revolted in 1848. The Italians are, it is said, at the eve of a revolution for the same purpose. When it required, in the North American colonies, almost two hundred years to realize a free, independent, stable government, among men who were comparatively free, at least in regard to the management of their municipal affairs, how doubtful must be such revolutions among people who, like the Spaniards or Italians, or even the Germans, have been for centuries *subject* to strong monarchical rulers!

The colonies had, as early as 1778, adopted the appellation, "UNITED STATES OF AMERICA." Still the present constitution, although framed by a convention composed of delegates chosen by the legislatures of the states, was *ratified and adopted by the people:* hence the words, "We the people"—that is, *the aggregate of families*, forming society and nations. It makes, indeed, but little difference whether this act of the free, independent people is called a sovereign act or not. A nation, as such, is master of its destiny. There is no society without a certain rule or organization. Cannibals, also, obey their chiefs. The family state is the beginning of social organization, and requires it for the purposes of support and education. It is, within its domestic limits, as independent as a nation within her political boundaries.

That the people, by their votes, and not by the states, have adopted the constitution, is an important fact in regard to the validity of the covenant, because on this fact, not the state governments, not Congress, *but only the people*, have to decide. Mind that no single state can leave the Union without the permission of the whole people or nation.

The preamble expresses the main objects of the constitution. First, A MORE PERFECT UNION. This was, as we have seen, most desirable. The new state governments cleaved with the same obstinacy to the national business as the English government, from the fear that Congress might become too powerful; from which cause sprung up a separate party, the republicans, opposing the federalists. This fear is unfounded, if we concede to Congress but *national* political business. You must remember that the business managed by states or Congress is called political or public business, which I shall, in a separate letter, endeavor clearly to explain. This Union has now been, after much trouble and a bloody war, achieved, by adopting the present constitution, which gives to Congress the *national* business, leaving to the states the *municipal*, and to society, or the people at large, the *free, non-political* affairs to manage.

The declared aim of the constitution is, further, to ESTABLISH JUSTICE. This is the supreme and ultimate object of all political organizations. St. Paul, as you know from his first letter to Timothy, had already said, "The law [or state] is not *made for the righteous, but for the lawless*," etc. This means: if men would always act right, there would be, of course, no need of states, Congress, courts, sheriffs, troops, jails, etc. But this not being the case, we have to organize society, in order to establish and realize justice, on account of the lawless, and thus INSURE DOMESTIC TRANQUILLITY and PROMOTE THE GENERAL WELFARE. On this account, Congress has also to take care for the COMMON DEFENCE. It is a part and the consequence of the establishment of justice, and its execution, at home and with regard to foreign nations. If all this is well done, the BLESSINGS OF LIBERTY will most certainly be secured to ourselves and our posterity; while the reverse, as injustice and lawlessness, will sow the seeds of discord, civil commotions, general misery, and despotism. The blessings of liberty consist chiefly in being *unsubject*—that is, in full possession of the rights of self-government, so that man is not hindered in regard to his industrial pursuits, culture, and management of his public affairs. No organic law, that I am acquainted with, protects people in this regard better than our federal constitution. For such a rational liberty, however, very few men comparatively are yet prepared. The majority mistake liberty for licentiousness.

The men who framed this constitution could hardly have introduced it by a better preamble. It shows best what a clear and practical conception they had of their task. They have erected a monument of their wisdom, which, although made for their time, and the actual wants of their society, composed of very heterogeneous elements (Americans, Indians, Europeans, and Africans), is, notwithstanding, a perfect pattern of an organic law for all states and nations, as we shall often have opportunity to notice. I promise you that you will admire it the more, the longer you live.

This brings me to the end of my second letter, which I close with the wish that it may give you a sharp appetite for the following.

LETTER III.

Congress. — Works in three Channels. — Legislature. — Grants. — Republics. — Monarchies. — Government preservative, not progressive. — Scarcity of Solons. — Senate and House of Representatives. — Two-Chamber System. — Qualification of Members of the House of Representatives. — Voting and electing, a Right of Families. — Congress biennial. — Qualification, twenty-five Years of Age. — Negroes, their counting. — Number of Representatives. — Census. — Large Legislative Bodies. — Vacancies filled by the State Executive Action. — Speaker. — Impeachment. — Importance of the House of Representatives. — Ladies. — Decorum.

We come now to the examination of the institution erected by the constitution. It works in three divisions, called the legislative, executive, and judiciary, which constitute the political institution called United States. A similar fabric is that of a state; also the subdivisions of states, viz., counties and towns or townships, work by these three channels. Properly speaking, the people, or the aggregate of families, form society, and neither the states nor the United States, which are separate institutions set up for the benefit of society. But it is in common use to call society after the names of the political divisions. You will, however, do well to distinguish society from these political institutions, because, if your mind is in the habit of doing so, you will readily distinguish social rights and affairs, from political, and be able to judge with precision on encroachments of governments — especially of the legislative branches on individual and social rights, to guard and protect which is the duty of the political institutions.

ARTICLE I.

Of the Legislature.

SECTION I.

"All legislative powers herein granted shall be vested in a Congress of the United States, which shall consist of a senate and house of representatives."

Mind, now, that every word of the constitution is law. This being the case, it was written by its authors with a care and clearness unsurpassed since by similar productions, which is one of the causes why it has required but little or any amending during eighty years. Legislative powers mean political business given in trust to a legislative body. In the word "granted" is the main difference between republics and monarchies. In the latter form of government the management of the public affairs is claimed by the princes as a property or crown right, coming directly from God. Still originally both kinds of governments have only the same business to do.

You will easily perceive that the debating on the laws by two distinct houses is calculated to prevent inconsiderate and hasty legislation, one of the greatest social calamities.

The federal government is not intended to be a progressive machinery, or to run a race with society, philosophers, and visionaries, but merely to conserve and protect the main object of all governments. The progressive element belongs to society and individuals, and never to state institutions, as many, especially Europeans, think; their office is to prevent confusion and embarrassments on the grand onward road of humanity. To frame for this purpose laws is exceedingly difficult. There have been a very few real Solons in the world. There are in our large nation not a hundred men fit for legislating. Two legislative chambers are considered sufficient to avoid errors in law-making—nothing to say here of the veto-power of the president. We have seen that the senate in the Congress of 1856, checked the passage of a clause in the army appropriation bill, repeatedly approved by the majority of the house, which was an open violation of the constitution, and which would have, if passed, annulled the army and impeded the execution of the laws in Kansas, and jeoparded the public peace there and the existence of the Union.

There are many men who pretend to be well informed, of the opinion that a constitution is something like a vane, and open to all kinds of interpretation, to suit people, just like the Bible; but you will not hesitate to consider this a mistake. The Bible is in itself no law, but a mere book, written and suitable for all moral purposes of life, while a constitution is an organizing law, made for a certain district and for certain special purposes, and therefore subject to a limited or circumscribed definite interpretation. It may be abused, like everything, the Bible included, but should not be arbitrarily interpreted *by authority;* for there are certain rules established for logical interpretation. These a jurist should know.

SECTION II.

"1. The house of representatives shall be composed of members chosen every second year by the people of the several states; and the electors in each state shall have the qualifications requisite for electors of the most numerous branch of the state legislature."

Very properly the constitution does not introduce a separate form of voting, but leaves the states free to take care of this business. But it is desirable that the laws on voting should be in harmony with the rights of society. As society is composed of families, it is but just that to these only, as the constituents of society, belongs the right of voting and electing, or the suffrage right.

The constitution presupposes that common sense, honesty, and patriotism, found in all classes of society, may be considered by the voters as the principal qualifications of their lawmakers, and not property, professional requirements, or caste, as is the case in Europe. The future will show whether the liberal, humane spirit which pervades this document in this instance, and all others, is right or not. No doubt that the voting laws, as I remarked, and the salary of the legislators, the numbers of the members of legislatures, and party and faction spirit, have an immense influence upon the working of legislatures, and may defeat the best constitutions. It is therefore the duty of all good citizens to be vigilant and understand the constitution well to prevent its abuse. Our Congress is, as you see, biennial; the British Parliament is septennial. This long term favors aristocracy; the short term, democracy.

"2. No person shall be a representative who shall not have attained to the age of twenty-five years, and been seven years a citizen of the United States, and who shall not, when elected, be an inhabitant of that state in which he shall be chosen."

American society being partly a product of immigration, requires laws in regard to the political qualifications of immigrants. The seven years' citizenship belongs to this kind of legislation. Official absence of a citizen does not deprive him of his rights as a citizen of the state where he comes from.

"3. Representatives and direct taxes shall be apportioned among the several states which may be included within this Union, according to their respective numbers, which shall be determined by adding to the whole number of free persons, including those bound to service for a term of years, and excluding Indians not taxed, three fifths of all other persons. The actual enumeration shall be made within three years after the first meeting of the Congress of the United States, and within every subsequent term of ten years, in such a manner as they shall by law direct. The number of representatives shall not exceed one for every thirty thousand, but each state shall have at least one representative; and until such enumeration shall be made, the state of New Hampshire shall be entitled to choose three; Massachusetts, eight; Rhode Island and Providence Plantations, one; Connecticut, five; New York, six; New Jersey, four; Pennsylvania, eight; Delaware, one; Maryland, six; Virginia, ten; North Carolina, five, and Georgia, three."

The representation and taxation ought to be regulated according to the inhabitants of the several states, and not according to the population of the United States. Those bound to service for a number of years, as sailors, etc., ought to be counted. Indians not taxed are excluded because they live in tribes, a kind of state. The three fifths of all other persons are those bound to service for life, or slaves, forming a distinct race not included within the regular political organization, like the before-mentioned Indian tribes.

The words "by adding three fifths of all other persons," are wrongly understood by some commentators and the abolition party. Their proper meaning, adopted by Congress, is that five slaves count as but three persons, while five free negroes in free states count as much, viz., five persons. Those free negroes do not vote themselves, but in making up the census they count like white persons, while in a slave state five negroes pass only as three persons. An example will show that this proviso is in favor of the free states, and not in favor of the slave states. Suppose there are in a free state

1,000,000 white and free colored persons,
100,000 servants or persons bound to service for a term of years,
———— this gives
1,100,000 whole number of free persons.

And in a slave state—

1,000,000 white and free colored persons,
100,000 slaves counting only
60,000 after deducting two fifths, leaving
————
940,000 whole number of free persons.

Thus a slave state may lose by this operation one or more representatives in Congress. It follows that this clause diminishes in the slave states the "whole number" at the rate of two fifths in regard to the slave population, compared with the free negroes and whites elsewhere. The federal constitution is as liberal as possible, and is only illiberally interpreted to please or suit parties.

When this clause was made by the convention there were more inhabitants in the middle and southern states than in the eastern. It would not be agreed to at present, because it deprives the slave states of about thirty-five members in Congress.

The enumeration here mentioned is the business known by the name of census. Congress, having nothing to do with municipal affairs, has no interest to ascertain, for its own use, more than the number of the inhabitants in order to control and regulate their representation in Congress.

Still Congress has assumed the right to inquire every ten years for everything people possess. There is no grant for that, and wisely not, because it belongs to municipal governments to make census for statistical purposes of this kind. It is supposed that a statistical state census, by the agency of the well-informed town officials, is more reliable than that made in the vast territory of the United States by United States marshals, appointed every ten years for this purpose at random. You see here how necessary is a strict adherence to the words and spirit of the constitution. Its framers were exceedingly careful not to interfere with the business of states, counties, and towns. At present all states take from time to time a census. Congress may be placed in possession of the number of the state inhabitants at short notice by telegraph. Of course the ratio of representation has been altered at each census. The difference between the present time and that of the constitution is interesting in regard to the progress of the population of the several states.

The electoral votes of the United States are at present as follows:

State	Votes	State	Votes
Maine	8	Delaware	3
New Hampshire	5	Maryland	8
Vermont	5	Virginia	15
Massachusetts	13	North Carolina	10
Rhode Island	4	South Carolina	8
Connecticut	6	Georgia	10

New York	35	Alabama	9
New Jersey	7	Mississippi	7
Pennsylvania	27	Louisiana	6
Ohio	23	Kentucky	12
Indiana	13	Tennessee	12
Illinois	11	Missouri	9
Michigan	6	Arkansas	4
Iowa	4	Florida	3
Wisconsin	5	Texas	4
California	4		

The whole number is 296; 176 in the free states, and 120 in the slave states. It shows a great preponderance of some states.

Large legislative bodies are useless for their proper purpose. The proper legislative business of Congress has not increased with the population, because it is national, not local. The grants of the constitution remain to-day what they were eighty years ago. The same wisdom which was required then to make the laws for the carrying out of the constitution is sufficient at present for the same purpose. The more state governments the less territorial Congressional business. It is different with the finance and the executive. Upon the administration of the laws the increase of population has some influence also in the Union. That our senate is a more respectable body than the house is owing to its smaller number. We have few fit men to fill our overnumerous legislative bodies. The house of representatives would answer better to its purpose if composed of the same or only double the number of the senate. Large legislative bodies become invariably corrupt and turbulent.

"4. When vacancies happen in the representation from any state, the executive authority thereof shall issue writs of election to fill up such vacancies."

Here also the constitution leaves the care of the elective business to the state governments; who, acting not in an understanding with each other, differ in regard to the mode of filling vacancies. In states where an absolute majority is required for an election often much delay is caused.

"5. The house of representatives shall choose their speaker, and other officers, and shall have the sole power of impeachment."

Impeaching means accusing for official malversation. You will learn later that the senate is the court of impeachment. All officers, the president included, being responsible or accountable, there must be a court and an impeacher or accuser. In choosing the speaker the absolute majority rule has been adopted, that is, the candidate must get the absolute or real and not merely the relative majority.—This rule presents no difficulty if there are but two candidates. But in the reverse case the election may remain for weeks and months doubtful, as we have witnessed several times. There should be a remedy for such delay which is merely owing to party. The power of impeachment, though rarely effectively used is yet an important check upon the judicial and executive officers.

These few provisions form the basis of the organization of the house of representatives of the Congress of the United States, one of the most august legislative bodies in the world, not excepting the English parliament, because it is the most independent legislative assembly, whose character and authority is entirely its own work. This, according to all appearances, the members of this house, alas, too often forget. The sessions being public and the debates promptly divulged by the press, the influence of the conduct of their members upon the morals of the people and upon the authority of the government at home and abroad must be immense.

We will still hope that the honest noble zeal with which George Washington labored in legislative bodies for society, may serve in the future as an example for all representatives.

Excuse me, my dear children, if I should not treat my subject pleasantly enough. But before I conclude this epistle, I can not repress the remark that the influence of the ladies upon these assemblies in regard to decorum, may be more effective than the most stringent laws, provided they are well informed of the actual duties of the legislators.

LETTER IV.

Senate. — Organization. — Each Senator has one Vote. — No Right of the State to instruct them. — Election by the States. — One third of the Senators to be chosen every second Year. — Temporary Appointments. — Age of thirty Years. — Vice President, President of the Senate. — Impeachment. — Election. — Annual Sessions of Congress, and the Parliament in Great Britain. — Difference between Congress and the House of Parliament in Great Britain. — Senate an executive Council. — British private Council.

WE come now to the senate, whose members, from old Roman recollections, represent themselves to our mind as a grave and awe-inspiring assemblage of Solons. Let us see what the constitution provides about them.

SECTION III.

"1. The senate of the United States shall be composed of two senators from each state, chosen by the legislature thereof, for six years, and each senator shall have one vote."

This plainly shows that the senators vote and act as individuals, because each has one vote. They have not to vote in the name of the state who elects them. Having no peerage, as the English, to form a house of lords, this mode of electing a second chamber of the national legislature, was adopted as the best. It is even against the tenor of this proviso that state governments may instruct the senators how to vote. As the law stands, one may vote for or against a measure, as he thinks best. The mode of election is again left with the state government; it is, generally, done by joint ballot of both houses of the state legislature, who serve here merely as electors, and not as legislators or instructors as to what shall be done in Congress. There is nothing to do by Congress except the carrying out of the powers specified by the constitution. Petitions and memorials may serve to inform the members of the wishes of the citizens. The states, as such, have no influence upon the business of Congress, just as the Congress has none upon the administration of the states.

"2. Immediately after they shall be assembled, in consequence of the first election, they shall be divided as equally as may be, into three classes. The seats of the senators of the first class, shall be vacated at the expiration of the second year, of the second class at the expiration of the fourth year, and of the third class at the expiration of the sixth year, so that one third may be chosen every second year, and if vacancies happen by resignation or otherwise during the recess of the legislature of any state, the executive thereof may make temporary appointments until the next meeting of the legislature, which shall then fill such vacancies."

"3. No person shall be a senator who shall not have attained to the age of thirty years, and been nine years a citizen of the United States, and who shall not, when elected, be an inhabitant of that state for which he shall be chosen."

"4. The vice-president of the United States shall be president of the senate, but shall have no vote, unless they be equally divided."

All these are plain provisions. The vice-president has a casting vote, as it is called; he may become president in case of vacancy. This is the reason why he is elected by the people.

"5. The senate shall choose their other officers, and also a president pro-tempore, in the absence of the vice-president, or when he shall exercise the office of president of the United States."

This also is plain, and it remains a great desideratum that the speaker of the house of representatives also should not be entirely dependent upon the absolute majority vote. The house has the right to make the necessary rules in this regard.

"6. The senate shall have the sole power to try all impeachments, when sitting for that purpose, they shall be on oath or affirmation. When the president of the United States is tried the chief justice shall preside; and no person shall be convicted without the concurrence of two thirds of the members present."

The president of the supreme court takes the place of the vice-president, on account of his right to succeed the president in case of vacancy.

"7. Judgment in cases of impeachment shall not extend further than removal from office, and disqualification to hold and enjoy any office of honor, trust, or profit, under the United States, but the party convicted shall nevertheless be liable and subject to indictment, trial, judgment, and punishment, according to law."

This all is plain.

SECTION IV.

"1. The times, places, and manner of holding elections for senators and representatives shall be prescribed in each state by the legislature thereof; but the Congress may, at any time, by law, make or alter such regulations, except as to the places of choosing senators."

This clause empowers Congress to control the state governments to prevent factitious legislation, interfering with the activity, and even existence of Congress.

"2. The Congress shall assemble at least once in every year, and such meeting shall be on the first Monday in December, unless they shall, by law, appoint a different day."

This clause requires no explanation.

The framers of the Constitution have, in a certain measure, imitated the English parliament, which is also divided into two houses, one of the commons, the other of the peers — those are created by privilege, the commoners are elected. The great difference between this parliament and our Congress is not in names, but in business. The English parliament is the national and municipal legislature, uniting within itself that business which priorly belonged to the kingdoms (and parliaments) of England, Scotland, Ireland, and Wales; our Congress is only the national legislature, equally divided between the senate and house of representatives. The senate, however, serves also as an executive council of the president, for like purposes a separate body under the name of privy council, exists in Great Britain. The fewer members of the senate have therefore more business to perform, than the larger number of members of the house. Having now never heard a complaint that there are too few senators for their business, it follows that the number of the members of the house may be profitably curtailed for the better despatch of the legislative business. The house began working with sixty members, a great advantage for the Union. Our Congress does not, as the English parliament, represent local interests, privileges, castes, classes, clergy, crown-rights, etc., but has only to mind that business which is clearly defined and expressly granted to it by the Constitution; the responsibility of both houses is alike; they control and check each other, to avoid errors in law-making. Thus there is some likeness in the external form of our Congress with that of the British parliament, but their proper business, legislative duties, and responsibility, differ widely. This difference should caution us not to adopt or imitate English laws.

All these provisoes are just and plain, and necessary for the activity and stability of Congress. We shall soon come to more interesting subjects.

LETTER V.

Election Returns. — Quorum. — Order of Sessions. — Rules of Proceedings. — Decorum. — Expelling of Disorderly Members. — Journal. — Yeas and Nays. — Factitious Legislation should be Resented. — Adjournment. — Compensation. — Privileged from Arrest. — No Questioning for any Speech. — Speeches for Party Purposes. — Members of Congress excluded from Offices. — Exalted Mission of Congress. — Influence of Ladies.

WE have to examine the framework of our political national fabric a little longer.

SECTION V,

Contains dispositions which may be adapted to all kinds of meetings, for church or charitable purposes.

"1. Each house shall be the judge of the elections, returns, and qualifications of its own members, and a majority of each shall constitute a quorum to do business; but a smaller number may adjourn from day to day, and may be authorized to compel the attendance of absent members in such manner and under such penalties as each house may provide."

The majority must govern; this requires a proviso for a working number or quorum. This proviso prevents the minority from doing business, and sufficiently proves the independence of our national legislature. In Europe generally the governments prescribe the rules of the houses, qualifications, etc.

"2. Each house may determine the rules of its proceedings, punish its members for disorderly behavior, and, with the concurrence of two thirds, expel a member."

Members of the American Congress should never be guilty of indecorous behavior. It must have caused pain to George Washington to admit this clause and subscribe it as a president of the convention. The debates about the political business granted to Congress should be of the most courteous, dignified, and temperate kind. The houses, of course, have also the right to resent contempts, the same as the courts. They have even extended their power to punish disorderly behavior for offences not committed as senators or representatives, which were considered entirely inconsistent with the senatorial dignity and trust. There seems to be then no lack of laws to prevent, or punish such disgraceful scenes, which we witness so often in Congress and out of it, wherein members of Congress are the actors. But laws make no gentlemen, good mothers do.

"3. Each house shall keep a journal of its proceedings, and from time to time publish the same, excepting such parts as may, in their judgment, require secrecy; and the yeas and nays of the members of either house, on any questions shall, at the desire of one fifth of those present, be entered on the journal."

This proviso shall render the members of Congress more mindful of their responsibility. Suppose a faction in Congress would refuse the constitutional appropriation for an established branch of the government, as for instance, the army or navy, on mere party, that is, private or factitious grounds, and not on national grounds, all those who should be injured by such an act may claim damages from the United States; which, in their turn, should take recourse against such factitious members of Congress proved as such by their votes, and the journals of the respective houses. The existence of the people in the United States, as a nation, may be jeoparded by factitious legislation. As the executive is amenable to the law and subject to impeachment, so ought to be factitious members of legislatures responsible with their persons and property for their participation in unconstitutional and injurious legislation not guided by justice. Hence the necessity of recording the yeas and nays.

"4. Neither house, during the session of Congress shall, without the consent of the other, adjourn for more than three days, nor to any other place than that in which the two houses shall be sitting."

By this clause the members of Congress are kept sedate and at work.

SECTION VI.

"1. The senators and representatives shall receive a compensation for their services, to be ascertained by law, and paid out of the treasury of the United States. They shall, in all cases except treason, felony, and breach of the peace, be privileged from arrest during their attendance at the session of their respective houses, and in going to and returning from the same; and for any speech or debate in either house, they shall not be questioned in any other place."

The usual compensation of $8 per day, besides a mileage to the seat of Congress, going and returning, has been changed of late to an annual salary of $3000 per member. It will make the sessions shorter and the despatch of business slower. The more lucrative the seats in a legislature are, the more they will be coveted and abused by mere speculators. I remarked in another place that there are exceedingly few persons fit for this business. This kind of business should be made as little attractive as possible. The less tampering with the laws the better. Our strength is not in laws—but in virtue and self-control, superseding political laws.

The privilege of speech and debate refers merely to the act of delivery. If a member of Congress publishes a speech, and it contains a libel, he is liable for it. There should be but little speech-making in such a legislature as Congress, where certain delegated business is to be performed, and not, as in Great Britain, a lordly king and a proud wealthy aristocracy is to be kept eternally in check. You may easily observe that almost all speeches, the maiden speeches included, in Congress, are made for party and personal purposes, not required by the actual business. Such harangues and oratorical feats may be in place in Great Britain, where society is subject, all popular rights must be conquered, and the crown has been, by the law of inheritance, in the possession of an immense executive power and patronage since time immemorial. But with all such things, no one in Congress has anything to do. There all is plain, settled, prescribed business. Nobody can entertain any serious doubts about it; and if this should be the case, the United States supreme court is authorized to settle the question. For what purpose are then with us bitter and angry harangues? The constitution gives no cause for them, our best public men have never indulged in them. As our form of government differs from the forms of European governments, so should our manner of managing public affairs differ from theirs. Ours should be plain, business-like, and free of rhetoric bombast, passionate and violent language. It will be the case if the public, and especially the ladies, condemn this style.

"2. No senator or representative shall, during the time for which he was elected, be appointed to any civil office under the authority of the United States, which shall have been created, or the emoluments whereof shall have been increased during such time; and no person holding any office under the United States, shall be a member of either house during his continuance in office"

The second part of this proviso is peculiarly American, for in all European constitutional states the state officers, ministers of the crown included, are elective or official members of the parliaments. This renders our Congress the more independent, and therefore alone responsible for their acts. What a most enviable position for a real good national legislature!

Let us pause here a little, and indulge in the hope that our Congress will become more and more true to its exalted mission, delineated in so masterly a manner in this beautiful organic law.

LETTER VI.

Bills of Revenue in both Houses. — British Imitation. — Veto. — All Presidents have used it. — Its Advantages in Regard to Factitious Legislation. — Repassing Bills. — Punishment of Unconstitutional Legislation. — Two-third Vote. — Parties. — How to get an Office. — Electors. — Political Brokers. — Strict Morality in obtaining Offices nowhere. — How they are bestowed in Monarchies and Republics. — Faction, its Danger. — Abolitionists a Faction. — Custom in England that Ministers resign when defeated in Parliament, to be imitated in the United States.

THE following section shows how the congressional laws are made by propositions or bills:—

SECTION VII.

"1. All bills for raising revenue shall originate in the house of representatives; but the senate may propose or concur with amendments, as on other bills."

This is an imitation of the British parliament. In practice, it is confined to bills for levying taxes, and not to other bills which may indirectly produce a revenue, as laws concerning the mint, postoffice department, public lands, etc.

"2. Every bill which shall have passed the house of representatives and the senate shall, before it become a law, be presented to the president of the United States. If he approve, he shall sign it; but if not, he shall return it, with his objections, to that house in which it shall have originated, who shall enter the objections at large on their journal, and proceed to reconsider it. If, after such reconsideration, two thirds of that house shall agree to pass the bill, it shall be sent, together with the objections, to the other house, by which it shall likewise be reconsidered, and if approved by two thirds of that house, it shall become a law. But in all such cases the votes of both houses shall be determined by yeas and nays; and the names of the persons voting for and against the bill shall be entered on the journal of each house respectively. If any bill shall not be returned by the president within ten days (Sundays excepted) after it shall have been presented to him, the same shall be a law in like manner as if he had signed it, unless the Congress by their adjournment prevent its return, in which case it shall not be a law."

This proviso, which creates the veto-power of the president, and defines the same with great accuracy, has been often denounced as one which interferes with the independence of the legislative branch of the government. But it has been exercised by all presidents from Washington to Pierce, and considered so wholesome, that it has found a place in almost all our state constitutions, even of the latest date. There is no doubt that considerate presidents and governors may, by means of this veto-power, best prevent inconsiderate legislation. It is also required for the protection of the minority. On such opportunities, and in their annual messages, they may urge and broach sound doctrines, which do not so easily make themselves heard in legislative bodies, ofttimes too numerous and noisy for legislative purposes.

The intrigues and power of parties and factions, extraneous influences (the lobby) of interested and designing persons, limited time of the sessions, and carelessness, may be the origin of laws, which, when executed, would promote more harm than good. On this point of legislation the executive must be the best judge. There could not occur an unconstitutional law in our country if this veto-power were exercised with more circumspection. In a self-governing society, a few, simple, general laws are desired for the common welfare. From this view, so often laid down in the messages of our better presidents, the veto-power has been created in the constitution. Its history proves that it always has been used justly by our presidents. In this regard our executives have an important duty to perform. They will do it rightly if they start from the point that our governments are only required for the realization of justice; that they have to protect and conserve the rights of self-government and liberty; that they have not to meddle with non-political, social affairs; that they must move strictly within the limits of the constitution, and neither allow partisan legislation nor indulge in the realization of ideals and moral problems, which must be left to the exertions of those whose proper duty and avocation it is to occupy themselves with such subjects. Bad laws create more evil than can be remedied by their repeal. Considerate and just laws are veto and repeal proof.

None of our constitutions or statute-books contains a proviso on the punishment of those who propose or approve of unconstitutional laws. A due sense for justice makes one desirable to check such legislation, which is, if not criminal, highly disgraceful under written constitutions. We can not be careful enough in selecting the members of Congress and in legislating, to save the reputation of our system of governing. There is in the English parliamentary transactions between the ministry and the houses a custom, that the first resign when they are defeated by a vote on the bills brought in by them. This can not happen in Congress, because government does not propose bills. This English custom is based upon the assumption, that the king can not err and is therefore not responsible, also not, when proposing a bill by his responsible ministers. In the untoward case, however, that such a bill should not pass, it would be against good aristocratic taste, to carry on the government with a ministry exposing the king to a defeat in the parliament. Something like such a custom should prevail in Congress and states, in cases, when a law has been declared unconstitutional by the judiciary. The executive, who has signed such a law, should then resign at once, to save the people the humiliation to be governed by a constitution-breaking executive, whose main duty is to see, that the constitution is preserved and together with the laws faithfully executed.

"3. Every order, resolution, or vote, to which the concurrence of the senate and house of representatives may be necessary (except on a question of adjournment), shall be presented to the president of the United States; and before the same shall take effect, shall be approved by him or being disapproved by him, shall be repassed by two thirds of the senate and the house of representatives, according to the rules and limitations prescribed in the case of a bill."

This, as you will see, is a mere extension of the preceding clause. Rules and resolves concerning the internal affairs of each house come not within the scope of this provision.

Let us now take a short review of the sections we have perused. They contain the rules for the organization and working of the Congress. The constitution says not a word of the parties or the ways and means of making a candidate for Congress, and what a party-candidate has to do to get into a place or office of influence and emolument. The constitution presupposes that the people or electors, and nobody else, shall be the source from which officials spring up. But this is not the case in reality. It is obvious, that all our elections are managed by parties, which, from usage, are the agents of the people and candidates in all election affairs. We may compare them to the brokers who are stepping in between sellers and buyers to realize a bargain. Those parties, or political brokers, leave for the people nothing to do at the ballot-box, which is called the palladium of our liberty, but to approve their party-candidates, or, to throw their votes away, as the phrase is, because, as matters are, a no-party candidate will never command a majority of the votes.

History proves, that there is no state (and I fear that there never will be one), where the ways and means to office and influence or power are such as they ought to be, according to justice and morals. In monarchies birth, station, connections, armies, courts favor, and what is called loyalty to the ruling party, smoothes the path to office and preference; in democracies a hundred artifices of popularity, party, even faction, open the road to power. Bribery with its golden key unlocks many doors to offices everywhere. Talent and merit, if not patronised by royal or public favor or party, remains behind. The press, another palladium of our liberty, is also the willing helpmate of partisans or the servile instrument of princely courts. Of course, in democracies many noble principles are set forth in platforms to strengthen the parties, and to recommend them to the favor of the people; still all this activity of parties is not legalized by law or the constitution, and, consequently, thus far, Congress depends entirely upon a power, that of party, which is irresponsible, although it assumes the management of the most important right of a free people, that of voting. I am aware that party is a part of the people, still it is not the people. When the force of party is turned against the law and constitution from selfish or even treasonable motives, party becomes faction. Of course, faction must be directly dangerous to the stability of the political fabric and constitution, while parties, which have their origin merely in a difference of opinion about the existing laws, are harmless. Genuine party never plots, but faction does; party shuns violence, but faction seeks and craves it. The abolitionists form a faction and not a party, because they act with violence against the laws and constitution, burn this document, ignore the Union and the constitutional compromises upon which it rest, oppose with arms in hand the officers of the government, refuse constitutional appropriations on party grounds, and may finally destroy the political structure, if not checked by the common sense of the law-abiding people.

I believe that we have nothing at all to fear from our officers in regard to liberty, or, what is the same, in regard to the stability and safety of our political institutions, even admitting that they often abuse their offices for selfish purposes; but we have everything to fear from factions, which spring up in our midst, and from unprincipled party influences in our legislatures. The officers change their places, but leaders of parties and factions do not; they take a strong hold upon the mind and passions of man, and, if reckless, will not rest until a constitution which bars their plots is broken down.

I write from experience, that, upon the activity of parties and factions, women have an immense influence. Read, my dear children, the history of the French Revolutions. The worst scenes of the first Revolution were enacted under the auspices of infuriated viragos. If they had taken the part of peace, order, and propriety, the lives of thousands, wantonly butchered, would have been saved. We all admit that the influence of women upon the character of American society is all-powerful and most beneficial. What would society be, everywhere, without it? Women form one half of society. God's plan can not be, that one half of human society shall be in public social affairs a blank. Their influence is in the direction of decorum, taste, and urbanity. If it is general, this character will be stamped upon our public affairs too. It is in want of a more universal influence of woman upon society, that the management of our public affairs seems to be so undignified and tasteless. Party helps to offices and power. "Party," so said Swift, "is the madness of the many for the benefit of the few." There is no greater slavery, no more corrupting condition, than the blind devotedness to party. If I vote for a party candidate, I do it because I believe him to be the fittest man for the place; but, this done, I watch his course with the independence of a freeman, and, if it should turn out to be wrong, oppose him with all lawful means. On the other hand, I support an officer or legislator elected by another party, with the same unbiased independence, if he is right. I beseech you, my sons, to act likewise as citizens. In regard to party promises, or platforms, or resolves, the constitution and established justice must guide your judgment. Only those platforms are worth noticing which are truly constitutional.

The constitution is our political theory, which may be corrupted or destroyed by a wrong practice. Every voter must be clear before he decides on a candidate, whether the party by which he is proposed rests, in regard to its aims, on the constitution or not. About special laws—as, for example, whether a naturalized citizen may be admitted to vote in five, or ten, or twenty years—there may exist a great variety of opinions, for such objects depend upon expediency, circumstances, and general principles of justice, but not upon the constitution itself. But whether Congress has the power to enact prohibitory laws in regard to the settlement of the territories or not, is a constitutional question, and not one of mere expediency. If such a power be admitted, Congress may to-day exclude certain classes of Americans, to-morrow catholic Irishmen, and again, protestant Germans, from settling and cultivating wild lands in Kansas and elsewhere, and setting up states.

I warn you, my sons, especially never to be the slaves of party, and always to judge carefully and soberly on the so-called party platforms, whether they are strictly constitutional or not; because, by supporting an unconstitutional party by your votes, you make yourselves guilty of a treason against the constitution, the foundation upon which our social happiness and national welfare rests.

LETTER VII.

Congressional Business or Powers. — Political Institutions. — United States, States, Counties, Towns, Cities, Villages. — Conflicts between them. — Supreme Court the Arbiter. — Kansas Troubles. — Direct and Indirect Taxation. — Paying Debts. — Estimates. — Tariffs. — Direct Taxation unpopular. — Protective and Prohibitive Tariffs.

We have now arrived at that part of the constitution which tells us what business properly belongs to Congress, and what not. There is more life, more interest, more matter of fact.

The public affairs committed to the care of Congress are called powers of Congress, because they are granted, or given in trust. Properly speaking, these affairs are alike all over the world. Governments, of whatever form, should never assume more business than is required for the realization of justice. To define the limits of the authority of Congress, a special list of the political business granted to it was necessary, to distinguish it from other political business reserved for the states. The framers of the constitution have made this list with great care and a due appreciation of the great difference, as we have already noticed, which exists between national and municipal political affairs.

I shall try to make this difference plain enough. The political institutions — as the United States, states, counties, towns, cities, and villages — are cut out of the same everlasting material, viz., society, which without them would be nothing but a confused maze. However, man being so much given to quarrelling, it can not fail that conflicts or disputes will happen about this political business, whether it may be done by towns or counties, states or Congress. But, under written constitutions, and in unsubjected society, they should never partake of a serious or disturbing character, especially while it is the office of the judiciary to decide on such conflicts.

The argumentation depends, then, upon the reading and interpretation of the constitutions. The federal constitution is so plainly worded, and its purpose (the organization of the national political business) so clearly set forth, that such conflicts have, up to this time, rather partaken of the nature of common lawyer cavilling, easily set aside by the supreme court. The Kansas troubles make an exception, because faction raised arms against the constitutional territorial government of Congress. Let us see what business belongs to Congress.

SECTION VIII.

The Congress shall have power—

"1. To lay and collect taxes, duties, imposts, and excises, to pay the debts and provide for the common defence and general welfare of the United States; but all duties, imposts, and excises, shall be uniform throughout the United States."

It is obviously a mere consequence of the establishing of a government, that it must possess the power to raise revenues for its support. Without it there would be no government at all. Taxes, duties, imposts, excises, were revenues in public use in Great Britain and other countries at the time of the framing of the constitution. At present, the terms duties and imposts are synonymous. Revenues are of two kinds, either direct or indirect. The first are generally called taxes; incomes from customs, public lands, the mint, etc., belong to the second class. The difference between the two is, that direct revenues or taxes are levied upon persons and property; while indirect taxes are derived from the use or consumption of certain commodities, and chiefly from imported articles of luxury, fashion, etc.

Direct revenues are based upon certain estimates, corresponding with the wants of the government; indirect revenues are collected by tariffs, and bring either more or less than the government requires, according to the amount of imposts: if more, they are superfluous, which may lead to profligacy and abuse of power; if not sufficient, the credit of the government may suffer from the want of means. Direct taxes are said to be more or less odious, because they can be counted; while indirect taxes are borne more easily, because they can not be readily ascertained by the consumer. Monarchs were and are in favor, and the inventors of, indirect revenues. In the United States, direct taxes must be apportioned in proportion to the population of the several states (see Section ii., No. 3).

The United States treasury is at present, in the main, filled by the customs, an arrangement which excludes the idea of absolute freedom of commerce. Thus, we are so little accustomed to pay a tax for Congress, that a taxation on this account would be unpopular, as the phrase is. The wording of this clause plainly shows that the framers of the constitution wished not to tie up the hands of Congress in the care for its financial resources, so that our federal government is at liberty to act according to time and circumstances, which, together with public opinion, have a great influence upon the finances of nations. Of course, this part of the public business is the cause of a treasury department with a secretary at its head, customhouses, collectors, sub-treasurers, and a large number of offices for the collecting, controlling, and disbursing of the revenues.

It is self-evident that laws on customs revenues ought to be made with a view to benefit the home and not foreign industry, as long as such customs are raised from a similar view abroad. This is required by the principle of mutuality in social affairs. The natural order of things is freedom of industry, of which commerce is a branch. It is impossible to determine, with mathematical accuracy, the just limits of such customs, especially on account of the influence of foreign customs systems. This has, therefore, been the cause of violent party disputes — one party (the whig) advocating protective and even prohibitive customs; the other party (the democrats) free trade. A middle course, between those extremes, is, under prevalent international circumstances, preferable.

LETTER VIII.

Contracting Debts. — States to pay as they go. — Regulation of Commerce at Home and Abroad. — Law of Mutuality. — The Self-preservation of Nations.

We continue our reading. The Constitution allows Congress:

"2. To borrow money on the credit of the United States."

This is a needful proviso to raise a revenue temporarily — for instance, in time of war, or if suddenly the imports on luxuries, etc., should fall off. Public economists maintain that mere municipal governments, as our states, should be deprived of the power to borrow money, and "pay as they go," because they can in their ordinary walk of business never be exposed to a necessity of borrowing money, while Congress, as the manager of our national affairs, may in consequence of an untoward event, as aggressive war, rebellion, etc., be involved in difficulties with foreign nations, requiring such temporary expedients to furnish means for the common defence.

"3. To regulate commerce—
a With foreign nations.
b And among the several states.
c And with the Indian tribes."

Three distinct objects are here committed to the care of Congress, which are as such pointed out in print. Those few lines have given rise to frequent debates, often of a very irritating character in Congress.

The intention of the constitution is plain enough, if we read it as the organic law defining the national political business, and not as one written for merchants and traders. Then the words to regulate commerce with foreign nations, or with our *quasi* nations, the states, at home, and Indian tribes, can not mean that Congress shall tell traders, where to get goods, or to fight the Chinese to force them to buy tobacco from us, or build canals or roads for the transportation of goods, etc.; never, they simply define a plain business, belonging to all national governments, to make treaties or certain rules or laws by which commerce in its threefold direction, clearly pointed out, shall be regulated and protected on land and water. Hence treaties about coasting-trade, fisheries, equality of duties, Danish Sound dues, police over the oceans, ocean harbors, and navigable inland waters, crafts and seamen, pilotage, salvage, ports of entry, embargo, lighthouses, safety of passengers (incidental) on board ship, etc., are exclusive business objects for Congress, whose authority is exhausted as soon as the case ceases to be a national one, when the municipal authority takes its place. Local internal improvements have no connection with this clause. It follows from this clause that no state government has the power to make commercial regulations with foreign governments, or with a government of one of the states, or with Indian tribes. The words "to regulate commerce," have no meaning without the words which follow. In such an abstract manner there is no government on earth wise and powerful enough to regulate commerce. The framers of the constitution were not the men guilty of such a folly. Still party has taken hold of this provision to make capital out of it. Partisans have inferred from those words, "to regulate commerce," that the power of Congress to regulate commerce, is unlimited.

This clause, namely, the duty of Congress to regulate the commerce between the confederated states, is the main source of our internal commercial liberty, one of the greatest boons of our confederation, and the very cause of the wonderfully fast-spreading culture of the land, because no state can enact constitutionally laws levying taxes upon trade, as the states do in Germany, although confederated, and as the Dutch and Swiss republics did, and the latter perhaps still do. Bloody revolutions have been the result of such commercial checks and burdens, guarantied by this clause of our noble constitution, which so endears our Union to the solid mass of the people, and which renders it a desirable home for all industrious men. What feelings would take the place of this love of our country, should the industry of the Boston merchant be checked by custom lines around every state? should Louisiana have power to tax New York city, and the state of New York New Orleans? This most precious liberty of commerce, for which fanatics and factionists care little, is the result of the clause giving Congress the right to regulate commerce among the several states. Further, in consequence of this proviso, neither our own states nor foreign governments can meddle with our Indian tribes. Without a good deal of fanciful reading and cavil this clause can not be misunderstood.

Fancy delights in considering human society as one family. It is so in abstraction, but not in reality, which shows that it is composed of different races, and these are divided into different independent nations, represented by peculiar governments, acting like persons, that is, taking good care of their *self.* No person, no family, can exist otherwise. It is much the same with nations as such. But if this is done according to the law of mutuality, the essence of justice, expressed by the Christian sentence, Do unto others as you wish they may do unto you, persons and nations will exist co-ordinately and comfortably together. To preserve this comfort, persons and nations must be on their guard against trespassers and trespassing. Suppose a European nation and their government were much more depending upon the commerce with our nation than we upon theirs, and their government opposed to ours in theory and practice, then this law of mutuality and due regard to ourself and comfort, imperatively require to regulate this intercourse from our side so that we should not strengthen by it the hostile force and attitude of the foreign government, in order to avoid our own national suicide. This, to balance right, requires wise, delicate, and resolute statesmanship.

LETTER IX.

Naturalization and Bankruptcy Laws. — Foreigners. — Declaration of Intention to become a Citizen. — Congress, and State-citizenship Laws. — Family Suffrage. — American Woman's Influence. — Credit. — Congress not true to their duty. — Legislation of the several States on Bankruptcy Suppletive. — France. — Germany. — President Buchanan's Message on a Congressional Bankruptcy Law. — Congressional Committee report against it. — Denies the Power of Congress.

We come now to the "foreigners." Congress further has the power :—

"4. To establish a uniform rule of naturalization, and uniform laws on the subject of bankruptcies throughout the United States."

For the sake of brevity, two business objects have been inclosed in this clause, which have nothing in common. The second sentence concerning bankruptcies would never have found a place in the constitution, if Congress were indeed the regulator of commerce, because as such this body could make as many laws concerning bankruptcies, banks, drafts, commercial partnerships, protests, exchange, discount, as it pleased, incidentally to the foregoing clause. Aliens must be Americanized. The colonies were a creation of immigration; that immigration from Europe would fill the vast regions of the United States, was foreseen by the sagacious framers of the constitution. To give uniformity to this national business, Congress was empowered to legislate upon it.

Hence, the naturalization laws, by which, of course, were excluded titles, orders of nobility, allegiance to foreign governments or princes, and a certain time fixed, five years' residence in the country, temporary business absence not included, and required a declaration of the intention to become a citizen, etc. State legislatures have altered the time of five years, and reduced it, in regard to voting, to one year and less, producing a kind of conflict with the laws of Congress, which has become a bone of party contention.

The federal constitution, and the laws of Congress in this respect, seem to have operated well, while state legislation has led to voting abuses, especially in consequence of the general suffrage law. Viewing emigration, and its political consequences, from a simple natural social standing-point, we must be inclined to admit that the establishing of a family, and home, is the universal beginning of the real exercise of citizen rights, and presumptively qualifies better than a law can do to voting. If a naturalization law could start from this natural basis, the matter would be easily set right, and state interference prevented. I admit that the voting by families is yet unpopular, but if American women would look into the matter, and insist upon such a voting law, it would soon be carried, and prove to be one of the greatest social political improvements of the time, and remain for ever popular; for it is just, necessary, natural, and common sense, as the family state itself, while the general suffrage law is a mere arbitrary measure.

The second part of this clause attributes to Congress the care for a general bankrupt law.

The framers of the constitution were well aware of the immense importance of the confederation in regard to the expansion of industry and commerce. They knew further, that commerce without credit is impossible, and that credit will degenerate into swindling, and lose its moral force without the support of uniform stringent laws. The idea of having throughout the Union a general law on the subject of bankruptcy, sprung up from a true, honest, and statesmanlike appreciation of the confederation. To such an appreciation, however, Congress never has come, never has aspired. This assemblage is far from answering to its true constitutional purpose. Very few of its members take the constitution for their rule of action. Thus Congress has tried repeatedly to enact a uniform bankruptcy law, but it always failed, so that this clause, thus far, is not exhausted by legislative action. The state legislatures have supplied this deficiency, which, of course, produces a variety of systems where uniformity is desirable. In South Carolina, executors of estates have a right to help themselves if they have claims against them before all other creditors; they can pay any creditor they please, according to the *dignity* of the debt; a man dying, or failing, may there prefer one creditor to another, etc. If now a citizen of another state is not aware of this anomalous state of things, and belongs not to the dignified creditors, he will suffer losses, while a uniform congressional law should protect him from such.

The opinion is at present adopted that this grant is not an exclusive one, and that thus the state legislatures may enact bankrupt laws which would be unconstitutional if this clause should be exclusive. But this seems to be not true, for if this opinion be right, all other grants in this clause would be as little exclusive, for they are all made in the same manner and tenor. The fact is, Congress has had, up to this time, no good will, or energy enough to establish a uniform bankruptcy law, therefore, the state legislatures were obliged to supply the deficiency temporarily. As soon as Congress would enact one, then all state laws in this regard would cease to be valid.

You see how much work is still left for us by this noble constitution. If the prevalent, virulent and speculative party spirit will pervade Congress longer, it will never be wholly executed.

France, with thirty-five million inhabitants, has a uniform law on this subject; and I observe that there was, in 1857, a convention sitting in Germany to make one. No doubt that our constitution has suggested the idea. So I hope it will be now soon realized, for the benefit of the public and unfortunate honest debtors at home.

President Buchanan having, in his first annual message to Congress, suggested the necessity of enacting a uniform general bankruptcy law, Congress appointed a committee, who reported that the subject, especially with reference to banks, belonged to the states to legislate upon. This may have been satisfactory to this committee, but is adverse to the constitution, and something like insubordination or revolution. A business intrusted wisely by the people to Congress, can not, by their agents, be intrusted to the states without causing confusion and anarchy.

LETTER X.

Coining Money. — Its Value. — Standard of Weights and Measures. — Mints. — Assay Offices. — Decimal Coinage. — Counterfeiting. — Punishment. — Post-Offices. — Post-Roads. — Roman Custom. — Mail Lines. — Competition. — Internal Improvement Policy.

We glide from power to power, or business to business. Congress has the power :—

"5. To coin money, regulate the value thereof and of foreign coin, and fix the standard of weights and measures."

The subjects of this provision are truly national, and thus justly belonging to Congress. For a general commercial intercourse, a certain standard medium of exchange is indispensable to represent property. Mankind have adopted for this purpose the most valuable metals, gold and silver, having an intrinsic standard value, not affected by laws or art. To legalize this standard, and coin and mint, accordingly, money, is the business of Congress. Consequently, Congress has erected mints, assay offices, etc.

Justice requires uniform laws for standard weights and measures, and even international arrangements for a mundane uniformity in such things.

That Congress has not succeeded until lately to make the national legal decimal coinage exclusive, proves that upon the circulation of money, usage exercises a more powerful influence than laws.

Within these few words lies the trust of the national monetary affairs. It is not fair, from the side of the state governments to circumvene this proviso by allowing associations to fabricate paper money, which is actually like coining.

"6. To provide for the punishment of counterfeiting the securities and current coin of the United States."

This grant is a sequel to the preceding. The crime of counterfeiting is declared a felony, punishable by imprisonment, fine, etc.

"7. To establish post-offices and post-roads."

This proviso has given cause to many disputes. The meaning of the constitution obviously is to give Congress the right to establish post or mail lines, as we should express it at present. That for this purpose offices and officers are necessary, is a matter of course. There are roads wherever a mail line is needed, so that Congress is saved the trouble of building one. But this never was the meaning of the framers of the constitution, which is here worded in the old European law language. The Romans built roads for government use, with posts or relays, straight through the provinces, without regard to the communication, commerce, and correspondence. Our post business is no such thing, but a mere forwarding or express-line business, and properly speaking, no political business at all. It belongs, at present, naturally to those who form express and railroad lines. No government is instituted for the forwarding or express business, or the diffusion of knowledge, or the facilitating of social intercourse; free men do not require such things from their governments. Europe inherited such institutions from the Romans, and the governments found it to their interests, to make the forwarding of the letters of their subjects a source of revenue, and, at the same time, keep the contents of the correspondence under secret and open surveillance. It is managed thus by the English government, was transplanted to the colonies, and left with the Congress, to keep it there consolidated. Congress saw fit also to forbid private competition, which stamps the business as a monopoly. Upon such nonpolitical business time exercises a paramount influence.

The forwarding of correspondence by mail or telegraph should be open to competition, and consequently to constant improvement. There is an invention spoken of to transport letters in tubes, by the pressure of air. If practicable, Congress will feel the injustice of monopolizing the letter-forwarding. By taking the words "establishing postroads" in the obsolete European or Roman sense of the business, the idea has sprung up that Congress has a right or is bound by the constitution to construct roads and improve rivers, generally called internal improvements, for the transportation of the mail; and has given cause to party disputes, and vetoed laws. It has happened that the presidents generally were against this internal improvement policy, and Congress, the house of representatives especially, in favor of it. Viewing the matter in the light of the present age, Congress has the right to establish post or mail lines, with offices and officers, without forbidding free competition, and designate the roads over which these lines shall pass. If Congress were authorized to build roads, the word build or construct would have been used instead of "establish."

LETTER XI.

Sciences and Useful Arts. — Copyright. — Patents. — Progress of Science. — Ripening of the Understanding. — Locke. — Smithson. — His Legacy Anti American. — Political Patronage of Arts and Sciences in Europe. — Goethe. — Fourierism.

We come now to fresh fields and pastures, the sciences and arts, and shall immediately see what the noble framers of the constitution thought of them. The law gives Congress on this point the power:—

"8. To promote the progress of science and the useful arts, by securing for limited times to authors and inventors the exclusive right to their respective writings and discoveries."

Is this all? you will perhaps ask. Could they not say a word or two of national education, national universities, national agricultural bureaus or colleges, national scholarships? No, my dear children; they preferred not to say a single word about these things, because they could not afford to consider them as national political affairs, for which alone they had the power to make a constitution. But eminently wise men as they were, they took good care for justice in regard to the products of arts and sciences and the property rights of their authors in the Union. They had at this time made a great step forward. There are still governments which leave those rights but little protected.

The consequence of this clause are the patent-office and copyright laws. The wisdom of controlling this business in Congress is obvious. Authors, artists, and inventors divulge their works, not with the intention to lose by it, but for their and others' benefit. But the act of publication would be mere loss if the law would not secure their property rights. This instance is again a proof of the immense value of our Union for the welfare of individuals and society at large. You have seen that by certain grants to Congress the liberty of commerce has been secured in the Union, binding to it the numerous trading-classes. You meet here a grant which links the literary, artistic, and mechanical public to the confederation. This policy benefits directly and indirectly the agricultural class. Who and what are then the men, my dear children, who can dare to speak, nay, to think of the dissolution of this Union! Can it be men who ever read this constitution, oı witnessed its working? A government has, strictly speaking, no force to effectually promote the real progress of science and arts, however ample the financial resources should be at its disposal; because this progress is dependent upon circumstances over which men have very little control. The real progress of science is the ripening of the understanding. This is a work of exceedingly slow advancement, as Locke has already observed. Useful occupation, early industrial habits, study, that is, select reading, good domestic example, improve the understanding more than doctrines, theories, novels, etc. Political officers, who are too often mere instruments of party, can do here nothing that society may not do as well and better; because arts and sciences belong to free social business, and not to political. To tax one for the purpose of raising the school-money for another would be unjust, it being beside doubtful whether such a support is indeed for his benefit and that of society or not. Education is a part of the destiny of man. We must not organize destiny. The more liberty and variety in education the better. Circumscribed schooling and instruction does not make better men. I wish not to be taxed for the schooling of a Robespierre, or to raise a fund for speculators.

The Englishman Smithson did not understand our constitution; otherwise he would not have bestowed upon Congress a legacy for the diffusion of knowledge; because Congress has nothing to do with such business. He, of course, a European, was not aware that we commit the care of that to writers, editors, publishers, preachers, lecturers, speakers, liberal wealthy men, amateurs of arts and sciences, associations, or, if you please, to everybody, nurses and mothers included. Congress would have acted upon truly American principles in declining this curious stipend, which is but a national bore. It is impossible that even our governments, constantly coming fresh from the people as they are, can keep pace with our free society in such things.

Our press is absolutely free; not so in Europe. It divulges events, discoveries, ideas, and projects, with a rapidity so great that stable formal governments in a race with it will always be behind time. To bring schools and sciences in contact with party is most objectionable. Still, all this is entirely different in Europe, which we are too prone to imitate in such things. The political patronage bestowed there upon sciences and arts is a part of that general favorite and pension policy peculiar to all monarchies, which is calculated to make the talent loyal and submissive. If it dares to be independent it is suspected, neglected, and even persecuted. Beside, my dear children, sciences and arts serve satan as much as God; bogus as much as truth; error and superstition as much as reason. Goethe, a highly gifted and prolific writer, as you know, says pertly, "Books are written to show our errors." My letters may also contain some: try to find them out. In what light do then appear books or sciences and arts originating with governments? to show their errors? Do we organize governments for this purpose?

This provision of our constitution is required by justice, and is sufficient for all practical purposes.

All publications at public expense, emanating from the patent-office, etc., are simply unconstitutional and exceedingly unamerican. You will excuse this word. But our society is unique; something *per se;* and chiefly in consequence of our excellent constitution, which expressly starts from the principle that the government shall not interfere with the social affairs, but only take good care for their protection; and never intended that Congress should become a book-publishing concern, or look out for teaching languages, for arts, seeds, pruning, gardening, fishing, camels, etc. The question what is useful and necessary in regard to sciences and arts, belongs to society to decide. She will judge fairly according to time, circumstances, and the laws of nature. For this very purpose we want to be free, in order that talent and its world-ruling influence may not be crippled nor led astray by the force or patronage of governments. "People in the United States are willing to bow to the sway of mind. We have done with the remnants of by-gone times, when bodily strength or military prowess and skill conferred wealth, distinction, and worldly greatness, and was rewarded by privileges, caste, primogeniture, nobility, crowns," etc. But the influence of mind must not be hostile to order and established justice. Under our federal constitution are widely opened all facilities for the expansion of the mind, the availability of talent, and the culture of sciences and arts. These flourish best when not stimulated or subsidized by governments. Those which can not grow upon the broad field of liberty and under the protective shelter of a constitution like ours, are useless for society, although they may find a place among imported exotics in the luxurious conservatories of the rich, who can pay for them.

In every respect the federal constitution has been framed to make her time-proof, and therefore she keeps wisely clear of scientific ideals, speculations, Parisian fraternity, socialism, Fourierism (by-the-by a very old ism), and all similar schemes.

We have to guard her like a jewel against the rough hands of tampering, wicked politicians.

But let me stop, that you may not feel alarmed about the length of my letters.

LETTER XII.

Inferior Courts. — United States District Courts. — Piracies. — Felonies. — Law of Nations. — Ocean Police. — Branches of the Ocean. — English Law curiosity. — War. — Letters of Marque and Reprisal. — Captures on Land and Water. — Justice the end of Wars. — Court of Nations. — Jurisdiction of Congress. — War defensive or aggressive. — Property of Neutrals.

WE lapse again for a little while into lawyer business. The constitution requires of Congress:—

"9. To constitute tribunals inferior to the supreme court."

This is a necessary proviso; for the good administration of justice requires a judicious distribution of the judicial business among graduated courts of law, for which purpose certain judicial districts are set up, to limit the jurisdiction of the courts. Hence we have United States circuit and district courts.

"10. To define and punish piracies and felonies committed on the high seas, and offences against the law of nations."

To the Congress belongs the jurisdiction over the vessels and the citizens of the Union upon the oceans and high seas, just as other governments exercise the same right, in regard to the vessels of their subjects, because the oceans are common for all, and therefore, the Congress has to enact all criminal, police, and other laws, concerning the ocean navigation, and crimes committed thereon. The oceans terminate where the creeks and inlets begin, included, within any county. Branches of the ocean, as the Long Island sound or East river, are under the jurisdiction of Congress, which is important in regard to ferries, buoys, lighthouses, fortifications, quarantines, harbor-line regulations, business belonging constitutionally to Congress. As our Congress, in the spirit of the constitution, has always been careful not to interfere with the jurisdiction and the business of the state governments, it has not made use of this grant in regard to offences committed on board merchant ships, lying in the waters of the United States, leaving the cognizance of such cases to the state officials. I here make you acquainted with an English law curiosity. The common law courts and the admiralty hold their concurrent and alternate jurisdiction where the tide ebbs and flows; one upon the water when it is full sea, the other (common law) upon the land when it is ebb. He who will commit a felony, and prefer common law justice must wait until the water ebbs.

You will excuse me if I am not able to tell you exactly what means the phrase, law of nations, for there is no such thing. Still certain usages, recognised from time to time by goverments of different nations as rules, have received this name.

"11. To declare war, grant letters of marque and reprisal, and make rules concerning captures on land and water."

If all governments would consider the realization of justice their principal aim, there would be an end to all war. But not a single government, even ours not entirely excepted, has up to this time acted upon this principle. Thus we must be prepared for war, in order to realize justice by the force of arms, if reason does not prevail in the national councils. The friends of peace have proposed a court of nations, similar to our United States supreme court, in regard to the differences among nations; but governments, which consider their business a property right, which they may improve by conquest, never will submit their difficulties to such a court, nor obey its decisions, even if they could be enforced. The decisions of our supreme court can be enforced by the army and navy of the United States.

War may be either one of redress and punishment, or of self-defence. We can never have a war of conquest as long as we obey our constitution. By means of letters of marque, merchant-vessels are transmitted into men-of-war, to increase our naval force. Of course, all war business is, or ought to be, a part of the realization of justice on a large or national scale.

On the subject of privateering or cruisers bears the question whether private property of neutrals and others on the sea shall be free or subject to be captured or plundered by privateers or men-of-war. Our government has insisted upon it that it shall be free. But the English government has, up to this time, not consented to it. We can not give up the right of fitting out private vessels as men-of-war in time of war, but neither such vessels nor regular vessels of the navy should be made use of for the plundering of private property, as little as armies should be thus used on land, or, in other words, governments should stop fighting. If they will not cease warring, then private property on sea or land will bear the brunt, because it is impossible to prevent this by treaties.

LETTER XIII.

Armies. — Appropriation of Money for them Biennial. — The United States disliked by Monarchs. — Necessity of Protection. — Navy. — Not exactly needed for the Protection of Commerce. — The Hanse Towns without a Navy. — Land and Naval Forces. — Militia. — Crimean War. — Serf Soldiers. — Discipline. — Training of the Militia. — Equal confidence in Congress as in State Governments. — Christian brotherly Love. — Priests.

CONGRESS is further authorized :—

" 12. To raise and support armies; but no appropriation of money to that use shall be for a longer term than two years."

The first part of this clause, compared with the following proviso concerning the navy, plainly shows that the framers of the constitution were not in favor of a standing army, the main prop of despotism and governments by inheritance. Congress shall, in case of war, raise and support armies, as many as are needed, while in the thirteenth clause the grant is to provide and maintain a navy without regard to war or time. An army requires arms and other materials, drill, and systematic organizations. Hence a war department, secretary of war, arsenals, and a number of offices and officers. Our government is, on account of its form, disliked by the property or grace-of-God governments, and, if not managed with exceeding prudence easily exposed to diplomatic intrigues and troubles, in spite of all assurances of friendship, treaties of peace to the contrary. Our polity naturally isolates us. This state of things requires due vigilance about our common defence. Congress has seen fit, from the beginning of its existence, to keep a small standing army, in virtue of this clause, for the protection of our coasts, forts, and boundaries, which may serve as a nucleus for the formation of armies in case of war. With this view the military academy at West Point has been established. Railroads, telegraphs, steam navigation, in one word, progressive Time may, however, produce frequent changes in such measures. A free people must be trained for self-defence. Military appropriations shall be biennial to keep them under the strict control of each congressional session. Such appropriations must be unconditional, in order to avoid clogging in the public service.

"13. To provide and maintain a navy."

The war of the revolution ushered our navy into existence. The exercise of the police over the oceans and the before-mentioned jealousy of foreign governments seems to require one. It is not so much needed for the protection of commerce as is proved by the merchant fleet of the German Hanse Towns which carries the largest amount of tonnage after that of ourselves and Great Britain, without the protection of a single man-of-war. A navy must be provided for in time; and this is the cause of a separate department, with a secretary of the navy at the head of the navy yards, and a large number of offices and officers. A naval academy is connected with it.

"14. To make rules for the government and regulation of the land and naval force."

This is a consequence of the preceding grants. As a general thing the English regulations have had much influence over this branch of the national business. Our public ships in our own waters, and wherever they sail, are under the jurisdiction of Congress. Justice, as good as mortals can have it, would save us from all war which plunge society in debt. Saltpetre would cease to be villainous. More justice and less villainy will do.

"15. To provide for calling forth the militia to execute the laws of the Union, suppress insurrections, and repel invasions."

The militia, you see, is not such an insignificant institution as it appears to be, when mustered. It is the real strong arm of the government, and wisely placed at the disposition of the central government, when needed for the common defence and to insure domestic tranquillity.

All citizens within a certain age are by duty, their own interest, and law, obliged to fill the ranks of the militia. American mothers must be resigned to see their husbands and sons rally under the national standard. They expect their homes to be protected by them. It is their duty to nourish patriotic feelings and to share the burdens of war. A patriotic militia, thus supported, at home, is invincible. The war in the Crimea has shown the difference between free soldiers and serf soldiers. The abolition of Russian serfdom may have something to do with the improvement of the army. A call of the president of the United States to arm for the common defence, will be answered by millions of brave men and stout hearts. There are no better teachers of patriotism, honor, and gallantry, than good mothers. You may learn this from the biography of Washington.

"16. To provide for organizing, arming, and disciplining the militia, and for governing such part of them as may be employed in the service of the United States, reserving to the states respectively the appointment of the officers, and the authority of training the militia according to the discipline prescribed by Congress."

This is the last of the six provisoes in regard to the common defence. The jurisdiction of Congress over the militia begins when it is mustered at the place of rendezvous. All expenses are borne by the national treasury for the militia called forth by Congress. The commander-in-chief has to decide all minor differences in regard to service. It is desirable that all state officials and citizens in general should cheerfully assist Congress when executing those grants, to ensure prompt results in case of common danger.

Congress is composed of the same material as state governments. Presumptively, as much wisdom, patriotism, and experience rule there as in state governments, or counties and towns. There is not a single reason why we should harrass our Congress with such mistrust or jealousy as European subjects treat their rulers, and by the grace of God princes. Still it has often been the case, and has even given rise to considerable party trouble.

The main object of the constitution placing the national business in the hands of Congress, promoted by legal order or justice, is the general welfare and prompt concentrated action when circumstances demand. Before thirty odd states, loosely bound like the old Dutch provinces, decide one single measure, Congress, as it is installed at present, can have already executed thousands. This is the strength derived from a judicious organization and location of the public affairs.

The bellicose propensities are easily excited in free men. The aim of Jesus was to supplant them by brotherly love and charity. Follow his precepts more than those of his priests, who too often forget that by prudence, forbearing, and a strong sense of justice, we, in our times, may easily avoid all resorts to arms.

LETTER XIV.

District of Columbia. — Exclusive Legislation over it and Forts, Magazines, Arsenals, Dock-yards. — Paris. — German Diet in a Free City. — Legislative Powers concerning all National Business. — Sophists and Cavillers.

WE come now to the clause which creates a curious little, but very wisely-devised empire.

In accordance with it Congress has—

"17. To exercise exclusive legislation in all cases whatsoever over such district (not exceeding ten miles square), as may by cession of particular states and the acceptance of Congress, become the seat of the government of the United States; and to exercise like authority over all places purchased by the consent of the legislature of the state, in which the same shall be, for the erection of forts, magazines, arsenals, dock-yards, and other needful buildings."

This is the origin of the District of Columbia. The desirable independence of the federal government from state, made the erection of such a ten miles square empire necessary, to be governed by Congress. The wisdom of this proviso is so obvious that those versed in politics—that is, the art of organizing society for the ends of justice, were astonished, that the French attempted, so late as 1848, to again establish a national republican government in Paris, where, if not protected by a powerful garrison, it may be at any time overthrown. Without such an arrangement a state, in whose limits Congress would sit, would acquire an undue preponderance. Even in monarchical Germany, the diet, as is called the present show of a national Congress, meets in an independent free city, from the same reasons.

The clause speaks for itself.

Congress is further empowered—

"18. To make all laws which shall be necessary and proper for carrying into execution the foregoing powers, and all other powers vested by this constitution in the government of the United States, or in any department or office thereof."

By this provision, Congress has the power to put in motion the different wheels of the government by acts or laws. Without this power, the constitution and its grants would be inoperative. Where this organizing has to stop, may be sometimes doubtful; still no interpretation should obstruct the carrying out of the plans of the constitutional grants. They are sufficiently specified for all practical purposes. Sophists and cavillers must always be put to rest by the authority of the judiciary, because for such men no constitution is conclusive. We have now examined the positive part of the constitution, specifying the business which shall be done by Congress, through the indicated channels. It is imperative for each to fulfill its trust, so that no legislative business may be transferred to the executive or vice versa.

In my next letter we come to the negative part, that is, which prohibits Congress to perform certain business. As simple as this seems to be, yet it required centuries before we arrived at this result; and what is still more remarkable, that, up to this time, a very few agree about what business is national or federal, and what not. Hence the great necessity for every citizen to investigate this subject thoroughly. Meanwhile let us faithfully stick to this constitution and our Union.

LETTER XV.

Interpretation of the Grant. — Congress, the Agent of the people, who remain the Proprietors. — Rights of Self-government. — National Bank. — Precedents. — Shoemaking in Time of War. – Expediency. — National Banks in England, France, Russia, Austria, Prussia. — Public Debts. — Washington. — Jackson. — Good Temper in Public Affairs. — Pulpit. — Ladies.

Before we proceed to the reading of a new section, I will add a few remarks to my last letter. The business entrusted to Congress has been granted or delegated by the people, who remain the original proprietors, while the officers act as their agents. When it is doubtful whether an expedient to carry such a granted business or power be proper or necessary or even constitutional, those who have to remove this doubt should not only consult the words of the constitution, but also the rights of self-government.

There was a time when the federal government under Washington thought it necessary to establish a national bank for the regulation of the finances and collecting the revenues, &c. Some doubted its constitutionality, while others believed the reverse and supported their opinion by referring to the eighteenth clause. Now, banking, by itself, is a private and not a political business, required for the convenience of commerce, not for the realization of justice; still it may be, that at certain times, when the public finances are deranged in consequences of war, such a bank, authorized by the national government, may be necessary and proper for carrying into execution certain treasury or financial measures, and thus far it would be entirely constitutional. Upon all such things time exercises its all powerful influence. A decision in favor of such a bank in time of general distress and paralyzation of business, however, should not be considered as an imperative precedent for all times to come, and the government should part with such an incidental financial auxiliary as soon as possible, because, as before mentioned, governments generally have as little connection with banking, as with farming and shoemaking. But in time of war why should not our government resort to shoemaking for the soldiers too, if there is no other way to get this necessary clothing? If such a case should be the cause of party disputes, and the supreme court decide that the shoemaking by the government be constitutional, would common-sense men set up this decision as a precedent for all time to come, according to which Congress can carry on shoemaking for ever at pleasure? Government itself is a mere expedient, and oft-times an exceedingly inconvenient necessity. If now, at a certain time, people all-wise, and good, and honest, should agree to dispense with all government, and a few voices should object, upon the ground that government was a necessity by precedent, what would common sense say to that? Precedents often rest upon no better grounds than fashions or customs. Disputes must, at a certain time, come to an end. It can not be supposed that the decisions will then be not in harmony with the existing facts, circumstances, and laws. But all those facts and circumstances do not happen exactly a second time again. This is the cause of the mutability of legal decisions and of the short validity of precedents. Peculiar circumstances make a national bank necessary in England, France,

Russia, Austria, and Prussia. There the governments are, to use this expression, living upon debts, for which purpose they use the financiering help of subservient banks, endowed for this purpose with monopolies and privileges.

Such precedents are, of course, of no value for us. Besides such a national bank with us would inevitably interfere with private banking or with the liberty of industry, one of our most precious social rights, which to protect, and not to molest, is a chief duty of government and the express aim of our constitution.

Increase of business has, of late, created a necessity for a department of the interior with a secretary at its head. A postmaster-general has been from the beginning of the government at the head of the postoffice department. The main channels have been for the same reason subdivided, as the treasury into sub-treasuries. But the origin of this extensive political machinery is in a few lines of the eighth section, whose simplicity and precision makes the constitution easily applicable to time and circumstances.

The grant to raise armies will, I am afraid, remain necessary for all time, as long as men have strong passions for violence and evil, and are destitute of self-control. Still the manner of executing this grant may, in a few years, entirely differ from that of our time. The less detail there is in a constitution about such grants the better. To cavil about incidental expedients is gratuitous and unbecoming if only everything is fairly and honestly managed. In this regard, public affairs do not differ from private affairs. Washington was as right in his time, when approving a national bank, as Jackson was later, when disapproving it. To make party capital out of such incidents is wrong.

We are in need of a good temper in our political affairs. Where shall we get it when even the pulpit is turned into a party hot-iron blast? I am not mistaken when I claim it from the American women. I wish they may, with their faculty of quick perception, consider themselves the social pacificators by the grace of God and the laws of nature.

LETTER XVI.

Migration and Importation of Persons. — Importation of Slaves declared Piracy. — Slave Labor, disposing of, in the States. — Habeas Corpus. — Rebellion. — Invasion. — Middle Ages. — Rogues. — Charles I. — Attainder and "Ex-Post-Facto" Bills. — Habeas Pursam.

LET us pursue now our reading.

SECTION IX.

"1. The migration or importation of such persons as any of the states now existing shall think proper to admit shall not be prohibited by the Congress prior to the year one thousand eight hundred and eight; but a tax or duty may be imposed on such importation not exceeding ten dollars for each person."

WHEN the first negative proviso was written down, there were in all the states, prior colonies, bound laborers or slaves kept. The framers of the constitution were, by their constituents, and especially the northern states, induced to insert into the constitution that Congress, in consequence of the policy over the oceans, should not prohibit the importation of slaves before 1808, in order to gain time to dispose of their slaves. After this time, Congress saw fit to prohibit the same under the penalty of piracy. This law is at present in force. Within the several states Congress has nothing to forbid in this regard. The states where slaves are kept have tolerated the trade with them. It is the only way to dispose of bound labor force, and make it useful where needed. Of course this disposing of bound laborers is an incident of the system. It is the business of the slave states to make the needful regulations in this regard. In forbidding the importation of Africans, Congress has cut the Gordian knot, and parted at once with all the matter in regard to the foreign slave-trade. In regard to immigration of free persons, Congress has no power to interfere, it being the natural right of man to migrate, and because it belongs to the states to legislate on this subject. For this very reason there is no passport system legal in the Union, and every one is at liberty to wander and migrate as he pleases, also with his servants, bound or free. There are some, especially the leaders of the abolition party, who maintain that this clause indirectly empowers Congress to forbid slavery in the territories, which politically to organize is its duty, but this is obviously a mistake. As a general thing, nobody is naturally a friend of labor, either bound or free. Also this section, and others of the constitution in connexion with bound labor, are not partial for slavery. They but contain, as a matter of course, the provisions necessary in regard to it from a national view. The prohibition of this labor in the United States must originate with the states.

"2. The privilege of the writ of 'habeas corpus' shall not be suspended, unless when, in cases of rebellion or invasion, the public safety may require it."

This privilege, which consists in the right of any person to take out an order of a judge or court, on behalf of a prisoner illegally arrested, to investigate into its causes by the competent authority, to promote, if possible, his discharge, was—in the middle ages, swarming with barons, earls, counts, dukes, and kings, all assuming, with sword in hand, lordly or sovereign rights of government or jurisdiction over their vassals or subjects—of more importance than now, but may be still of some good service in certain instances. However, in consequence of the change of circumstances in favor of liberty, the great improvement of the laws in regard to damages, the better organization of the courts, the unlimited publicity with the help of the press, this privilege, as a general thing, is more useful for the rogues to slip through the meshes of the law than for men really illegally imprisoned. Such is the influence of time. The high praises bestowed now upon this habeas corpus right are rather suspicious, while in the feudal times of Charles First they were deserved and in place.

"3. No bills of attainder or 'ex post facto' laws shall be passed."

Such bills would realize injustice, but not justice; for the first would allow a judgment to pass without a trial, the latter would make an act criminal which was not criminal when committed. At present an attempt to make such laws would be resented by a general outburst of indignation. It is impossible to carry one through the stages of legislation whether this clause be in the constitution or not.

Such atrocities are past. They are gone with the feudal barons and knights. But in their places have sprung up political financiers, speculators, politicians by trade, etc., whose mischievous schemes to defeat requires the utmost vigilance, and the creation of a new privilege, perhaps, called "habeas pursam," to recover fraudulent taxes, etc.

LETTER XVII.

Negative Provisoes. — Capitation Tax. — Free Commerce and Navigation between States. — Appropriation Laws. — Title of Nobility. — Presents to Officials from Foreign Princes.

Let us go straight through the negative or prohibitive provisoes now.

"4. No capitation or other direct tax shall be laid unless in proportion to the census or enumeration herein before directed to be taken."

A similar provision is contained in the second section of the first article. It is but just.

"5. No tax or duty shall be laid on articles exported from any state."

Export duties are generally unjust. Such a tax would neutralize a main object of our Union, liberty of commerce, and would never be submitted to by our people after they have tasted so long the sweet blessings of liberty in this respect.

"6. No preference shall be given by any regulation of commerce or revenue to the ports of one state over those of another; nor shall vessels bound to, or from one state, be obliged to enter, clear, or pay duties in another."

This is all in harmony with a "perfect union" and the liberty of industry, whose promotion the framers of the constitution had especially in view, in contrast with Europe, where the reverse order of things prevailed at the time when the colonies freed themselves.

"7. No money shall be drawn from the treasury but in consequence of appropriations made by law; and a regular statement and amount of the receipts and expenditures of all public money shall be published from time to time."

This is an important proviso. If the appropriations are made only for the necessary national political business, with due regard to economy, no government can be cheaper than ours. But this is actually not the case. The officials in republics are responsible to the people, and under an array of checks, which, by themselves, are well enough. Still, when the checks of all checks, honesty, is wanting, corruption will easier creep in than in monarchies, where the personal interests of the monarch and the security of his dynasty make it imperative to him to control the finances strictly. It is the general opinion at present, that our public affairs in Congress, states, and their subdivisions, are managed too expensively or not honestly. If true, it is not owing to the constitution.

"8. No title of nobility shall be granted by the United States: and no person holding any office of profit or trust under them shall, without the consent of the Congress, accept of any present, emolument, office, or title of any kind whatever, from any king, prince, or foreign state."

This whole section is truly American, and entirely anti-European. But it is so just, time has sanctioned and approved those provisions it contains so universally—their aim and principles are so well appreciated by mankind—that even strong monarchical governments are forced by public opinion to respect them. Still, monarchs and their courts can not well exist without titles of nobility, badges, orders, and the like. The reacting effect of our simple free institutions would be more powerful, even in this regard, if our public affairs were managed with more Washingtonian honesty and dignity. To promote both, high salaries are far less commendable than integrity, and a strict vigilance of the people in regard to the business in public trust. Self-governing people must above all try to do themselves what they conveniently can. If our government is, indeed, a mere hazardous experiment as some, especially Europeans, say, it is time to undeceive them.

LETTER XVIII.

Checks upon State Legislation in regard to Treaties. — Alliance. — Money of Metal and Paper. — Attainder. — Ex-post-facto Laws. — Contracts. — Nobility. — English Banking. — State Banks. — Merchants make their own Paper Money. — Clearinghouses. — Political Defaulters. — Homes, where best.

We come now to a section containing checks upon the state governments, to prevent them from meddling with political business not belonging to their sphere. You will readily appreciate the propriety of it.

SECTION X.

"1. No state shall enter into any treaty, alliance, or confederation, grant letters of marque and reprisal, coin money, emit bills of credit, make anything but gold and silver coin a tender in payment of debts, pass any bill of attainder, ex-post-facto law, or law impairing the obligation of contracts, or grant any title of nobility."

The objects mentioned here are either reserved for Congress (as treaties, coining of money, etc.), or are generally unjust and inadmissible in a society politically well organized. The prohibition of state bills of credit, or state paper-money, redeemable at a future day by the states, is necessary to prevent the embarrassment of the national finances and general circulation. At the time of writing the constitution there existed a flood of such depreciated state paper-money, causing much inconvenience in commerce, and ruin. Some say that bank paper-money put into circulation upon state authority is also prohibited by this clause. It will most certainly cause the same disastrous effects of state bills of credit, if irredeemable and not readily convertible into gold and silver. Those in favor of the English banking system succeeded under the plea that the people like paper money and are in need of it, in maintaining it thus far. The state bank system has been made a party issue. What influence it has upon the solidity of commerce, foreign importations, the prices of all things, the home industry, the circulation of coined money, mercantile crisis, and the national finances in general, is not easy to ascertain. Congress has not, as yet, interfered with the bank paper-money circulated on state authority. If it should, then the matter will be thoroughly sifted.

So much is true, that merchants, as a class, are not in need of bank paper-money; because they everywhere make their own paper money, called drafts, notes, checks. According to the statistics of clearinghouses and bankers, mercantile business amounting to fifteen millions is settled or balanced with the help of about one million of specie money. *The best and most solid bankers and banks decline to have anything to do with emitting paper money.*

Laws impairing the validity of contracts are the acme of injustice. States or their courts have to enforce contracts, if needful, but not to help break them. On this account states should never be defaulters. We have, alas! good grounds for complaint against several of our state governments for such faithless, dishonest conduct. Swindling corporations and associations follow in their wake. By it they undermine public morals, impair the state authority, encourage fraud, and promote injustice and general embarrassments. Women should consider well before consenting to a home in a state or city which has been a defaulter.

LETTER XIX.

Honesty. — Checks upon State Legislation in regard to Imports, Duties, Exports (under control of Congress), Tonnage, Soldiers, Navy, Treaties, War. — German National Congress at Frankfort. — Greek Confederations. —United States and States separate Business Concerns. — Wicked Men. — Well-informed Women.

Honesty is the best policy also for states. Let us see what is further forbidden-ground for the states.

"2. No state shall, without the consent of the Congress, lay imposts or duties on imports or exports, except what may be absolutely necessary for executing its inspection laws; and the net produce of all duties and imports laid by any state on imports and exports, shall be for the use of the treasury of the United States; and all such laws shall be subject to the revision and control of the Congress."

The restrictions laid upon the state governments in this clause are necessary consequences of the Union and the establishment of a national government, and are required for the protection of the liberty of industry. The different agents of our public affairs should scrupulously avoid any violation of their trusts or powers. Thus only will they command the respect of the citizens; because these submit themselves cheerfully to the laws, and respect obediently the public authorities, if they are executing the laws faithfully and honestly. It is plain that there can be only one sort of imposts or customs; otherwise the same article might be taxed by each state, and its whole value soon absorbed by taxation. Something like this has existed in European countries, and may still take place under the name of excise, octroi, etc. Our state governments are thus forced to resort to direct taxation, which, in its turn, obliges them to be economical, if they are not allowed to borrow money.

"3. No state shall, without the consent of Congress, lay any duty of tonnage, keep troops or ships-of-war in time of peace, enter into any agreement or compact with another state, or with a foreign power, or engage in war, unless actually invaded, or in such imminent danger as will not admit of delay."

If state governments were allowed to keep troops, Congress would be under the necessity of having constantly an overwhelming force to keep the state governments with their troops at bay. When, in 1848, the German national Congress at Frankfort had debated and resolved awhile without an executive force at their disposal, the state governments, tired of their debates, marshalled their armies, dissolved this Congress, and made an end of German national unity. A similar destiny awaited the ancient Greek confederations. This would also happen in the United States under similar circumstances. Without a strict adherence to the provisions of this clause, the United States would be Europe to-morrow. No state, as such, has a right to control Congress, or to exercise any authority under the general constitution. No state tribunal has a right to interfere with the seizures of property made by federal revenue-officers in conformity with the laws of Congress. State laws have no operation upon the rights or contracts of the United States. The United States and the states are throughout to be considered as entirely separate business concerns. The governments of Great Britain and France can not be more distinctly separated from each other than the federal government from the state governments. All resolves and acts of the state legislature or executive, all propositions and recommendations in messages of our state governors on business belonging to Congress are improper, unconstitutional, and entirely gratuitous, betraying a meddlesome spirit and very little appreciation and knowledge of our political system and organic law.

If all governments would aim at nothing but the realization of justice, never meddle with any business which is not strictly political, and never interfere with each others' affairs, a serious misunderstanding among those public business concerns would be as little possible as a misunderstanding between two neighboring farmers or merchants, if they act upon the same plan, that is, mind their own business. However, for plotting and intriguing men, there is, alas! no help in laws, though made by a hundred Washingtons; none in compromises or treaties, though written with the blood of millions of patriots. Those wicked men are the cause of the complaints about the complication of our political system and machinery.

Well-informed women can here do much good for society. While they are excluded from direct participation in the public affairs, they may cultivate harmony and promote the interests of the country the more surely. If they are not Viragos — would that there were none in the United States, even to promote the temperance fanaticism by violence — they may wield the social balance of power.

I do not flatter; you, my daughters, know me too well in this respect. Make, then, a good use of your real woman's rights: there are bogus woman's rights abroad.

LETTER XX.

Executive. — President. — Vice-President. — Their Election. — Term of Four Years. — No Titles. — Santa Anna. — Vulgar Political Papers. — Respect of Public Officers. — English Grumbling. — Second Term. — Swiss Presidential Election.

We have now to examine a few simple provisions concerning our president or executive. Laws require execution. It is wise to separate this business from the legislative; it may then be done more considerately and effectively, the patronage and power which public business produces divided, and a wholesome mutual check created between the great branches of the government.

ARTICLE II.

Of the Executive.

SECTION I.

"1. The executive power shall be vested in a president of the United States of America. He shall hold his office during the term of four years, and, together with the vice-president, chosen for the same term, be elected as follows:—"

An office which is merely ministerial, that is, has to execute what others have ordained, as that of our president, is better filled by one head than by several. Our federal laws are discussed or enacted by a college or assembly, with the help of committees, and executed by one responsible man, in Greek called a monarch. This brings unity, energy, and precision in this business. That ambition may not creep in and spoil the man and business, he serves only four years, and therefore must be elected. The simplicity and business-like character of our constitution appear pre-eminent in omitting all titles, in this instance also. There was no example of such a singleness on earth, when this constitution was set up. Our next door neighbors have not learned from this constitution, otherwise Santa Anna would not have assumed the title of highness.

Still, our president has just the same business to perform about which kings and emperors make so much ado for nothing. While we are not given to empty titles, we should, however, not deny the president, the elected responsible head of our federal government, his due respect. I know that you, my daughters, and a great many of your sex, do not like the political papers on account of their systematic vulgar attacks on the president and other officers, just as if they were the common mark for the missiles of malice and bad taste. A public officer who is not respected, is without real authority. Englishmen have good reason to grumble, and if they please, ridicule their obsolete feudal state-affairs and wigged officials; but is there any thing obsolete or ridiculous in our political system? As long as our president acts constitutionally, and as well as he is able to do, with the help of his numerous advisers, he deserves general respect. The licentious vulgar press corrupts the taste of the masses, and is the cause of villany and mob violence.

According to the wording of this clause, the president shall hold his office during the term of four years only. Washington, and several other presidents, have been elected for a second term. With the increase of the population, the parties have gained strength. Party influence may now be coveted by a president in favor of his re-election. At present, Washington would not have consented to a re-election. This is the cause why some wish that the absolute one-term system, either of four or six years may be adopted. The constitution being silent about a second term, or re-election, we have to understand it as being in favor of one absolute term, which, no doubt, is right; for if not, one person may as well, from four years to four years, be re-elected to the end of his life.

The Swiss, probably to avoid the excitement which accompanies our presidential elections, have, in their new constitution of 1848, (a good imitation of ours,) made the heads of the departments elective, who then chose one of their number as president. This, however, is against the principle which serves as a guide in appointing officials. Those who act merely as clerks, and not as representatives of the government, should never be elected. Our constitution is, in this regard, perfect, and has been, thus far, misunderstood by the Swiss.

LETTER XXI.

Electors. — How Chosen. — Qualification of Presidential Candidates.

THE constitution disposes further :—

"2. Each state shall appoint, in such manner as the legislature thereof may direct, a number of electors, equal to the whole number of senators and representatives to which the state may be entitled in the Congress; but no senator or representative, or person holding an office of trust or profit under the United States, shall be appointed an elector."

"3. [As amended.] The electors shall meet in their respective states, and vote by ballot for president and vice-president, one of whom, at least, shall not be an inhabitant of the same state with themselves; they shall name in their ballots the person voted for as president, and in distinct ballots the person voted for as vice-president, and they shall make distinct lists of all persons voted for as president, and of all persons voted for as vice-president, and of the number of votes for each, which lists they shall sign and certify, and transmit sealed to the seat of the government of the United States, directed to the president of the senate; the president of the senate shall, in the presence of the senate and house of representatives, open all the certificates, and the votes shall then be counted; the person having the greatest number of votes for president shall be the president, if such number be a majority of the whole number of electors appointed; and if no person have such majority, then from the persons having the highest numbers, not exceeding three, on the list of those voted for as president, the house of representatives shall choose immediately, by ballot, the president; but in choosing the president, the votes shall be taken by states, the representation from each state having one vote; a quorum for this purpose shall consist of a member or members from two thirds of the states, and a majority of all the states shall be necessary to a choice; and if the house of representatives shall not choose a president, whenever the right of choice shall devolve upon them, before the fourth day of March next following, then the vice-president shall act as president, as in the case of the death or other constitutional disability of the president. The person having the greatest number of votes as vice-president, shall be the vice-president, if such a number be a majority of the whole number of electors appointed, and if no person have a majority, then from the two highest numbers on the list the senate shall choose the vice-president; a quorum for the purpose shall consist of two thirds of the whole number of senators, and a majority of the whole number shall be necessary to a choice. But no persons constitutionally ineligible to the office of president shall be eligible to that of vice-president of the United States."

This is all plain. Still the action of the electors is forestalled by the parties, which are now better organized than at the outset of the federal government. They preconcert the legal elections, and propose the candidates, so that the activity of the presidential electors is in the main a mere form, for the loyalty to party forbids the electors to make a change in their creed or policy.

"4. The Congress may determine the time of choosing the electors, and the day on which they shall give their votes, which day shall be the same throughout the United States."

This arrangement is calculated to prevent fraud, at present the vote is to be cast throughout the United States on the first Tuesday of November.

"5. No person except a natural born citizen, or a citizen of the United States at the time of the adoption of this constitution, shall be eligible to the office of president, neither shall any person be eligible to that office who shall not have attained to the age of thirty-five years, and been fourteen years a resident within the United States."

It is considered unquestionable that the chief executive officer should be a citizen of the United States, and a native. There never has been a president elected younger than forty years. Mr. Pierce was forty-nine years old when elected, and so was Mr. Polk; all other presidents were over fifty, and some over sixty years old at the time of election. The fire and ambition of youth is little suitable for an office like that of our president. He must be a tried man, otherwise he will either not bear the burdens of this office, or become a mere instrument in the hands of designing men. This, according to the results of the elections, people seem to appreciate well.

LETTER XXII.

Presidents advanced in Age. — Mrs. Phelps. — Mrs. Strickland. — Mrs. Willard. — Mrs. Howe. — Mrs. Hale. — Presidential Vacancy. — Acting President. — Non-election. — Salary. — Honesty of the American Presidents. — Oath. — Spirit of Urbanity.

It is, perhaps, superfluous to mention, that although a citizen, thirty-five years old, is eligible as president, there never has been so young a man elected. Our presidents were, as you know from history, all advanced in age, a proof that people are well aware that business experience, and knowledge of the world are, besides honesty and common sense, indispensable qualities of a president of the United States. I should have inclosed this remark as a P. S., in my last letter, but did not prefer to imitate here your letter fashion, my daughters, much as I admire letters written by ladies, for they alone understand well how to write them. I have waited long enough for letters on the constitution from a Mrs. Phelps, Mrs. Strickland, Mrs. Willard, Mrs. Howe, or Mrs. Hale, but think the time has now come to try my skill. Let me then go on:—

"6. In case of the removal of the president from office, or of his death, resignation, or inability to discharge the powers and duties of the said office, the same shall devolve on the vice-president, and the Congress may by law provide for the case of removal, death, resignation, or inability, both of the president and vice-president, declaring what officer shall then act as president, and such officer shall act accordingly, until the disability be removed, or a president shall be elected."

In this regard, the law is that the intermediate president of the senate, or the speaker of the house of representatives, shall be president. In regard to non-election, the constitution is silent. But the law is just, and required for the preservation of the Union, and the regular management of the public business.

"7. The president shall, at stated times, receive for his services, a compensation, which shall neither be increased nor diminished during the period for which he shall have been elected, and he shall not receive within that period any other emolument from the United States, or any of them."

The salary of the president is twenty-five thousand dollars, and that of the vice-president eight thousand dollars per annum. In spite of the peculiar liberty especially enjoyed by the opposition party of showering clouds of calumnies daily upon this functionary, there is no instance on record that one of our presidents has abused his station to accumulate money from spurious resources. Some of them died poor. They were among the best of men.

"8. Before he enters on the execution of his office, he shall take the following oath or affirmation :—

"I do solemnly swear, (or affirm,) that I will faithfully execute the office of president of the United States, and will, to the best of my ability, preserve, protect, and defend the constitution of the United States."

You will notice with great pleasure that the form of this oath or affirmation is made acceptable to the members of whatever denomination or confession.

The spirit of urbanity and liberality breathing through this organic law is not so much appreciated at home as it deserves. What true and noble humanity filled the mind and heart of those who framed it. It stands still alone among and above the numerous constitutions since made in Europe and America.

I feel happy to be at the head of a family, whose members, without exception, feel thankful to the great and good men who devised the constitution.

LETTER XXIII.

Presidential Functions. — Commander-in-chief of the Army and Navy and Militia. — Opinions of the Heads of the Departments. — Reprieves. — Pardons. — The Union a Government, no League. — Prompt Protection analogous to Police. — State Governors Commanders-in-chief. — Treaties. — Consent of two-thirds of the Senate. — Jefferson. — Hamilton. — Removal from Office. — Treaty with France. — French and English Alliance. — Slave Treaty. — Vacancies.

We shall now hear something about the proper business of the president.

SECTION II.

"1. The president shall be commander-in-chief of the army and navy of the United States, and of the militia of the several states when called into the actual service of the United States; he may require the opinion, in writing, of the principal officer in each of the executive departments, upon any subject relating to the duties of their respective offices, and he shall have power to grant reprieves and pardons for offences against the United States, except in cases of impeachment."

This is plain without comment. The phraseology of the first part of this clause seems to pre-suppose a United States army separate from the militia. If so, our little army is all right. As matters are now, it seems that we can not much longer enjoy our civil liberty without an army of the United States, because we are fond now of enforcing our will with weapons, instead of confiding to the ballot-box. Look at Kansas, California, etc. He who is at the head of the executive must be commander-in-chief of the forces subservient to the executive. The second clause pre-supposes different executive departments, as of war, navy, treasury, state, interior, with proper heads, as advisers of the president.

Our Union being constituted as a government, and not as a mere league, the executive acts, in all cases belonging to its sphere, analogous to the usual state executives, police included. Should foreign nations attack our territory, molest our citizens when travelling abroad, or stop and destroy our ships on the oceans, in all such cases it is the duty of the executive to defend our interests, rights, and honor, with all disposable means at hand, without waiting for legislative action, because, for this purpose, we have executives. They are instituted parts of the government, acting within their sphere independently. The state constitutions make their governors commanders-in-chief of the militia, and navy too, which, if it refers to war, seems to clash with this section, in some respect at least.

"2. He shall have power, by and with the advice and consent of the senate, to make treaties, provided two-thirds of the senators present concur; and he shall nominate, and by and with the advice and consent of the senate, shall appoint ambassadors, other public ministers and consuls, judges of the supreme court, and all other officers of the United States whose appointments are not herein otherwise provided for, and which shall be established by law; but the congress may by law vest the appointment of such inferior officers as they think proper in the president alone, in the courts of law, or in the heads of departments.

Instead of a separate council, as in Great Britain, the constitution designates the senate as the adviser of the president, in certain instances. Our history shows what importance has been given to the heads of departments, as for example, under General Washington's presidency on the National bank question. Jefferson, then secretary of state, was against such a bank, Hamilton, secretary of the treasury, in favor of one. The first became thus the patron of the democrats, the second that of the whigs. And ever since, the local partisans respectively oppose or approve of such a bank, because Jefferson was against and Hamilton for it. The executive concurrent activity of the senate is, fortunately, not so distinctly apparent. The president, not the heads of the departments, is responsible for his official acts. In monarchies, the prince is not responsible, but the heads of the departments. When the better performance of the public affairs require it, the president may delegate his authority, namely, in time of war.

The pardoning power can properly be exercised only by the executive, because it has directly nothing to do with the law and sentence. As the laws of procedure are at present, indeed, more in favor of the accused than of society or the accuser, it should hardly ever be exercised, because it invariably interferes with established justice and the judiciary. This pardoning power is a different thing in monarchies, where the laws are made more in favor of the king and state than the accused. The advice of the senate divides or lessens the responsibility of the president.

A treaty is a compact made by nations through their governments. It would have been an anomaly to give the treaty power to the executive exclusively, while all our laws are made by an assemblage of legislators; hence, the advice and consent of the senate. The house of representatives has nothing to do with treaties, but may be required to enact in consequence of treaties financial laws, without giving them the right to alter such treaties. President and senate appoint diplomatic and other public officers, without concurrence of the house. The clause is well devised. The small branch of the legislature is well adapted for a state council. The appointing power includes the removing power; it is lodged with the president according to a sound doctrine, for the constitution is silent on it. If the concurrence of the senate was required for a removal from office, this part of the responsible office of the president would or could be surrounded with vexatious delays, obnoxious to the public service. To trouble the senate with advising about the appointment of postmasters, and the like officials, would be superfluous, because a refusal would be probably resented by a delay in nominating. Engagements for offices in state or private relations, depends much upon personal acquaintance, qualifications, and inclination of favor. The president must be at liberty to appoint officials who correspond with these requisites. This is the custom everywhere.

If a convention or treaty with a foreign government concerns a certain business, the first ceases when the latter has been achieved. The French government found it in its interest from national jealousy, to support the American colonies in their struggle for independence against England, and entered into a treaty with them about it, with this struggle terminated the treaty. There is nothing entangling in such special arrangements, just as little as in a mutual support of neighbors in case of a conflagration. But a treaty like that known under the name of Bulwer and Clayton treaty, which stipulates that the Isthmus shall remain for ever as it is, and neither occupied by ourselves nor the English, anticipates business, events, and changes, over which we must have free control at all times, and is, therefore, eminently entangling and undiplomatic. Turkey was wantonly attacked by the Czar; France and England allied themselves to help the aggressed. This successfully done, according to sound doctrine, the alliance should cease. If it is prolonged by intrigue, one of the parties will feel the consequence of the blunder in season.

Our government entered into a treaty with England, France, Spain, etc., to stop the slave-trade in Africa, by keeping the coast blockaded for this purpose. While we keep watch on the coast, the English, French, and Spaniards, carry on the trade under another name, or indirectly. Such a treaty is false diplomacy. Its object ought to be reached at home. With the import of slaves ceases the export alone.

"3. The president shall have power to fill up all vacancies that may happen during the recess of the senate, by granting commissions which shall expire at the end of their next session."

The business order requires such a proviso. If a temporary officer should be rejected by the senate, justice and propriety, or comity, require that the president should not appoint him again during the recess of the senate. If he does—the constitution does not distinctly forbid it—the house of representatives, keeping the purse-strings, may withhold the appropriation, and thus dispose the president to agree with the senate. It is the practice that the president can not create the office of minister during the recess of the senate without its consent.

So far as I am acquainted with the business connection between our presidents and the senate, it has always been of a friendly character. Why should it be otherwise under such a constitution?

LETTER XXIV.

Messages. — Ambassadors. — Commissions. — Chateaubriand. — Impeachment of President, Vice-President, and other Officers, for Treason, Bribery, or other high Crimes and Misdemeanors. — Pensions.

SOON we shall have done with our mighty president and then turn a new leaf, and make acquaintance with the grave federal judiciary.

SECTION III.

"1. He shall, from time to time, give to the Congress information of the state of the Union, and recommend to their consideration such measures as he shall judge necessary and expedient; he may, on extraordinary occasions, convene both houses, or either of them, and in case of disagreement between them, with respect to the time of adjournment, he may adjourn them to such time as he shall think proper; he shall receive ambassadors and other public ministers; he shall take care that the laws be faithfully executed, and shall commission all the officers of the United States."

The custom of written messages originated with President Jefferson. It affords a timely opportunity to lay down a certain plan for legislative action, based upon necessity, business experience, and principles, necessary for large legislative bodies, whose members, too often, bring but vague notions about the constitutional public business to Washington and other capitols. These messages and the reports of the chief heads of the departments are considered our most valuable papers. They best prove the abilities which have managed our public affairs. In return, Congress has the right to call, at any time, for information and executive documents.

He receives ambassadors, dismisses, or rejects them too, as he sees proper. The care that the laws be faithfully executed would be a useless phrase without the power of instantaneous removal in the case of malpractice.

Many of these ministerial provisoes, adapted to present usages are subject to the reforming influence of time. If the government should prefer to appoint only consuls, and dispense with ambassadors entirely, as, indeed, superfluous in a good political system, according to the opinion of the latė ambassador, Count Chateaubriand, who said, "le tems des ambassades est passé et celui des consulates arrivé," our constitution would not be against the adopting of such reforms.

SECTION IV.

"1. The president, vice-president, and all civil officers of the United States, shall be removed from office on impeachment for, and conviction of treason, bribery, or other high crimes and misdemeanors."

This clause does not exclude or prohibit removals on other grounds—and thus ends the article which makes our four years king.

Salaries and pensions are an important item in our age, where every man of a little wit strives to make a fortune as fast as possible. Civilians and soldiers also love to accumulate. Good services ought to be adequately remunerated, either by fees or annual salaries. The first are prescribed, in regard to the latter the rule is, that they preclude all fees and extras for office outlays, travelling, etc., if not expressly reserved. There are a number of offices which require very little regular office attention, and are honorable and influential, which should be therefore unsalaried. All town (mayor) and county (overseer) executives belong to this class. The occupiers should imitate the example of Washington, who never accepted a salary, but only his outlays restituted; mere ambitious speculators would be thus kept off, and retired citizens of standing induced to devote their time to such functions. The English fashion of allowing high and low aristocratic lazy officials to appoint deputies, who do their work, should be discarded with us, because it produces sinecures and an inclination to extort.

Is it impossible to organize the common defence of our Union without the help of the European pension system? We have no standing army in the proper European sense of the word, but only some troops to guard the forts and boundaries, who are comparatively well paid. We pay per head over one thousand dollars, while Great Britain pays about four hundred dollars, France, one hundred and fifty dollars, Austria, one hundred and ten dollars, and Russia eighty dollars, army and naval expenses. To keep the large armies in Europe in such pay as ours, would exhaust the resources of the wealthiest nation at once. Therefore they make their use of pensions, orders, badges of nobility, certain offices reserved by law for soldiers out of service, etc., to make it acceptable and popular. Moreover, the princes, when fighting against each other, to promote their interests and that of the aristocracy and opium dealers, make their soldiers believe they fight for civilization and Christianity. *En passant*, it must puzzle the government in London, fighting for civilization and Christianity, when General Outram, after the occupation of Lucknow, declared in a public proclamation to the people of Oude, that the government had not the least idea of making war against the religion of the Hindoos! Again, while we have nothing to do with such things, is it, I ask, impossible to provide for the common defence of this home of the proud freemen of America, without the pension system, invented by European princes of the school of Machiavelli, to keep standing armies, that is, human machines without whose prop their thrones would fare like that of the king of Oude?

I wish we could, for soon will civil pensions in the Union and states become fashionable too. There would then be a degrading, corrupting precedent, less in the country.

LETTER XXV.

Officers, their desire to earn Money like the rest. — Parties kept together by monied interest. — Majority in Elections. — Right to the Spoils. — Opposition to the Party in Power. — Court Favor in Monarchies. — Election Expenses. — Difficulties in filling Offices. — Catherine de Medicis. — Chancellor Hopital. — Selling of Offices. — Swiss sell Offices. — Self-government curtails Offices. — Paul. — Parties outside the Constitution. — Platforms. — Logrolling. — Party should cease in Congress when sworn in. — Presidential Patronage. — Political Martyrs a Nuisance. — Factitious Speaking. — Demagogues.—American Women. — Benjamin Franklin. — Office-seeking.

Before we part with the chief of our Union, the successor of Washington, I must write a word or two more on his business. It is his duty to appoint a large number of officers, who must be paid for services. These, naturally, are as fond of making money as the rest of us. Liberty of industry produces industrious, speculative, perseveringly accumulative business men. Wholesome and well-executed laws make man trusty, generous in credit, giving, expansive, and associative. Despotic and arbitrary governments, on the other hand, cripple this spirit in man, make him sly, beggarly, distrustful, hoarding, in one word—Chinese. We should then not expect that our officers to be less speculative than the rest, nor should we grumble if many are eager to get an office. This desire for office and money is the sole cause of parties, and the glue that makes them cohere or stick together. Principles never do such things, for there seldom agree two men about one. But about an office, with a good salary, thousands may have the same opinion and sharp appetite. To get at the offices in our republic we must be in the majority; to get that we must organize or join a party. When one party has succeeded to be in the majority in the presidential election, it has, as the phrase is, a right to the spoils—that is, offices, salaries, emoluments, etc.; because it is the custom that the president of the victorious party elects among his party friends the officers for the offices in his gift. This, however, is the reacting cause, why, from that moment, the party left in the minority, and, of course, out of office, rallies and strains every nerve to recover the lost fleshpots—of course, an impossible thing without clubbing and party organization. This is natural. It is the same in Europe with one great difference, that the party in power is permanent; because the chief of a monarchical government is hereditary, and retains therefore loyal officers for life, while others, not loyal, never can get any office at all. There is, of course, little excitement about office. Court favor takes the place of party. There are no election expenses—which often amount with us to considerable sums, as ten per cent of the salaries and more. They are one of the causes of raising the salaries of late. The charges of the political brokers, I mentioned in another letter, are now much higher than previously.

In republics and monarchies prevails the same difficulty about the filling of offices with the right men. One of the best French statesmen, Mr. Hopital, chancellor under the profligate Catherine de Medicis, preferred the selling or farming out of the offices, to deprive the vicious court of the occasion to fill them with its creatures. In several Swiss cantons the same policy has been adopted to preclude hungry office-seekers, and stop their hunting for office.

The best help promises self-government, self-control in this difficulty. If each is his own governor in the right direction, he, of course, needs none to govern him. St. Paul understood this perfectly well. Virtue and godliness makes man free, self-governing, independent. No doubt about that, my children.

I remarked, in another place, that our parties are outside the pale of the constitutions; they are ignored by them; they can not alter the constitutions. Their platforms, promises, resolves, stump speeches, etc., at election times, have merely an eye upon the majority, which promises offices, salaries, jobs, etc. They may exercise a great influence upon the making of laws and their execution, if the officials are partial, unmindful of their obligation and office oaths, and winking at partisan iniquity. Logrolling laws are inseparable from spurious political business.

LETTER XXVI.

Judiciary. — Supreme Court. — Inferior Courts. — Salaries. — Appointed during Good Behavior. — Judiciary a Product of State. — Elective Judges inclining to favor Mobism. — Public Morals under an Elective Judiciary.

As there is a necessity of distributing some kinds of judicial business among certain districts, called towns, counties, etc., so there is a necessity of giving a certain class of quarrels and disputes and crimes to Congress to settle them according to the laws. Also, the courts established by Congress have nothing to do with ideal justice or with the realization of moral problems, but only to execute the laws, or to decide what is right or wrong. These laws may be sometimes repugnant to the feelings: still, if they are enacted by the legislative bodies in due form, they must be executed and obeyed as long as they are valid. What kind of judicial business shall belong to Congress you will learn by the following:—

ARTICLE III.

Of the Judiciary.

SECTION I.

"1. The judicial power of the United States shall be vested in one supreme court, and in such inferior courts as the Congress may from time to time ordain and establish. The judges, both of the supreme and inferior courts, shall hold their offices during good behavior, and shall, at stated times, receive for their services a compensation, which shall not be diminished during their continuance in office."

This is the third branch of the institution called federal government or government of the United States. We have seen that the president appoints these judges with the advice and consent of the senate, which is sound doctrine, because the judiciary is the product of the state institution, and not of society. It is against the well-understood principles of politics to make the judiciary dependent upon popular elections. The federal constitution is in this regard not so well appreciated at home as it ought to be. The truth is, people are in need of justice, and erect for this purpose an institution called state, with a constitution. Out of this institution comes the judiciary, in order to make it entirely independent of the people, of whose acts and deeds and obligations it shall judge. It is a state right or duty of government to provide a judiciary; because the principal aim of this institution is the realization of justice, which most of the people who come in business contact with the judiciary do not like at all. Public morals will unavoidably come to a low ebb in states where the judiciary is elective. The constitution creates the United States supreme court, but leaves it wisely to Congress to organize it and the needful inferior courts, according to time and circumstances. The supreme court held at Washington is the highest legal authority. It construes and adjudges the constitution and the laws of the United States supremely. What belongs to the laws of nations comes under the sole cognizance of this tribunal. It has ever borne a noble character and enjoyed universal confidence in the United States and abroad.

Some complain that transactions before this court are too expensive and too long protracted. This is applicable to all courts organized after the English fashion; because they act not under strict codes of procedure, but under their own rules. Still, it is in the nature of cases coming under the jurisdiction of this court that they are complicated and therefore time-absorbing.

The appointment of the judges during good behavior should be also the rule for the municipal judges.

LETTER XXVII.

National Judicial Business. — Court of Claims. — Checks upon State Wars.

LET us continue our reading.

SECTION II.

"1. The judicial power shall extend to all cases in law and equity arising under this constitution, the laws of the United States, and treaties made, or which shall be made under their authority; to all cases affecting ambassadors other public ministers, and consuls; to all cases of admiralty and maritime jurisdiction; to controversies to which the United States shall be a party; to controversies between two or more states; between a state and citizens of another state; between citizens of different states; between citizens of the same state claiming lands under grants of different states, and between a state or the citizens thereof, and foreign states, citizens, or subjects."

From this array of business which belongs to the competency of the supreme court, claims against a state by citizens of another state, or by citizens or subjects of any foreign state, according to the eleventh amendment to the constitution, are excluded, because such claims do not partake of the character of national affairs, inasmuch as a state when sued takes the place of a private person or corporation. But it is desirable that provision should be made for a court adjudging such controversies, wherein the state is defendant, as a substitute for the mere pleasure of the legislature in such instances. Congress has felt the necessity of such a court and created the United States court of claims, which should be a real independent court, and not a mere committee, as it stands at present. Neither the supreme court nor the lower tribunals are above law, but only the interpreters in regard to the final meaning of the law, without willing anything. This is a power inherent to all courts.

It has been maintained that a state can not be sued by a private person, because it is inherent in the nature of "sovereignty" not to be amenable to any private person. This may hold good in Europe, but even there not generally, because the continental governments have designated by law certain courts before which claims raised against them or their treasuries, and refused, may be tried like all other claims. Even in Great Britain, which is in all these things much behind time, the chancellor has some authority to decide on such claims. A monarch, called sovereign—a thing we have not—who pretends that he got by the grace of God the right to manage the political affairs of the people as his property, is very likely to pretend, too, that he can never do wrong, and, of course, can not afford to be sued. Our governments have nothing in common with this specious doctrine. They are agents, and when they, as such, bind the state, the state must suffer to be sued like other bound people who refuse to fulfil their obligations.

This section makes the supreme court the arbiter between independent states; and this eminently-wise arrangement is the reason that there can not be from any cause, however provoking, a war between the several states. Yes, my dear children, fond as some of the male gender are of fighting, there can be no war between Massachusetts and South Carolina, or between Michigan and Ohio, or California and Oregon. The supreme court is the arbiter in all our more or less wicked state-troubles. What an inestimable blessing, then, is our Union for a large branch of the human family! Where is the like? Without this constitutional guaranty of peace there would be eternal fighting between our parties. Hence the opinions and decisions of the supreme court are cheerfully considered as entirely conclusive and final by the people.

The house of representatives excels in such speculative or log-rolling law propositions, against which most of the presidents have battled with their vetoes successfully. It is significant that the same popular branch of Congress is indifferent in regard to laws which bear upon the better administration of justice, as the adjustment of claims, regulation of the territories, etc. Large legislative bodies seldom answer to their real purpose. The members of the legislative bodies who transact the national business from mere party views, violate their constitutional duty and oath. Party may help one to a seat in Congress, but when sworn in party influence should cease.

The patronage of our president amounts, at a general estimation, to eighty odd millions of dollars. There is much attraction

in such a sum. We have not to complain that matters are so. Governments are a necessary evil, required for the lawless and disobedient, or, as a theologian would say, are the result of sin. The burden can only be relieved by self-government. The more of that the less of public business, offices, salaries, taxes, etc.

You see, my children, why we have parties, and will have them as long as there are offices. The rotation in office, promoted by frequent elections, checks the tendency to become hereditary, but increases party virulence. Factions, by trying to enforce their plans and platforms, implicitly admit that they are useless in the ordinary way of political business.

Martyrs for party purposes are a nuisance in the United States, because there is no hinderance to joining or forming parties on principles. If an inconsiderate speaker on party issues gets whipped, he is as guilty as the inconsiderate whipper. A factitious or rebellious speaker commits a glaring contempt of law much more dangerous to society than a mere contempt of a court.

But why write to you, my children, and you, my daughters, especially, on such things? My reasons are, as you may suppose, not to entangle you in party affairs, very commonly but very wrongly called politics, but to show you exactly what they are, that you may be able, in exciting times which grow upon us, to converse understandingly on them and inform your children about them. Further, to explain to you what kind of men those are who make the regular managers of parties, often called politicians by trade, or demagogues; and to show what real difference there is between public and private life, and how speculations in offices may turn out to be visionary and often ruinous to families.

If I succeed in that, I shall feel myself well rewarded. The American women should be in public affairs what the senate is to the president, friendly counsels to their husbands and sons. Those may, in the end, if meritorious, as certainly be called to offices of trust as Benjamin Franklin, who never had anything to do with party on this account, and was almost constantly in the service of his country.

LETTER XXVIII.

National original Jurisdiction. — Appellate Jurisdiction. — Sovereign scruples. — Jurisdiction makes no Subjects. — Jury Trial of Crimes. — Place of Trial. — Abolitionists. — Magna Charta. — Runneymede.

THE constitution farther ordains:—

"2. In all cases affecting ambassadors, other public ministers, and consuls, and those in which a state shall be party, the supreme court shall have original jurisdiction. In all the other cases before mentioned, the supreme court shall have appellate jurisdiction, both as to law and fact, with such exceptions, and under such regulations as the Congress shall make."

This clause places consuls and ambassadors justly on the same legal footing, and designates the supreme court as one of original jurisdiction, that is, of the first resort. Some say that this provision brings the states within the sovereignty of the Union, but this is not the fact, because lawsuits do not alter stations, they merely refer to doubtful obligations or the right or wrong of a case, and the bearing of the laws upon it. The dubious case alone goes to the decision of the supreme court and not the state or government. The word sovereignty, obsolete with us and not occurring in this constitution, irritates unnecessarily the feelings of zealous state-rights champions and partisans, who make political capital out of it. Jurisdiction makes no subjects, but means only the authority given to a court over certain civil and criminal cases in a certain district. There is no court for a man who shuns lawsuits and evil deeds.

"3. The trials of all crimes, except in cases of impeachment, shall be by jury, and such trial shall be held in the state where the said crimes shall have been committed; but when not committed within any state, the trial shall be at such place or places as the Congress may by law have directed."

This clause, together with two amendments, which you will find annexed to the constitution, but do not properly belong to it, ordains that in crimes committed against the laws of the United States, a trial by jury shall take place, just as in all other trials of crimes committed against state laws. This clause has been unjustly misapplied by the abolitionists for party purposes. There is a clause in the constitution to which I shall devote a separate letter on account of its celebrity in the annals of our political parties, which ordains that fugitives from service shall be delivered up to him who justly claims them. The Congressional law based upon this clause, does not prescribe an indictment or trial by jury, usual in crimes, but a simple ministerial or clerical examination of the claim, to prove the identity of the claimed fugitive servant, whereupon the return of the same is ordered, or, in the reverse case, the fugitive is free. And this, the law commonly called the fugitive slave law, very properly ordains—because there is no crime at all in question, but a mere breach of an obligation which all over the world is treated as a mere police or civil case. Your servants do not commit a crime when taking French leave from your house. But the abolitionist party objects to this procedure, as depriving the fugitive from labor or service of the privilege of the trial by jury, or, in other words, they insist that such a fugitive ought to be indicted and tried like a criminal. Even you, my dear daughters, will discover that behind this partisan manœuvre is hidden the intention to abuse the trial by jury in favor of the guilty party, the fugitive from service, so that of this trial by jury I might repeat the same that I remarked on the habeas corpus privilege that it is apt to be used to relieve the guilty rather than protect the innocent according to law. People at Runneymede, when they had conquered the magna charta from their lordly prince, probably never thought that the privilege of jury trial would be, as our abolitionists do, insisted upon in such instances.

These letters open a deep insight into the administration of established justice, the bulwark of civil liberty. The federal constitution appreciates it well; her framers well knew that state institutions are useless burdens if they do not bring a prompt administration of justice according to law.

But it seems as if the present generation has lost much of the innate sense of justice. A restoration of it can do no harm.

LETTER XXIX.

Treason, no Attainder. — Forfeiture. — Kansas. — Utah. — Madness, its fair play. — Rebellion. — Vigilance Committees. — Major André. — Washington and his Steward. — Justice.

YOU will learn now what the constitution says about treason.

SECTION III.

"1. Treason against the United States shall consist only in levying war against them, or in adhering to their enemies, giving them aid and comfort.

"2. No person shall be convicted of treason unless on the testimony of two witnesses to the same overt act, or on confession in open court.

"3. The Congress shall have power to declare the punishment of treason, but no attainder of treason shall work corruption of blood, or forfeiture, except during the life of the person attainted."

These provisoes are taken from an English statute, whose severe and barbarous features our constitution has obliterated. By the corruption of blood is meant the destruction of all inheritable qualities, so that no one can claim anything from a person attainted, that is, accused, or through him. The war must be actually levied to constitute treason. There never has been a person accused and convicted of treason since the establishment of the constitution, except lately in Kansas and Utah. As we are situated, enjoying as we do the largest amount of natural liberty man may claim, overwhelmed as we are with privileges and arrangements securing freedom, it is madness to resort to brute force in our Union in regard to private or public affairs or offices. But even madness, often the precursor of destruction, will have, now-a-days, fair play. It is party, the madness of the many for the benefit of the few, which only can be capable of treason.

Of course, treason aims a blow at the state institution or government. Rebellion goes not so far — but is an insurrection against lawful authority. Under this category comes the vigilance committee of San Francisco, however necessary its organization may be for the community. Revolution implies a radical change in the government, such one as has been successfully tried by the

North American English colonists. All these movements are symptoms of social diseases. Their main cause is — utter neglect of justice.

Major André, of revolutionary memory, was found guilty of treason, and punished by death, according to law. When General Washington heard that his steward at Mount Vernon had given relief to English troops, he reprimanded him, although he saved, by his comforting the enemies of the country, the home of his noble master from devastation, because he had, in the eyes of Washington, acted rather treasonably. Justice, the first of all virtues, commands: give each his due and injure none. By supporting the English, the steward had injured his country. So thought Washington. His steward thought that he acted prudently and according to circumstances, and, besides, in accordance with the religious precept: "love your enemies." But Washington held that justice, according to law, is first and paramount. And this is perfectly true, also in regard to all moral and religious duties; because without justice there is no real morality, no real charity, no real religion. Without it the practice of religion is in constant peril from the side of ignorance, violence, organized superstition, priestcraft, fanaticism, etc., as the history of our religion sufficiently proves.

Society in the United States has done well enough although governed with a very little regard to established justice. But what would this country be, if our states never had been defaulters, if their governments had administered the affairs strictly according to the constitutions, and set an example of prompt justice, honesty, and fidelity to obligations at home and abroad, if all the courts were always the unflinching executors of the laws and the terror of the abettors of crimes? What startling immorality has been produced by the corruption prevalent in our legislatures! how many families have lost their all by crises, the effects of wanton legislation and mismanagement of our public institutions!

My children, never approve or join a party which has treasonable tendencies against our Union. This is the ardent wish of your affectionate father.

LETTER XXX.

Public Faith. — Natural Rights of Citizens. — Acts. — Records. — States are exclusive. — Clanish Nationalities. — Union Sentiments. — Privileges and Immunities Mutual. — Missouri Compromise. — Fugitives from Justice, their Extradition. — Treaties. — Mutual Control shared by the Women. — Sharpe's Rifles. — Slip-shod Sermons.

We come now to miscellaneous matters incident to and consequent upon the establishment of the United States government.

ARTICLE IV.

Miscellaneous.

SECTION I.

"1. Full faith and credit shall be given in each state to the public acts, records, and judicial proceedings of every other state. And the Congress may, by general laws, prescribe the manner in which such acts, records, and proceedings shall be proved, and the effect thereof."

In consequence of our Union the several states have been stripped of the predicate foreign. And this is, indeed, the only loss these districts or institutions have suffered by it. It is one of the most conspicuous state-rights to be exclusive, foreign. Without our Union, Rhode Island would be a foreign country to Massachusetts, and Connecticut to New York. Our states have lost nothing else by it, rather gained every blessing desirable from state organizations. The laws and acts of foreign nations are not judicially taken notice of by other nations, but must be proved, like other facts, when they come under examination. Thus, without our Union, a marriage contract entered into in Massachusetts would not be conclusive in Georgia, and so vice versa. Our Union has equalized and domesticated our public affairs, they have thus acquired the character of common family affairs. Our Union has done away with those dynastic, clanish, European nationalities; and if, from custom, we speak and write in the European fashion, of a north or south, of a South Carolinian or a New-England man, it proves that neither ocean, nor distance, nor nativity, nor time, nor laws are able to destroy easily old habits. No business whatever, not even bound labor, should have the least biasing influence upon our Union sentiments.

This clause is calculated to endear the Union and strengthen our Union feelings. We shall presently meet more of the same noble, generous, and just nature.

SECTION II.

"1. The citizens of each state shall be entitled to all privileges and immunities of citizens in the several states."

The federal constitution aims at nothing but rational liberty. There is no liberty without order established by certain rules and mutuality. Liberty without order is anarchy, as order and rule without liberty is despotism. Where justice prevails, there is equality of rights before the law.

The clause before you expressly sanctions a just, mutual, equal relation among the citizens. It makes the whole vast realm of the United States one home for their citizens; it excludes all sectional preferences, distinctions, and divisions; it condemns the Mason and Dixon lines, Missouri compromises, etc. As we all have the same citizen rights, so we have the same obligations. We have men in our society with monarchical and tyrannical dispositions, just as there are republicans in monarchies. This inborn tyrannical disposition to enforce our rules and views upon others, who differ from them and prefer to live after their own, is curbed by this clause. It makes it impossible that the United States can be converted into a "societas leonina."

"2. A person charged in any state with treason, felony, or other crime, who shall flee from justice and be found in another state, shall, on demand of the executive authority of the state from which he fled, be delivered up, to be removed to the state having jurisdiction of the crime."

A state being organized for the main purpose of realizing justice, it obviously is one of its first duties to protect society against law-breaking men. To make a state a hiding-place for criminals is a monstrous idea, and diametrically opposed to its nature and purpose. Still the before-mentioned state privilege to be foreign, to have nothing common with other states, necessarily makes them a kind of asylum for criminals. This abominable abuse of the state institution at home has been, at once, destroyed by our Union.

Among foreign states treaties are necessary for this purpose. In regard to foreign states the difficulty consists in their peculiar policy. If they are ruled justly and do not stamp acts as crimes which are not such, and which in other states are, perhaps, laudable deeds, there nobody will fly from justice, except real felons or criminals, of whom alone this clause is treating.

You see, my dear children, what our Union is, and ought to be. Political affairs partake of the twofold nature of all things, that is, they may be managed wisely or foolishly. A strong, irresistible sense of justice, a manly, unwavering execution of the laws as they are, and a watchful eye over our own conduct and that of others, in regard to constitutions and laws, will keep things right. This mutual political control is one of the strongest pillars of republican forms of governments. The eyes of the officials can not be everywhere, but the eyes of the citizen can. Women, also, wield a large share of this control. Be careful, then, whom you admit to your fireside; frown upon the enemies and revilers of our Union; do not listen to the rebellious demagogue; do not applaud the tirades of a bold partisan by trade; do not give money for Sharpe's rifles, to be used instead of ballot-boxes; listen not to partisan, slip-shod sermons; never countenance treason, and rebellion, and crime, under whatever form and pretext. This will help a good deal to keep peace, and settle all differences in a just, honest, constitutional manner.

LETTER XXXI.

Man given to Lying. — Imperfect Laws. — Force opposed to Law. — Fugitives from Service and Labor, their Extradition. — Apprentices. — Sailors. — Bound Laborers. — Claim upon them for Outlay, to be respected and protected by all Civil Governments. — Property-right to Labor-forces. — Its Market Price. — Property-right of Parents to the Use of the Labor-forces of their Children. — Bound Labor is Personal, Serfdom is Glebose. Abolition Agitation is Glebose. — Englishmen and Russians are Glebose. — Territorial Feudal Rights. — Free Labor-force, increased by Immigration. — Gradually extending South. — Seigneurs. — Manor-born Subjects. — Labor in Spain and Portugal and the Southern States. — Jamaica. — Few real Free Men. — Immense Number of Laws. — Europeans are Subjects or Matter. — Captain Ingraham. — Austrian Emperor. — English King in the War of 1812. — English Abolitionism explained. — American Society Africanized by Abolition of Slavery. — Duke of Sutherland. — Property in Man.—Men of Property. — Loafers. — Hereditary Governments. — France. — Subordinate Races. — Difference between Monarchies and Republics. — Industry of the Southern People. — Savage Men, their Training by Industry. — Manumission of Bound Laborers. — Serfs sold with Property, and belong to it. — Judge Loring. — Travelling with Bound Servants. — Africa no Place for Culturing their Savage Inhabitants. — Not improved by the Greeks and Romans. — Frenchmen. — Bound Labor is under Municipal Government. — A Bound Laborer is no Citizen. — Territories. — Missouri Line. — District of Columbia. — Fanaticism in Law-making. — Party Press. — Boston Journal in favor of Constitutional Monarchy.— Canadian Paper prognosticating the end of the Union. — Nobility after Abolition of Bound Labor. — King Bomba, Emperors of France, and Austria, and Hayti. — Boston Notions. — American Women.

We come now to a clause which has caused serious misunderstandings, but without the least sufficient reason. Man is not only much given to lying, as Shakespeare has it, but also to doing wrong, without being naturally inclined to bear the consequences of either. There will always be laws which are not, in some respects, what they ought to be. Little is perfect in our world. Still in a society where man has all practicable means and remedies at his disposition, to express his opinions about laws, and to have them altered or repealed, and where every one who has the right of voting, virtually has a share in law-making—in such a society, I am going to say, the use of force against existing laws and their executors, is one of the most censurable and contemptible acts or crimes imaginable. Such an act characterizes the most dangerous enemy of social order. This use of force has happened oft times in regard to the congressional law, making the following clause operative:—

"3. No person held to service or labor in one state, under the laws thereof, escaping into another, shall, in consequence of any law or regulation therein, be discharged from such service or labor, but shall be delivered up, on claim of the party to whom such service or labor may be due."

This clause is the origin of that law which is generally known by the name of fugitive-slave law. It is applicable to all persons engaged to service as apprentices, etc., and must find a place in a constitution of a real confederation, whether there be a single bound laborer within its limits or not. If a sailor engaged to service in the state of New York escapes into another state, he may be claimed there, and ought to be delivered up. Such cases would happen daily if it would be profitable to prosecute them. However in regard to bound laborers such claims are of importance, because the party to whom labor is due has bestowed considerable expenses upon such laborers, by raising them, or remunerating others for those expenses. This constitutes a great civil or judicial difference between bound and free labor, so often lost sight of by sentimentalists and fanatics. The raising of a man, his support in healthy and sick days, the care bestowed upon him to make him a useful being, entitles to a return or remuneration, which should, as a property-right, be acknowledged by all legislatures in Canada and elsewhere, who aim at the realization of justice. It is a rightful claim to the person raised, upon which land has not the least influence. This return is given by the use of the labor-force of the servant or laborer, which to control and maintain is connected with great difficulties and risk, unknown in the employment of free labor. The right to this USE has, of course, a market value. It is but witty, or rather malicious, to compare a bound laborer with cattle, because not his weight, that is, muscles or bones, are in question, but merely the use of his labor-force, or the right to it, which also determines the price of free labor. When now the laws of all civilized nations expressly acknowledge a property-right of a parent to the use of the labor-forces of his children, what is there, I ask, abnormous in the claim of a man, who, with or without the sanction of state laws, has raised and trained a laborer from childhood at considerable expense and trouble, to his labor-force, being besides obliged to support him in all emergencies through life! Nothing can be plainer than that this claim is property, which ought to be protected by all governments.

With our bound labor system, land or soil, as mentioned, has nothing to do, as little as land has to do with shoemaking and spinning. It is a PERSONAL condition, something like that of a child relative to its parents. The condition of the Russian serfs and European subjects in general, depends, however, upon territorial rights. Free soil politics is an imported European article (as the whole Abolition agitation). If the Englishmen and Russians, etc., wish to become independent and self-governing men, they must first remove these territorial feudal rights; that is, they must cry for "free soil." This, of course, will bring down the royal and imperial landed crown-rights.

Up to this time Englishmen and Russians are property, and judged, and taxed, and sold as such with the land to which they belong. Whole provinces are accordingly acquired and disposed of, or conquered, while the soil in South Carolina is just as free as that in Massachusetts, Kansas, and Utah. Our bound laborers are not attached to dominions or soil *(glebæ adscripti)* like the European subjects and serfs. Our society is at present composed of the same elements as at the time when the constitution was made. People in the northern region, abundantly supplied with labor-force by immigration, found the risk of bound labor too great, and therefore sold their interest in it to the South. The same will happen under similar circumstances again and everywhere. Slavery is transient, liberty permanent. The free-soil talk can in a sensible American, who knows the difference between his country and Europe, only excite ridicule; for a little thinking must convince him that our bound labor is a mere personal condition or obligation recognized by State laws.

This is the reason why our bound labor system has, if well managed, not that deteriorating influence upon the culture of the land, as the European territorial subject and serf system. This is the reason why Russia begins in the thickly-settled, best-culti vated provinces, to abolish serfdom. It is profitless there. A European seigneur must see how he can get along with his manor-born subjects—the American master is at liberty to improve or dispose of his bound laborers as he pleases. The labor of our four million slaves is more profitable to society at large than the free labor of ten million people in Spain and Portugal. The world can go along without the latter very well, but can not exist conveniently without our cotton.

Good governments adjust accurately the laws to the actual exigencies and conditions of society, while bad governments supplant their visions and schemes, and let slide these conditions, and ruin society—vide Jamaica.

There are still very few real free men in our northern states, as is proved by the immense number of laws, lawyers, judges, legislators, etc.—for these are not required by real free men, as St. Paul says. There are still fewer such men in Europe, as the general state of subjection and bondage there proves. Almost all Europeans are subject, *or matter*, possessed by princes according to the laws of inheritance. Capt. Ingraham rescued a man from the grasp of his imperial owner, who will resign his property-rights as unwillingly as the English king did to the captured naturalized British-Americans in 1812, claiming that they never had ceased to be his property. Rights by inheritance are property-rights—nothing else. The British government and the subjects, dukes and counts included, partake thus of the character of matter.

These peculiar conditions of society in England explain why the English government is *at present*, in favor of slave abolition, since by this process it changes men into landed feudal crown-property, who priorly were the personal property of masters, and why, the queen, the lords, dukes, and the whole aristocracy, seem to favor this change, because all the privileged classes remain there as before, elevated and distanced from the new low crown-subjects. But let us see how such a change would operate with us. Our society differs in this regard entirely from that in Europe. When, with us, bound labor is abolished in the true sense of this word, all subjection is at an end; the freed bound servants stand upon the same platform with their prior masters; they acquire all political rights, and there being, in a great many districts, more slaves than masters, the latter would be, with their families, in the minority, and, of course, ruled by the majority, the liberated Africans. Thus, by abolition, society in the slave states would be Africanized.

What do you think of such a society, my children?

Would you like to live in a town, ruled by Africans, or per chance, by Chinese? Do you believe that the Duke of Sutherland with his lady would? I for one never could believe it.

There is much confusion of notions abroad about that what is called property in man. What I write in general on social affairs I take from nature and not from fancy and theories. The federal constitution, too, is organizing society as it naturally is. Society rests upon the idea of property. The child is the property of his parents, the father calls its mother his own, the wife claims her husband as her own. When sons and daughters break loose from the family they seek a new home, longing for the possession of beloved hearts and persons, also animals and vegetables exist by appropriating without ceremony what they need for their subsistence. Each must and will possess something. Industry is producing, man is accumulating by force of the desire to possess. A man of property is something, a loafer nothing. The patriarchal times are praised as the happiest, they were the period of full property in man. Who got disappointed in the possession of a wife or husband was an object of pity or ridicule. Most men prefer to be possessed by their governments (hereditary monarchs) to make them more stable and conservative. Look at France. Subordinate races submit without murmur to the dominion of superior races. Travellers report from Liberia that the emigrants fresh from the slave states are useful citizens, while free colored men from the free states are loafers. The possession of man is no slavery or barbarism, but the abuse of this possession. The father who claims his child as his property is no tyrant, but who maltreats it is. It is the same with a bound laborer. If treated right by a superior-raced man, this relation will make happy men. The main difference between monarchies and republics is that society or families cease to be possessed by the latter governments.

It is impossible that society in our southern states can exist in a state of civilization, that is, enjoyment of civil liberty, or real citizen rights, without keeping the Africans subject. There would be an end of social order and of subsistence by abolition. The industry which supports society there, and contributes so much to the comfort and wealth of the world, would collapse at once; cotton, rice, sugar, tobacco, and other products of the southern climates, would disappear almost entirely from the market. Never have Africans in mass been better treated by any nation than by the Americans.

Again, my dear children, men and republics are more the work of circumstances than of philosophical systems, constitutions, and laws. The circumstances here in question are — first, savageness and slavery in Africa; secondly, domestication, the first step to the culture of Africans in America; thirdly, their gradual liberation, and, perhaps, reshipment to Liberia, etc. There is more providence in these circumstances for schooling and training savage men than party politicians are willing to admit. Of course, no one will believe that bound labor will exist a single day longer than it is required and profitable, just as free labor is never employed one minute longer than it is profitable and needed. To control all these circumstances is the business of those who are surrounded by them, and of nobody else.

The personal character of our bound labor system has many qualities which make it preferable to the European subject and serf system. First, it allows an easy combination with free labor. There are 250,000 free colored laborers in the southern states, according to the census. Secondly, it facilitates manumission. About 4,000 bound laborers are without interference of states annually emancipated in our country. They now begin to spread civilization in Africa. Thirdly, our bound laborers may be easily transplanted to regions mere apt to their labor, and improved by travelling. The tampering with bound laborers, when travelling with their masters abroad, by busy-bodies, has cut off this source of labor-culture, to the great disadvantage of the bound laborer. A real abolitionist should cheerfully open his house, and city, and state to the masters with their bound laborers, to give the latter a better chance than that at home of comparing their situation with that of free servants and laborers. But it is in vain to expect such just and generous dealing with bound laborers from the side of English "pecora imitationis" in Boston and elsewhere. Nothing would promote more voluntary manumission than a fraternal, upright, gentleman-like intercourse between our fellow-citizens North and

South, and a stoppage of that clumsy English abolition and free-soil party movement whose greatest triumph consists in robbery, by seducing a bound servant to become faithless to his master.

Migration of bound laborers from place to place, or state to state, does not increase the number of slaves, of course. Slavery is a product of circumstances, just as liberty. Abstract notions never make a man free. Our world exhibits a social "tableau" of slaves, serfs, subjects, and a very, very few free men, comparatively. The policy of prohibiting, instead of regulating the importation of slaves or savage Africans to Europe or America, for domestication, is *from a mundane view*, still debatable.* Without transplanting these Africans to America or Europe and domesticating them, no culture will ever take hold on them. Neither Greek nor Roman local influence has altered Africa. I have not the least faith in the humanitarian efforts and successes of the French corporals and generals on this terrain. In the United States begins a new African history—that of African industry. Asia has been slave before, and remains slave after the introduc-

* The following passage is from the London *Times*, of July, 1858. This letter was written 1856 :—

"All this time, on the pretence of preventing the passage of slaves, we are actually preventing that free passage which undoubtedly would arise but for our interference, and which is the very thing wanted both for Africa and the West Indies. The best thing that could happen would be a spontaneous, though encouraged, assisted, and regulated emigration of negroes from Africa to the fields of labor and enterprise on the opposite shore. The African would go across, learn to work, live as well, save money, and return a wealthy and comparatively civilized man, and would become the means of civilizing his countrymen at home. He would bring back to Africa not only the money, but the industry and arts of his employers; and he would retain at home the new wants he had acquired in his period of service. The benefits of the West Indies are too obvious to enlarge upon, and all we have to observe is, that we don't think our countrymen and our possessions in that part of the world utterly undeserving of consideration.

"What we have described may not be a lofty principle, but it is something better and safer; it is the right course of nature, and the way in which mankind has hitherto been civilized. But it is prevented by the effort to which national pride has now committed us. We interpose our wooden walls between the vast reservoir of African labor and the channels of industry and civilization into which it is ready to run. Of course we are prepared to find any number of English politicians ready to maintain this or any other national hypocrisy. Such diseases must run their course, even if the climax should happen to be a severe one."

tion of Christianity. Europe has done with African slaves, but not with serfs and subjects, and never will do without them, as long as the present social institutions and conditions remain as they are. It will take a long time before our southern states, Middle Central America, and Brazil can do without bound laborers. Philanthropists never will alter this without causing general social confusion and ruin. The unprejudiced begin to open their eyes. In a few generations African bound laborers will be imported to Europe.

Who has eyes to see must perceive that from sheer want of those labor-forces the works of the old Spaniards in Central and South America crumble now to pieces, and Jamaica and Hayti are laid waste.

With us labor is wealth. Our renowned smartness consists mostly in the excellent use we make of all kinds of labor-forces. The possibility of starting a slavery party in Massachusetts, where there are no slaves, and of a free-soil party in a country where land is as free as the air, betrays the foreign and spurious origin of these parties—further, a great weakness and sickly impulsiveness in our character, and an unripeness in our judgment, which our national enemies know very well how to use to our immense disadvantage.

But, when shall bound labor cease? I answer: In due course of time. This apparently knotty question is easily solved by the causes which made it necessary. Once Time required it in America, Time requires it still in some parts, Time will abolish it, whether in one hundred or one thousand years must not in the least concern lawmakers. There is too much slavery and bondage abroad for good old Father Time to abolish. Think only of the bondage of superstition, of political party, of mammon, of libertinism, of intemperance, of false sciences, of thousands of vices and ignorances, all to be removed by good old Father Time! Think only how few know what is the right measure in eating and drinking, not to say a word about talking and writing! Why, therefore, be in a hurry in Boston with the abolition of slavery in Louisiana, while people in New Orleans complacently wait until Time has taught people in Boston and elsewhere the correct measure in eating, loving, writing, talking, preaching, and to respect and obey faithfully constitutions and laws made by and with the consent of their own representatives in Congress and state—those referring to the duties of the judiciary too! The treatment of Judge Loring at the hand of the government of Massachusetts is a greater stain on our national honor than African bound labor; for this is not of our own making, as is our federal constitution and its judiciary, but of British inheritance, as every person a little versed in history knows.

Keep, then, my children, in all questions concerning laborers, strictly in view, that our national government has not the least power to legislate on this labor any more than on free labor. A bound laborer, in a state or territory, is, as such, subject to the municipal laws of the state or territory. A bound laborer is no national man, no national property, no subject, no citizen, but a domesticated man, belonging to his master, like a child to his parents, or a wife to her husband and vice versa. The presidential party-dispute of 1856, would and could not exist, if all those belonging to the free-soil or abolition party would but read the constitution correctly and understood it well. If a bound laborer is not a national political subject, Congress, as the national government, has no concern with it, neither in states nor territories. It has the power to organize or regulate a territory, but not to legislate on the domestic affairs and laborers, or waiters, or chambermaids, or mechanics, or churches, or other municipal subjects. It is one of my principal objects in these letters to show that the federal constitution has not the least concern in the maintenance or abolition of bound labor; that Congress has not and never had the least power to legislate on it or to make Missouri lines or compromises; that neither the president, nor the United States court, has the least official influence in the matter; that petitions to Congress for the abolition of slavery, except from masters in the District of Columbia, are entirely out of place; that a Congressional election issue or platform on the ground of slavery or free soil is a spurious mockery of politicians by trade deserving a stern rebuke by the people.

I frankly consider the prohibition of bound labor in the northern state constitutions as injudicious, uncivil, and entirely superfluous in our Union, and indeed, against the best interests of the bound laborers, as I have noticed before. Fanaticism in lawmaking is a terrible curse to society. It has become fashionable, of late, in Congress and state. Unprincipled daily papers have much to answer for it. Our public men, even of some note, betray a deplorable wilfulness in these things.

Although I never feel alarmed by the utterances of strict party papers, whatever may be their tenor in regard to our political system, still it is prudent to notice them as signs of the times.

Please, my dear children, compare the following extract from the Boston Journal, a leading abolition or free-soil paper, with what I have just said of the peculiar character of this party. It reads thus:—

"We are decidedly of opinion that monarchy — hereditary monarchy — is by far the best form of government that human wisdom has yet devised for the administration of considerable nations, and that it will always continue to be the most perfect which human virtue will admit of."

A Canadian paper of the same stamp says: "The United States has about run its race as a republic. Its democracy is ripening into anarchy, the fruits of which will inevitably be despotism of some sort or other."

To carry out an abolition scheme, a monarchy for the southern states is inevitable. If the negroes shall be free citizens their masters must become heavily-privileged barons, counts, dukes, lords, and the like. In this, the opinion of the Boston journal is decidedly right. And to come to that, we want first anarchy, mentioned in the Canadian paper, rebellion against the existing laws, removing of the landmarks. To this abolitionism and free-soilism lead. You see how these kinds of "republicans" are making common cause with the dukes, queens, kings, and emperors in Europe. No better monarchists exist in Prussia, Austria, and England, than those "republicans."

What kind of a monarchy the Boston journal will establish for our administration, whether after the famous models of King Bomba, or Emperor Francis Joseph, after the fashion of the Spanish or English queen, or after the whims of their majesties Soulouque, or Napoleon III., is irrevalent, since we have already in our political system all that is good in a monarchical government — viz: one head as executive, and all that is good in a republican government, viz: the representative form blended with the democratic, surrounded by the necessary checks. Still all forms of governments are, of course, useless, if the laws are not executed with a good will. The first thing in most monarchical countries, that would happen with the Boston journal, if speaking there in favor of the republic, as it speaks in our republic in favor of the monarchy, is—*suppression*, closely followed up by *persecution* of the editors, printers, publishers, and all in the concern.

But let us turn away from such Boston notions. You have already experience enough in housekeeping to know that good masters make good servants. The exemplary good order, prevalent in the regions where our four millions of African slaves are held, obviously proves that they are well managed. The men, fellow-citizens of ours, who are doing this work, which is not an easy one, deserve our thanks and that of mankind. And all we, as their countrymen, under the shelter of the same constitution, have to do is, to let them alone, and not interfere with their own affairs, nor deprive them of their share of the common privileges of every citizen in the Union. This is but fair and just. The sensible and generous American women have an immense influence upon these things, for they are the managers of the domestic affairs everywhere.

LETTER XXXII.

Annexation of Texas. — Portentous in regard to the Union. — New States. — Their Admission into the Union. — Territory. — Land Surveying. — Indian Territory. — Indian Agents. — Indemnification. — Selling of Land. — Culture of Indians impossible in their own Country. — Acquisition of Foreign Country. — Florida. — Louisiana. — Mexico. — Division of States. — Overgrown Municipal States, as New York, Ohio, Pennsylvania. — Mutual Control and Power of Self-government lost therein. — France. — Monarchies with blended National and Municipal Business. — Increase of Free States compared with that of Slave States.

I SHOULD, perhaps, close my letters with number thirty-one, because I hardly believe that I shall be able to rivet your attention longer upon the constitution, after we have done with the fugitive slave law, which is common ground for writers and readers of both sexes. Still, I hope you will listen a little longer, as we come now to the annexation business, which, at the time, at least, when Texas was admitted into the Union, caused so much universal anxiety—such a sea of alarming prophecies about the downfall of our political fabric, that it is indeed a real miracle how the Union could survive this crisis. And behold, there it stands still, upon a broader and, I say, surer foundation than ever, provided American women will—what?—turn not European with the abolitionists and free-soilers. Read on, then, a little longer in patience.

SECTION III.

"1. New states may be admitted by the Congress into this Union, but no new states shall be formed or erected within the jurisdiction of any other state, or any state be formed by the junction of two or more states, or parts of states, without the consent of the legislatures of the states concerned, as well as of the Congress."

This section is a *new* political social feature—a *novus ordo seculorum.*

The rule is that a colony, settled upon an adjacent territory belonging to the United States, when she has reached a population of sixty thousand inhabitants, which entitles it to two senators, shall be admitted into the Union. As Congress has alone the power to transact business with foreign governments and the Indians, and as the acquisition of new wild lands or territory is made by the Union and for the same, so to the Congress necessarily belongs the whole disposition and regulation of the territorial affairs, from a national view. Therefore Congress has originated a land surveying and selling system, embracing the acquisition of the lands from the Indians, or adjacent governments, their indemnification, superintending, establishing of land-offices, Indian agents, bestowing titles to settlers, appointing governors, judges, and the necessary civil officers.

Congress has also tried to promote the culture of the Indians. Still, the official reports prove that little good has been promoted. The annuities paid to them in money and certain goods have produced but vice and laziness. Tribe after tribe dies off. The whole number of the Indians in the United States territories is little over three hundred thousand, at present. The twelve nations alone once numbered as much. This lesson proves what happens if governments meddle with the industry and culture (education and instruction) of society. If a similar plan should be adopted with the Africans their fate would be like that of the red-skins—destruction. The Indians can be as little cultivated at home as the Africans. They should have been for this purpose transported to Europe, just as the Africans had on this account to be brought to America. Without domestication abroad no savage ever will improve.

The constitution contains no prohibition of the acquisition of foreign territory, as happened with Florida, Louisiana, New Mexico; and this makes the utmost caution of Congress imperative not to transgress in this regard its powers. It should, as far as possible, always be done with the consent of the population in question; for we annex not the land, but men. Men, not acres, form the Union; men, not rocks, establish states; and these are made for men, and not for mountains and vales. It is but right that no state should be arbitrarily divided, since a state is a social institution, based upon a convention or compact, embodied in a written constitution and represented by a government. This, then, must be the organ by means of which a dismemberment of such an institution must be made. Any other procedure would be improper, arbitrary, and revolutionary.

The necessity of dividing states, with a fast-increasing population, will soon be felt, not only because municipal states containing more than about one million inhabitants are generally badly governed—it being then almost impossible to exercise the political mutual control of which I wrote in a prior letter—but also because such states acquire, in consequence of party organizations, too powerful an influence upon the national affairs. I refer in this regard to the list of electoral votes elsewhere. The state of New York commands in Congress as many votes as eight smaller states taken together.

This produces an undue preponderance in the national councils. Moreover, in the population of a state of about three millions of inhabitants the sentiment or feelings of nationality begin to become conscious and substance. This consciousness steeled the arms of the American colonists in their struggle for freedom and self-government. It will cause trouble in our Union. Factionists and intriguers will use it for selfish purposes.

There is a certain measure based upon the natural laws of

society for municipal and national state districts and organizations. This is a most important subject for the consideration of statesmen, debating societies, and patriotic citizens in general. The population in the states of New York, Ohio, and Pennsylvania has reached that number which renders a good republican municipal government more and more impracticable. History proves that the power of self-government is lost in states of too great a populat on. France, with thirty-five millions of inhabitants never will be a republic for a longer time than it requires to pull down the throne in Paris. She should be first divided into at least thirty-five state districts, for the municipal political business, with a central federal government like ours, for the national business, to become a stable republic. In a monarchy the municipal and national business is blended and centralized. It would be constantly thrown into confusion if not supported by a powerful soldiery, rich hereditary aristocracy, a hereditary dynasty, a wealthy state church, aud more such props, against which, if well combined, a discontented or oppressed people can not do much. But as soon as these artificial props give way, and especially the army turns traitor, the crown rolls into the street, where it is a plaything of the mobs. If you understand the federal constitution well you will better understand the history of bygone states, empires, and republics, especially those of France. From this history the noble framers of the constitution learned more than the Napoleons, Bourbons, and those who made constitutions after them.

This clause, I say, is without precedent, and the mother of nineteen new states, peopled by those whom it pleased to seek a shelter in this Union. What a beautiful social phenomenon; what a picture of human progress; what a triumph achieved by that simple honest common sense which has founded our Union!

Still, this exceedingly wise proviso, if not wisely executed with regard to the population, which naturally accumulates in favored localities, will, I repeat it, in the course of time produce trouble. Each proviso of a constitution is subject to abuse, as all other things in this world.

Remark here that when the federal constitution was framed every state tolerated slavery. Since that time two, only two states have been added sanctioning slavery, so that there are at present fifteen slave states, all counted, while there have sprung up seventeen free states at the time (1858) of writing this letter. This shows what course we take under our constitution. Our march is toward freedom on the path of justice and order.

LETTER XXXIII.

Territories. — Their Disposal and Regulation. — Three Periods. — Indian Policy. — Territorial Policy. — State Policy. — Kansas Nebraska Act. — Missouri Compromise not Constitutional. — Dred Scott Case.

THE following clause refers to the land belonging to the United States:—

"2. The Congress shall have power to dispose of and make all needful rules and regulations respecting the territory, and other property belonging to the United States, and nothing in this constitution shall be so construed as to prejudice any claims of the United States, or of any particular state."

Some say that this proviso should be restricted to the territory of the United States at the time of the establishing of the constitution, but I see not for what practical use, since the nature of the case requires a discretional power. Increase of territory was foreseen by the framers of the constitution.

In regard to government, society in the United States goes through three periods. The first is entire dependency of thinly-settled regions upon Congress, without any state-like organization of their own; it is called the period of the Indian policy. The second is the period of territorial organization, lasting until the population is large enough to be entitled to state representation in Congress. During this period the people make their own laws, but the executive and judiciary are appointed and paid by Congress. The third period begins when a territory is admitted into the Union, on the ground of a republican constitution, as an independent state. This once done, the state is an indissoluble part of the Union, except Congress should see fit to exclude it on constitutional grounds, as by adopting a monarchical constitution. If people, as the Mormon sect, should abuse their territorial rights, Congress may deprive them of such, and place them back under a government entirely depending upon Congress.

This clause has gained of late undeservedly much interest in consequence of the change produced by the act of Congress concerning the organization of the territories of Kansas and Nebraska. Up to the 34th Congress, by a law of Congress of 1820, it was declared that in all the territory north of lat. 36° 30′ not included within the limits of Missouri, slavery and involuntary servitude should for ever be prohibited. By this act Congress was involved in the slavery question, which, however, as a mere municipal business does not belong to its business sphere. To terminate the eternal, angry debates about this subject in Congress, it saw fit to abrogate in the bill just mentioned this geographical or sectional line, on the ground that the question of slavery should be left to the people to decide when they had formed a state and accepted a constitution. You, my dear children, will now be able to form for yourselves a pretty correct opinion upon this subject. We leave the constitutionality of the prior acts to the supreme court to decide upon, since there is not the least doubt that Congress, by virtue of the clause under consideration, has the right to repeal or alter such acts at pleasure. But so much is certain, that a Union divided by a political geographical line in regard to bound or free labor, commerce, religion or anything else, ceases to be a union or unit, but appears as a divided thing. This much-talked-of Kansas and Nebraska act will work rightly under the constitution, provided only real actual settlers have to manage the public business. These will, you may be sure, adjust their state constitution to the actual circumstances, and this is all they should do. But if there are men allowed to vote which are, by the abolition party or others, expressly hired for this purpose, the result will be different. That such mercenary votes are a fraud and illegal is obvious.

It is to be devoutly hoped that we shall not hear a single word more about bound labor in Congress. If the principle pointed out above of free settling of the territories by Americans, Europeans and Asiatics be right, it is self-evident that no American citizen can be excluded from any section of our territories, may he keep bound laborers or not. At least, the federal constitution, our supreme law of the land, does not contain a single word against this principle, as may be presumed considering its origin.

Allow me to ask here; would not the often-mentioned family-state vote at once prevent party outrages in such instances? would families be liable to be abused for fraudulent voting errands? have you ever heard of families going fillibustering? This proves what a great difference there is between the family and the usual personal suffrage, how the first naturally guaranties order, and the second produces all kinds of mischief and social corruption. Usurpers, like the Napoleons, understand this difference very well, and side with our demagogues. Congress has the power to make the laws on the suffrage in the territories. Why not use it?

Who has seen the managing of the voting in territories and new states will agree that it is impossible, in most instances, to distinguish *bona fide* settlers from fraudulent voters. The real *bona fide* settlers are families, because they are forced by nature to found a home. That legislature which first substitutes the family suffrage for the personal or general suffrage, relieves society of an evil which every patriot and good citizen deeply deplores. Its name is mob-rule.

As the parents are advising and helping their children when they are going the first time to housekeeping, so Congress supports the young settlements until the appointed time has come for the independent management of their own state affairs. This kind of transient regulation of territories must be in its nature discretionary, and should be borne with cheerfulness, and not resented by fierce demagoguism and treasonable revolt, as has been done in Kansas of late; for Congress acts for the best of society, and does, indeed, nothing but bears the first expenses of the local government, which the settlers have in their hands, by making their own civil and criminal laws.

I have perhaps dwelt too long upon these subjects, but you see what dangers are surrounding us, and will therefore not be tired if I repeatedly recur to important principles to better show their working in society.

Postscript.—After this letter was written, there appeared in the papers a notice of a judgment of the United States supreme court in the case of Dred Scott against his master, claiming his freedom on the ground that he had resided two years, by the act of his owner, in a state where slavery was prohibited by its constitution, and afterward in a territory from which it was prohibited by the Missouri compromise. The supreme court denies the validity of his claim, and decides the following points:—

First. Negroes, whether slave or free, that is men of the African race, are not citizens of the United States, by the constitution.

Second. The ordinance of 1787 had no independent constitutional force or legal effect subsequently to the adoption of the constitution; and could not operate of itself to confer freedom or citizenship within the northwest territory on negroes, not citizens by the constitution.

Third. The provision of the act of 1820, commonly called the Missouri compromise, in so far as it undertook to exclude negro slavery from, and communicate freedom and citizenship to, negroes in the northern part of the Louisiana cession, was a legislative act exceeding the powers of Congress, and VOID, and of no legal effect to that end.

In deciding these main points the supreme court determined the following incidental points:—

First. The expression "territory and other property" of the Union in the constitution applies "in terms" only to such territory as the Union possessed at the time of the adoption of the constitution.

Second. The rights of citizens of the United States emigrating into any federal territory, and the power of the federal government there, depend on the general provisions of the constitution, which defines in this, as in all other respects, the powers of Congress.

Third. As Congress does not possess power itself to make enactments relative to the persons or property of citizens of the United States in a federal territory, other than such as the constitution confers, so it cannot constitutionally delegate any such powers to a territorial government organized by it under the constitution.

Fourth. The legal condition of a slave in the state of Missouri is not affected by the temporary sojourn of such slave in any other state, but on his return his condition still depends on the laws of Missouri.

As the plaintiff was not a citizen he, therefore, could not sue in the courts of the United States. The suit must be dismissed for want of jurisdiction.

This decision settles an unsteady practice which has influenced party rancor and virulence. A slave is not born as a citizen, and does not acquire by simple manumission citizen rights, any more than an immigrant acquires such a right by mere immigration. The judgment is plain and just, and in regard to the increasing Mongolian immigration very seasonable.

LETTER XXXIV.

Guaranty of a Republican Form of Government. — Protection against Invasion and Domestic Violence. — Switzerland. — Hanse Republics. — Monarchs. —Greeks. — King Philip. — Amphyctionic Congress. — European Opinion of the American Political System. — Rev. T. S. Hughes's Opinion. — Dangers of our Republic to the whole World.

We shall soon be through the constitution. It disposes in —

SECTION IV.

"The United States shall guaranty to every state in this Union a republican form of government, and shall protect each of them against invasion; and on application of the legislature, or of the executive (when the legislature can not be convened), against domestic violence."

Harmony in a confederation requires that the forms of the government be of the same kind. Republics and monarchies never will form a real confederation. We see how the monarchs are treating Switzerland or the little Hanse republics in Germany. The Greeks, by admitting King Philip to their republican Amphyctionic Congress, sapped the foundation of their confederacy, ending in their subjection to the Macedonians.

Congress is by this clause pledged to guaranty free governments, the most simple, the most natural, and the best, if not permitted to be abused by lawless and unpatriotic men. The clause is plain by itself. Of the common defense, in case of invasion, we have read before. In case of domestic violence against the governments Congress shall also provide protection. As long as the trouble is merely local, and, of course, not endangering the state government, Congress has no right to interfere; for, in a well-governed state, where the executive has a sharp look upon the execution of the laws, there will always be force enough to assist the authorities in carrying out the laws in such instances.

European statesmen and writers hold the opinion, that in this constitution too little power is given to the federal government over the state legislatures, which they generally call provincial legislatures. But all who study the federal constitution with an eye and keen instinct for business will discover, that in the very little or no power at all Congress has over the state governments is the very strength of our system. The states, being all republics, have only to care for the good management of the municipal public business. This is or should be their ambition. Congress, on the other hand, is appointed to manage the national business well. Therein may its members exhaust all their ingenuity and ambition. If both institutions act their parts well, and the people are well able to control them practically, the American system of organizing society and managing their public affairs, must necessarily be the best men can devise. When one of those writers (Rev. T. S. Hughes, in his English History) says, that our republic is destined, for a time at least, to be the great disturbing force of Europe, if not of the world, and so potent for mischief, that it becomes a question whether it would not be sound policy for all European states to combine for the purpose of curbing its encroachments, and counteracting its designs, he little understood the merits of this system, and the pivot upon which it moves. All that Europe has to do is to let America alone. There is not the least danger that this republic will disturb Europe, unless forced to resent injurious meddling with their interest. Our internal troubles (there will be always some) will be trifling, if we do not neglect the voting laws and the distributing of society.

LETTER XXXV.

Amending the Constitution. — Check upon large States. — Public Debts. — Supreme Law of the Land. — Higher Law Reveries. — Religious and Moral Precepts. — Channing. — Philosophical Opinions and Truths, no Law. — Sharpe's Rifles.

THOSE who made this constitution were honest enough to admit it might not be so perfect as they wished to make it, and therefore provided how it might be improved.

ARTICLE V.

Of Amendments.

"1. The Congress, whenever two thirds of both houses shall deem it necessary, shall propose amendments to this constitution, or, on the application of the legislatures of two thirds of the several states, shall call a convention for proposing amendments, which, in either case, shall be valid to all intents and purposes as part of this constitution when ratified by the legislatures of three fourths of the several states, or by conventions in three fourths thereof, as the one or the other mode of ratification may be proposed by the Congress; provided that no amendment, which may be made prior to the year one thousand eight hundred and eight, shall in any manner affect the first and fourth clauses in the ninth section of the first article; and that no state, without its consent, shall be deprived of its equal suffrage in the senate."

The limitations indicated in this article refer to the prohibition of the introduction of slaves, and in the mode of levying a capitation or direct tax, not to be changed so long as slave property could be increased by importation, and to the representation of the states in the senate. The first and second restrictions are compromises, and the third a check upon the influence of large states, of which I have spoken before, but which requires a special law of Congress, also in regard to their influence in the house of representatives.

ARTICLE VI.

Miscellaneous.

"1. All debts contracted, and engagements entered into, before the adoption of this constitution, shall be as valid against the United States under this constitution, as under the confederation."

It is but just, since changes of the form of government do not rescind, change, or destroy the obligations between governments and citizens. This is often forgotten in revolutionary times, which invariably increase prior public debts.

"2. This constitution, and the laws of the United States, which shall be made in pursuance thereof; and all treaties made, or which shall be made, under the authority of the United States, shall be the supreme law of the land; and the judges in every state shall be bound thereby, anything in the constitution or laws of any state to the contrary notwithstanding."

This plainly settles all higher law reveries. I respect deeply all religious or moral precepts. They ought to be the fountain from which our legislators should draw their wisdom: they should be the rules of our life. But what is considered by Channing, in his writings on slavery, the duty of free states, spiritual freedom, etc., and by his followers, higher law, is no political authority, no law, to be executed, but merely a sentiment, an opinion, an ideal. Who is not satisfied with our supreme law, as it stands, and with the laws made under it, must, in this free country, not rebel against them, but quietly suffer them or expiate himself, as hundreds and thousands do in Europe, who do not like the established laws there. All other expedients are unworthy of a republican citizen and an honest man, notwithstanding anything to the contrary in the theological, philosophical, metaphysical, and poetical systems and doctrines. These are all very well in their way, but, if there shall not be confusion without end, LAW must be their guiding star as it *is* that of a good people. I love our federal constitution and our system of governing, because, under it, people may enjoy the greatest spiritual freedom, expand freely their noblest faculties, so far as circumstances permit. Let then the philosophers develop the truth, but not enforce their opinions with Sharpe's rifles. Every good thing has its proper time for use.

LETTER XXXVI.

Official Oath. — Religious Test abolished. — Party. — Unconstitutional Platforms. — Sliding Constitutions or Platforms. — Perjury. — Chaplains. — Object of Religion.— Separation of Religion from the State.— E Pluribus Unum.— Norvus Ordo Seculorum.— Religious Intolerance.— Ratification by a Majority of the States. — No Preference of, or Difference between, the Old and New States.

WITH this letter we have done with the constitution proper.

"3. The senators and representatives before mentioned, and the members of the several state legislatures, and all executive and judicial officers, both of the United States and the several states, shall be bound by oath or affirmation, to support this constitution; but no religious test shall ever be required as a qualification to any office or public trust under the United States."

Public officers, in order to give a guaranty of their honest intention, are placed everywhere under such a solemn obligation, although it is by some thought superfluous, under a written constitution, about which there can not be a mental reserve. We have seen that it is almost impossible to get a seat in Congress or an office, without the intervention of party. It may happen in a free country that a party acts upon a platform, which contains sectional, anti-union, or unconstitutional conditions. An unscrupulous man may slide such a platform, and by dint of smartness and hypocrisy, carry the election, so that he can pass the Rubicon of this official oath without a great deal of violence to his conscience; but if he accepts such a platform, swears the oath, as prescribed in this clause, and acts and votes according to the platform and lets slide the constitution, he obviously commits perjury. The chaplains of the legislature and Congress should often expose this danger of violating the supreme law on party grounds. They should do it as the monitors of the moral and religious precepts, alias called higher law. I hope to see the crime of perjury in regard to this clause, if not punished, always promptly resented by the people. Against this oath is the doctrine of instruction; under it Congress is not free, and perjury almost unavoidable.

The abolishing of the narrow-minded religious test is consonant with the pure and elevated principles of humanity, morality, and justice, upon which the constitution has been reared. We all know that the object of religion is to induce and bind man to a faithful performance of his personal and social duties. In this regard all sects and denominations should agree, however much they may differ in their rites and creeds. For what rational use is then such a test? It was, therefore, not only a novel, but, as time has proved, also a wise and just step forward on the path of humanity to exclude a religious test entirely from public offices, while it is even at present required by all foreign governments.

Our constitution has in this manner made religion a private affair, obviously considered as such by its framers, and separated it from state. For, if the government has no right to require such a test, it has no right to interfere with religious affairs at all.

Thus ends this most noble document! It has, as our national escutcheon truly states, successfully united a number of discordant states in one stable-confederation (e pluribus unum), and opened a new period in the history of mankind (novus ordo seculorum). It has, upon the rational principles of self-government, established justice and civil liberty; and is not only a master-specimen of a free political family compact, but also the first organic law, which effectively destroyed the modern Hydra: RELIGIOUS INTOLLERANCE.

ARTICLE VII.

Of the Ratification.

"The ratification of the conventions of nine states, shall be sufficient for the establishment of this constitution between the states so ratifying the same."

The ratification should take place in conventions of the people. A majority of the thirteen states was designated by the constitution sufficient for its adoption. Nine of these states ratified instantly, and thus began the confederation, four within a year afterward. There is not a vestige in the constitution favoring a preference of, or a difference between the first thirteen states of the Union and those later admitted to it, although some writers insist upon such a discrimination. They are led astray by the European notions of territorial sovereignty. And thus livé under its panoply in thirty-two states, twenty-six millions of happy men — they, at least, can be such, if they make a right use of their reason. May God protect this Union.

LETTER XXXVII.

Exceptions and Mob Commotions against the Constitution. — Bill of Rights. — Amendments. — Religious Establishment. — Freedom of Speech and of the Press. — Assembling. — Petition. — Great Britain. — Municipal Legislation. — Right to bear Arms. — European Legislation. — Municipal.— District of Columbia. — Quartering of Soldiers in Time of Peace. — Unreasonable Searches in Houses. — Grand jury Indictment. — Double Trials. — Process of Law. — Private Property for Public Use. — Municipal Legislation. — Speedy Public Trial by Jury. — Witnesses. — Counsel. — Trial by Jury in $20 Cases. — Blackstone. — Excessive Bail.— Enumeration of Certain Rights. — Powers reserved to the States. — Extension of the Judicial Power. — Electors. — Presidents compared with Crowned Heads.— Executive. — Judiciary compared with the Legislative Branch. — Stability of the Federal Constitution.

Against this constitution were raised strong exceptions, even mob-commotions, because it contained no bill of rights, &c. But we have seen that all general principles of justice (such as make up what is called a bill of rights) were carefully embodied in this organic law, so far as they were in harmony with its purpose—the organization of the Congress and defining of its business. To do more would not have been befitting, or would have been encroaching upon state constitutions, statute-books, or judicial codes. But this would not suit some wiseacres, and therefore a string of amendments was proposed, of which the following were approved by the good people. I shall pass them over with a few remarks, because they are irrelevant.

AMENDMENTS.

"Art. 1. Congress shall make no law respecting an establishment of Religion, or prohibiting the free exercise thereof; or abridging the freedom of speech, or of the press; or the right of the people peaceably to assemble, and to petition the government for a redress of grievances."

You will see at the first glance, my dear children, that this amendment is superfluous with us, while it may be appropriate in Great Britain or elsewhere. By abolishing the religious test the constitution has done more in regard to religious freedom than this amendment would do, if it stood alone. On the other subjects, even about the aberrations of the Mormon church, Congress has no right to legislate. To say a word about petitions is gratuitous and improper, our officials being our responsible agents and not our lords or royal proprietors, and, therefore, can and never will refuse to accept petitions on subjects belonging to their business-sphere. The main objects mentioned here belong to municipal legislation and not at all to Congress.

"Art. 2. A well-regulated militia being necessary to the security of a free state, the right of the people to keep and bear arms, shall not be infringed."

Good for Europe. We have read the dispositions of the constitution about the militia. Congress has no power to legislate on the keeping and bearing of arms, except in the District of Columbia.

"Art. 3. No soldier shall, in time of peace, be quartered in any house without the consent of the owner, nor in time of war, but in a manner to be prescribed by law."

Is also good for Europe. We have no soldiers in the European sense of the word. If our troops should be in need of lodging and board, somebody must pay for it. Of course, necessity in times of war knows no law, no restraint; but the right to indemnification after the war, no one can destroy.

"Art. 4. The right of the people to be secure in their persons, houses, papers, and effects, against unreasonable searches and seizures, shall not be violated, and no warrants shall issue, but upon probable cause, supported by oath or affirmation, and particularly describing the place to be searched, and the persons or things to be seized."

Very well for England and a statute-book of municipal laws, but superfluous here.

"Art. 5. No person shall be held to answer for a capital, or otherwise infamous crime, unless on a presentment or indictment of a grand jury, except in cases arising in the land or naval forces, or in the militia, when in actual service in time of war or public danger; nor shall any person be subject for the same offence to be twice put in jeopardy of life or limb; nor shall be compelled in any criminal case to be a witness against himself, nor be deprived of life, liberty, or property, without due process of law; nor shall private property be taken for public use, without just compensation."

This is entirely superfluous, and does not belong to the federal constitution; and, so far as partaining to it, has been provided for in the constitution. The maxim, that an accused criminal shall not incriminate himself, is equivalent to a prohibition of the confession of guilt, an utterly immoral and irreligious maxim, more calculated to accommodate and harden scoundrels than to promote order and realize justice.

"Art. 6. In all criminal prosecutions, the accused shall enjoy the right to a speedy and public trial, by an impartial jury of the state and district wherein the crime shall have been committed, which district shall have been previously ascertained by law, and to be informed of the nature and cause of the accusation; to be confronted with the witnesses against him; to have compulsory process for obtaining witnesses in his favor, and to have the assistance of counsel for his defence."

All this is municipal state-business, and does not belong to the federal constitution, and proves that this law was little understood by those who moved such an amendment.

"Art. 7. In suits at a common law, where the value in controversy shall exceed twenty dollars, the right of trial by jury shall be preserved, and no fact tried by a jury, shall be otherwise re-examined in any court of the United States, than according to the rules of common law."

Also entirely improper for this constitution. Such municipal law-details, as the sum of twenty dollars, never belong to any constitution at all, for they ought to be regulated by a statute according to time and circumstances. If those men, who urged such amendments, had had a seat in the convention, which framed the federal constitution, it would have been either never made, or become something entirely different from what it is, most certainly a book of several hundred pages old English law lore, copied from Blackstone, &c.

"Art. 8. Excessive bail shall not be required, nor excessive fines imposed, nor cruel and unusual punishment inflicted."

Such things must be left to the judgment of the legislatures, and will be taken care of just as well, if not mentioned at all in a constitution.

"Art. 9. The enumeration in the constitution, of certain rights, shall not be construed to deny or disparage others retained by the people."

Is a matter of course. The federal constitution applies merely to the organization of Congress, and nothing else, and can, therefore, not prejudice or alter anything in the social affairs and individual rights of the citizens, and in the public business of towns, counties, and states. And if, notwithstanding, Congress should transgress these limits, all it does would be unconstitutional, and null and void.

"Art. 10. The powers not delegated to the United States, by the constitution, nor prohibited by it to the states, are reserved to the states respectively, or to the people."

Is much like Art. 9, and entirely superfluous.

"Art. 11. The judicial power of the United States shall not be construed to extend to any suit in law or equity, commenced or prosecuted against one of the United States by citizens of another state, or by citizens or subjects of any foreign state."

I have spoken on this subject elsewhere. It is plain and self-evident also, without an express proviso.

Art. 12. This amendment I have inserted in Letter XXI. It alters the forms of the presidential election somewhat, but not materially (because the influence of the political parties neutralizes or paralyzes the action of the electoral college), as will be seen by a comparison of it with the *original* clause of the constitution, which I insert here:—

"3. The electors shall meet in their respective states, and vote by ballot for two persons, of whom one at least, shall not be an inhabitant of the same state with themselves. And they shall make a list of all the persons voted for, and of the number of votes for each; which lists they shall sign and certify, and transmit sealed to the seat of the government of the United States, directed to the president of the senate. The president of the senate shall, in the presence of the senate and house of representatives, open all the certificates, and the votes shall then be counted. The person having the greatest number of votes shall be the president, if such number be a majority of the whole number of electors appointed; and if there be more than one who have such majority, and have an equal number of votes, then the house of representatives shall immediately choose by ballot one of them for president; and if no person have a majority, then from the five highest on the list the said house shall in like manner choose the president. But in choosing the president, the votes shall be taken by states, the representation from each state having one vote; a quorum for this purpose shall consist of a member or members from two thirds of the states, and a majority of all the states shall be necessary to a choice. In every case, after the choice of the president, the persons having the greatest number of votes of the electors shall be the vice-president. But if there should remain two or more who have equal votes, the senate shall choose from them by ballot the vice-president."

All pains have been taken, as you see, to always get the right man at the helm of the federal state-ship. We can not be but satisfied, thus far, with all our presidents. Impartial history will, when comparing them with the contemporary crowned heads of monarchies, readily yield the palm to them. Their activity is limited by the laws of Congress. No doubt, that the executive and judicial branches of the federal government are, by far, surpassing the legislative branch, in the prompt and thorough management of their affairs.

The wheel of time sets facts and circumstances in motion. They are eternally changing. The mind demands new rules for them, but nature remains the same. The sun of Solon illuminates our paths to-day. The seasons sung by Homer, are still inspiring our poets. The child, the youth, the old, follow each other in the same order, as when Moses made laws for them. Almost as permanent and stable as nature, is our federal constitution. There is no clause in it, which may require a modification a century hence. I, for one, do not understand, how it could be essentially improved by amending.

Thus we have discussed one of the best state-papers ever made by men. It has caused me infinite pleasure to go with you over these grounds. They are laid out with great care. The seeds planted there, have grown into large, shadowy trees. May it be my lot and yours to live long beneath them.

LETTER XXXVIII.

Washington's Letter to Congress with the Constitution. — Duties of Confederated States and Individuals. — Consolidation of the Union. — Spirit of Amity and Mutual Deference. — Marriage. — No Industry secure without the Political Organization of Society.

After the acute politicians of the different states, headed by those of Massachusetts, had exhausted their stock of genuine English legal lore and native acumen in attempting to improve, by amendments, a constitution which they did not know by practice, with what result you have seen, it was addressed to the president of Congress and accompanied by a letter from General Washington, president of the convention which framed the constitution; from which the following extracts are taken. They show in a remarkably clear manner in what light the constitution was then viewed, and what were the objects of its formation:—

"It is obviously impracticable," so writes General Washington, "in the federal government of these states to secure all rights of independent sovereignty to each and yet provide for the interests and safety of all. Individuals entering into society must give up a share of liberty to preserve the rest. The magnitude of the sacrifice must depend as well on situation and circumstance as on the object to be obtained.

"It is at all times difficult to draw with precision the line between those rights which must be surrendered and those which may be reserved; and on the present occasion this difficulty was increased by a difference among the several states as to their situation, extent, habits, and particular interests.

"In all our deliberations on this subject we kept steadily in our view that which appears to us the greatest interest of every true American, the consolidation of the Union, in which is involved our prosperity, felicity, safety — perhaps our national existence. This important consideration, seriously and deeply impressed upon our minds, led each state in the convention to be less rigid on points of inferior magnitude than might have been otherwise expected; a spirit of amity and of that mutual deference and concession which the peculiarity of our political situation rendered indispensable."

How true! These few lines alone delineate the clear, practical, sagacious mind of this great and good citizen. As a young woman never should enter into the matrimonial compact without having before made up her mind to dispense with girlish fancies and habits, and begin a life devoted to the duties of the family state, where the earnest spirit of mutual deference, concession, compromise, and amity must preside, if there shall be union, that is, prosperity, felicity, and comfort at home: so should no single person, no people organized as a state, think of entering into a confederation without dispensing with selfish, anarchical, capricious, arrogant, unsocial feelings and pretensions; for only in such feelings consists what General Washington, in his letter, politely calls independent sovereignty.

Man is created a rational social being: we all depend upon each other. The political organization of society secures order, safety, and compass for our activity. There is no certain plan, pursuit, or career practicable without it. Why, then, should not all men of intelligence cheerfully obey the laws of their country, especially when made by their own representatives?

LETTER XXXIX.

Committees. — Appointed in the House by the Speaker, in the Senate by Ballot. — The Committee of Ways and Means. — Standing Committees. — Select Committees. — Committee of the Whole — Three times Reading of Bills. — Massachusetts. — Twenty-nine Standing Committees. — Accusations of Fraud, Corruption, Bribery. — Judiciary. — English Custom.

A MOST important part of the machinery by which the public business is performed, is the committees.

In all legislative bodies, the chief business is usually done by their committees. To these, all matters of business requiring investigation and consideration, are first referred, and by whom a report is made upon the subject, which report is the topic of consideration with the legislature. Committees in the house are appointed by the speaker, in the senate by ballot. In the house they consist of seven members each, in the senate of five. System in legislative work requires such an arrangement. The business before Congress is thus divided into classes, with an appropriate title for each, and appointing to each a separate committee. These classes are, with little variation, the same in both houses. By the seventh section of the first article of the constitution, it is provided, that all bills for raising revenue shall originate in the house of representatives; hence the house have a committee which the senate have not, styled "The Committee of Ways and Means." This committee is one of the most important parts of the machinery of legislation, and of the government itself; for in it are investigated all the moneyed affairs of the nation, and by it are digested and reported the various plans of revenue and finance for the support and credit of the government.

The principal committees in either house are: the committees on Foreign Relations, on the Judiciary, on Military Affairs, on Commerce, etc. These committees are called "Standing Committees;" while others appointed for particular occasion are called "Select Committees." Besides these, the whole house at times resolves itself into a committee, called the "Committee of the Whole." The object of this is to obtain greater freedom of debate, under a chairman appointed for the occasion. The rules of the house do not govern, but simply order is preserved as in common deliberative assemblages. When the Committee of the Whole have finished their discussions, they rise, and, like other committees, report to the house, the speaker resumes the chair, and the members vote in the house upon the acceptance or rejection of the report.

Every bill or proposition must be read three times previous to its passage, and each reading must receive the formal sanction of the house. Thus, before a proposition of a member may become a law, the bill has to pass three readings, a committee, the debate on the report of the committee, then it goes to the other house, where it passes through the same stations, and, finally, the scrutiny of the president. I should think those formalities sufficient for the purpose of getting good considerate laws; and still, how few are such.

This will suffice to give you an insight in the Congress and its working machinery to execute the powers of the constitution. A similar law-making machinery is at work in the several states and territories.

In Massachusetts there are generally twenty-nine standing committees appointed. They consist of two members on the part of the senate, and five on the part of the house. Each legislature has its own rules and orders on all such subjects.

The different legislative bodies are in the habit of examining accusations of frauds, corruption, bribery, etc., committed by, and referring to, members of such bodies, or by officials appointed by them—proceedings, however, which seldom produce the desired result. It seems that such investigations should be left to the judiciary, whose proper sphere it is to investigate illegal acts. The custom is of English origin, where the judiciary depends entirely upon the king, and is considered with jealous eyes by the parliament and people. Our judiciary is a part of the people and deserves full credit. These exceptionary inquiries are apt to undermine the credit of the legislative body, if the accused party is considered not guilty, even when indeed it is innocent. Better the law should have with us its regular course.

LETTER XL.

Knowledge. — Commerce. — Money. — Cotton.— Business is King. — Political Business. — Politicians. — Statesmen. — Genuine and Bogus Politics. — Commander Maury's Letters. — Dead Sea. — Telescopes. — Camels. — Whales. — Patents. — Patriotism. — Hard Times. — High Salaries. — Scarcity of Talent. — Consolidating Cities. — Political and Private, or Free Non-political Business. — What it is. — French Emperor. — Pennsylvania selling State Works. — General Welfare. — Canals. — Competition. — Railroads. — Public Debts. — National Political Business. — Congress. — Representative System. — Municipal Political Business. — State Legislature. — Executive. — Judiciary. — Organizer. — Subdivisions. — Counties. — Towns. — Representative. — Counties. — Political County Business. — Legislative. — Executive. — Judicial. — Overseer.— Supervisor.— County Court. — Representative. — Townships. — Political Town Business. — Threefold. — Mayor. — Aldermen or Selectmen. — Democratic Representative. — Working Districts. — State Failure. — Self taxation. — Hamburg. — Cities. — Villages. — Size of States, Counties, Towns. — Philadelphia. — New York. — Centralization. — Mutual Control. — European Large Places. — Monarchy. — Its Philosophy and Substance. — Japanese Cities. — Commodore Perry's Report. — Hakodadi. — Political Arithmetic and Geometry. — Measure for Private Affairs. -- Crisis. — Crash of the Largest Business Concerns. — Size of State Confederations. — Congress meddling with Non-political and Municipal Local Business. — American Ladies. — Character of Free Non-political Business. — Science, Arts, Culture, Religion, Commerce. — Society Progressive. — States Protective. — Monroe Doctrine. — Licenses. — Liberty of Industry in China, Japan, European States. — Publius. — Cantons in Switzerland Republics, when consolidated Monarchy. — Great Britain consolidated England, Ireland, Scotland, Wales. — Mr. D'Israeli. — Napoleon III. — Missouri Compromise. — Division of States. — Stability of Government.

At certain periods something, call it an idea, genius, or as you please, rules the affairs of mankind. Some say that, at present, *knowledge* rules the world, others attribute this honor to *money*, or *cotton*, or *commerce*. Is this true? In some respects, yes. But over knowledge, money, cotton, and commerce, there rules, no doubt, in our age supremely, a stern, logical, mathematical, exact, positive, and really tyrannical master, whose name is *business*. Its sway and rights begin now to be more universally felt, appreciated, and respected, and nowhere more than in the United States.

What are the thirty millions hoarded in the banks of New York without business? Mere dross. What are the ships in our harbors without business? Floating Spanish castles. What is all our knowledge, skill, enterprise, and industry, without business? A sickly thing in a crisis. Business is *king*. It is the godfather of practical knowledge. It is industry drilled and in march. Without hard thinking, exertion, perseverance, experimenting, diligence, and labor that sweats the brow—in one word, without methodical business, there is no true knowledge, no real wealth. Show me a single dollar, book, or other thing made by man, which is not the product of business. Mere knowledge is culture, too often unpractical, until business gives it tone, form, animation, and creative force. Mere gold is glitter. But let it be carried by business into the streets, streams, wheels, cars, carts, shops, factories, stores, offices, upon the highways and seas, and, magic-like, it will transform the most common, inert, hetereogenous, rare, and incongruous things and elements into a living, blissful, harmonious, mutually-benefitting whole!

The middle ages were dark, because business was either unknown or despised and persecuted. The sword and mitre were then king of the land. But business prevailed upon the sea, and soon conquered the land. Since, it has been coveted, privileged, respected, taught, and skilfully systematized in the house, market, and on the field; it is now conducted with the precision of the solar system, operating with the velocity of electricity, and working with the combined forces of races and elements. See how it presses the "dolce far niente" gents and "poco curante" lazzaroni-loafer-drones in Italy (a railroad in Rome!) Spain, Mexico, and elsewhere into its service! how it taps, I will not say stupid, but dark Africa, opens quaint Japan, finds its way into Chinese Tartary deserts, and wherever idleness or false power hovers about or unappropriated nature sleeps! Its sway is universal. Proud emperors and haughty queens, arrogant sabre knights and dull breviary monks bow before it, and become business men in their turn. Yes, business is king, and an honest, skilful business man the true nobleman of our age.

It is foreign to the scope of my letters to give you a full picture of the immense power and sway of this modern autocrat. All I can do is to say, that the earth, heavens, and sea are tributary to him; that all men are his subjects; and even the most abject loafer—that is, a being who shuns business—can not drag on his miserable existence without being a cause of business to others, perhaps jailors or hangmen, as the case may be.

I have, however, to confine myself to one business branch, viz., the political, which, to explain, requires quite a book. It would fill a library to tell you all about the diverse branches of business, from that of Rothschild down to the *filitier*, from the trunk railroad to the cartman, from the cotton-spinner to the needlewoman, from the miner to the pinmaker, from the planter to the fruit-vender, from the Appletons to the rag-picker, from the whaler to the oysterman, from the ocean telegramist to the news pedlars, etc., for each has its own sphere, science, system, history, manipulations, chances, and rights. Now, to understand the working of republican constitutions and parties, one must well know what is *political business* and what not, and what difference there is between *politicians* and *statesmen.* I most certainly would not trouble you so much with those things, if the happiness of families or society were not so closely connected with it. Think of California, Kansas, Utah, to say nothing of Mexico, Nicaragua, South America, Spain, Italy, Hungary, etc.

If the best men in all ages devoted their wealth, comfort, energies, and even their lives to *politics*, it must be something better, and of more importance to the human family, than what passes under this name in the newspapers and general conversation. What would be our Union, if Washington and his noble compatriots had devoted their lives exclusively to agricultural, mercantile, or manufactural pursuits? And what is their merit? They understood the art of politics well. They were real statesmen, acting for the general welfare, differing entirely from those who are at present called politicians—that is, mere placemen, or traders with the public affairs for their personal advantage.

When Mr. Commander Maury, in his valuable Letters to his Sons, advised them not to meddle with politics, he took, of course, this word in its improper sense; but when I have told you, my sons: Study politics well, that you may become masters of this art, and thoroughly acquainted with its bearing upon society, I used the word in its proper sense.

What public or political officers, *in their capacity at public expense*, are doing is public or political business, right or wrong. The examination of the water of the Dead sea, the exploration of the whaling grounds, the explanation of the best sailing routes, the looking through government telescopes, the riding on government camels, at government expense, and the records, maps and books published thereupon by the government; hospitality and fireworks at public expense, all this is public or political business. It will be admitted, however, that these examples, and all that is done by political officers, besides the realization of justice, is spurious or improper political business, because it is originally private business. Any traveller may taste the water of the Dead sea, any whaling captain may tell the world all about the feeding grounds of the whales and the best methods of catching them, etc., etc., and at very trifling expense, too, while our Congress has spent for such spurious political business, in two years, six millions of dollars! Is not this practice utterly wrong?

Congress is bound to protect private rights and business, but not to embark in it, or divulge whaling, fishing, manufacturing, and scientific arcanas. I have heard bitter complaints of the congressional whaling revelations, because stirring up uncalled-for competition. This *apropos*.

Patriotic and well-informed statesmen established our Union, and organized the federal government on sound principles, leaving the organization of the municipal affairs to their posterity. But their place is now occupied by speculators in politics. Are only "hard times" raising patriotic men? Is the flower patriotism not perennial, but only centennial?

They well know that the genuine political business, especially that belonging to the states, is not very lucrative, except the salaries are high and afford a chance for accumulation. The pretext for them is that talent is scarce and very high in price; that new offices are required for certain business, as for compromising or conciliation, insolvencies, banks, railroads, etc., which may be by the ordinary officials attended to as well. But their most successful operations consist in manufacturing bogus political business, which they do by drawing free social business into the sphere of states, for which purpose they even break down constitutional town, county, or city organizations, and consolidate them, as they call this operation, to get larger spheres for monopolizing gas and railroad companies, and all kinds of contracts and jobs beyond the possibility of a control by the people. These tactics are the cause of exorbitant taxes, debts, and inevitable corruption. Badly-governed New York city alone, consequently, pays as much in city taxes as a respectable well-managed kingdom in Europe in state taxes. To stem, now, this wrong current in public affairs so detrimental to society, I beseech you, and all men and women, to learn and understand well exactly what is political business and what is not.

In a society organized like ours, on the natural and rational principle of self-government, the following objects are private or free social and not political business, viz: industry, as commerce, manufactures, agriculture, speaking, lecturing, preaching, teaching, printing, painting, sculpturing, etc.: further, education in families not to be interfered with by church or state officials; instruction in schools, academies, colleges, universities, etc.; literature; religion; charity in regard to poor, infirm, sick, etc.; travelling; migration; communications by canals, railroads, etc. With these, and similar affairs, free governments have directly nothing to do, and should provide in regard to them only general laws, for the administration of justice when needed. A free state government indeed never should have the means for such business. In free society men are presumptively perfectly able to manage those objects alone; and this ability constitutes indeed the great difference between free and subject society. Subjects, as such, admit that they expect from their governments that they should do all for them. The French emperor said this, without reserve, of the Frenchmen, in his speech from the throne to the legislative body, in 1857, and therefore condescended to give advice about the fertilizing of the lands in Gascogne. How you would laugh if our president or one of our governors should indulge in such advice! Still, Congress meddles with similar things, as seed, books, etc.;

and states have embarked in the building of canals and railroads, and the manufacturing of salt, etc. This being no political business at all, the consequence has been imposition, fraud, corruption, extravagant expenses, high taxes, undue patronage, overindebtedness and bankruptcy of such states. I refer here only to Pennsylvania and New York. There is no probability that any of our states which aim exclusively at the realization of justice ever will be involved in debt or insolvency. The government of Pennsylvania is returning to sound doctrine and disposing of its state railroads and canals. All other states involved in similar speculations have to follow this example as fast as possible.

But you may perhaps object: does not this circumscribe the activity of governments too much? Is it not the duty of Congress to promote the general welfare? I am aware that these words occur in the preamble of the constitution. They have been made use of by speculative politicians of all parties for all kinds of schemes, and too often they have succeeded in carrying them out at enormous public expense. The truth is, however, that no government can promote the general welfare of society better than by paying its undivided attention to the realization of justice. If a government should build a canal on account of the general welfare, it must begin with injustice; because such a work would be built at general expense, to which all those who carry freight now forwarded on the canal, also have to contribute. The government breaks down, by its canal, teamsters and carriers, without offering any indemnification, and forces them besides to pay taxes for the canal and its indebtedness. Instead of protection and justice, this class of citizens and all those connected with the prior transportation business, are ruined by the state. Later some private citizens construct cheap and expeditious railroads, which supercede by competition the government canal. This canal being backed by state power requires the railroads to be taxed for its support—a tax which is called "discriminating duties." Thus begins and ends such a canal in injustice, simply because government meddles with a private business never belonging to its proper province. Private people among themselves are equal in regard to competition, but not private persons and governments. This applies to books, salt, academies, universities, hospitals, and everything governments undertake at public expense which does not properly belong to their sphere.

If all governments embark in private business, for example, railroad building, express lines, freight and passenger transportation on land and sea, they can not avoid running the race of competition together, as it happens between the Pennsylvania and New York state-works, between the New York and Canadian canals and railroads, between the English, French, and United States mail-steamers. This race, of course, is carried out with more or less recklessness, at the expense of the people who are thus saddled with debts and high taxes. Every one who argues fairly, and has a lively sense of what is right between governments and governed, will admit that on one hand the applying of the powerful forces of state institutions in such a direction is against the object and dignity of government, and, on the other hand, that justice alone produces the highest social happiness and welfare imaginable. For this we are exclusively indebted to the art of politics; because it teaches how to organize society for this elevated noble purpose.

I hope the time is near when our governments will vie with each other in regard to the best law codes, the promptest administration of justice, the greatest public order, economy, and safety, and leave their intelligent, enterprising, wealthy, and very speculative citizens at liberty to take care of the rest.

If you understand the nature of the non-political or private business well, I can be short in the description of the political business. This is two-fold — national and municipal — generally committed to the care of one institution, called a state. The American states, when framing the constitution, separated the national from the municipal business, and left the first to the functional care of Congress.

First. Of the national political business belonging to Congress we have spoken: it is exceedingly well specified in the constitution. It is managed by accountable and responsible representatives, and never by the people directly. After deducting this business there remains —

Second. For a state the business of *organizing* society politically, that is, for the ends of justice in municipal regard; setting up for this purpose a constitution, appointing a government, viz: a legislature, executive, and judiciary; dividing society into smaller political districts, viz: counties and townships, cities and villages; distributing the political business, viz: the legislative, executive, and judicial, among them; controlling it; organizing the state (executive) forces and finances; enacting all general laws, codes, and statutes. The state institution is also managed by accountable representatives, and as supreme sovereign organizer of society never should be what I call a working district. You will see that without states there would be no Congress. (In regard to the state officials, I refer to the letters on the constitution of the state of New York, in the second part).

Third. To the counties rightfully belong political local business of importance, and concerning people in several towns. It is, like the state business, legislative, executive, and judicial, and refers to important civil and criminal cases, prisons, penitentiaries, forming of associations under general laws, roads, bridges, inland harbors, county forces, finances, state elections, etc. There occur supervisors, sheriffs, judges, jurors, etc. This district is also a representative and working district. At the head of the executive, in imitation of the federal constitution, should be appointed a single responsible officer, perhaps called overseer.

Fourth. To the townships or towns rightfully belong the public local business of a more personal or detail character, as voting, census, measures, weights, common schools, sidewalks, streets, taxation, abating of nuisances, minor civil and criminal cases, police, etc., generally enumerated in the statute books.

The town organization force is but little developed. It may easily be used for hypothecation systems, for mutual insurance objects, and for various other purposes, even with the help of ladies' associations. This will be done if left more free by the busybody legislatures.

They are the principal working districts, where often the private and public affairs are blended. They alone are truly democratic. They make by-laws, which are executed by the mayor. Why should not, in uniformity with the federal constitution, every township have ONE executive, assisted by constables or policemen? They have selectmen or aldermen—the same thing in reality as representatives of the people—and assistants of the executive. The judiciary consists of town judges or justices of the peace, clerks, etc.

If you will examine the merits of a government, begin first with the towns (communes), and the management of their public affairs, before you devote much time to the reading of the constitutions of the states, and diplomatic documents, messages, and other state papers. These may all bear a high character, contain the loftiest sentiments, proclaim the soundest principles, still if the towns (cities, villages) are disorderly, full of rowdies, stained with crimes, overburdened with taxes, buried in debts, or in the hands of mobs or vigilance committees, then you may safely hold that the state institution itself is an imposture or a failure, whatever may be its name. If you will study the political character and public morals of our people, do not go to Washington when Congress is in session; spend no time in metropolises or large cities. No, go into a town and attend several town meetings, and see how the citizens, fresh from the field, anvil, and counting-room, converse, debate, speak and resolve, under a moderator, on their public affairs.

A general symptom of public corruption is public debts. France and Great Britain take here the lead. Spain owes seven hundred, Switzerland two million dollars. Including the political bank paper-money, the people of the United States have a large public debt, almost as large as Russia, viz., four hundred millions, a country where public corruption and profligacy are the rule.

If the towns are independent in their home affairs—under state control, of course—the spirit of patriotism and a brisk emulation among the townships will be kept alive, and a permanent home feeling and warm attachment created, from which will spring up those deeds of charity and munificence which are the true glory of a free country. The genuine blessings of liberty ripen there. A true home attachment can only grow up in such a town. And this is the reason why sensible citizens, after living a while, during the busy stage of life, in large cities, generally terminate it within the precincts of a town. A state constitution should contain the general organic dispositions on the formations of towns. It might be well to forbid the creating of public debts, and make self-taxation in towns the rule; it is better than assessing. Free men are well aware that public business and services cause expenses. In the free city of Hamburg, the principal taxes are raised by self-taxation. The citizens assess themselves, and state the amount of their property in writing. These statements are recorded, and a tax-roll made out. If a fraudulent estimate is discovered, a revision of the case takes place at the expense of the citizen, and if there is fraud proved or neglect prevalent, he moreover exposes himself to punishment for thus violating his duty as a citizen. It is said, by all who know Hamburg, that this self-assessing never gives cause to complaint, and acts admirably well. It is the only just and respectable manner to raise taxes among free men. We may still learn something from Europe.

Exceptions from this districting are incorporated cities and villages. If the towns are well organized, and, when growing too populous, conveniently divided, the incorporation of cities, only leading to bad centralization, may be obviated entirely. Most European cities were priorly fortresses, and therefore densely built up.

It is self-evident, that if in the towns and counties the laws are well executed, society will be in order, and that if not, neither the states proper nor Congress can do much to avert the evil resulting from a bad execution of the laws.

It is further obvious, that for a good performance of the necessary political affairs, it is indispensable to make those districts of the right proportionate size, that is, neither too large nor too small in regard to population. The best business men can not perform a task which is not adequate; therefore, the right proportion we may learn from history and experience. A republican state, to preserve its character well, should not contain much over one million of inhabitants, equal to two hundred thousand voters or families; a rural township not much over ten thousand inhabitants, equal to two thousand families; a city-like built township not much over twenty thousand inhabitants, equal to four thousand families; and a county not over five urban or ten rural towns.

The real cause of the downfall of republics and of their expensive and corrupt administration, is their imperfect organization with regard to size, population and business, depriving the citizens of the facility to control the latter and their officials well. *Their mutual social control must be preserved under all circum-*

stances. In monarchies the prince takes studiously the self-control out of the hands of the people. He fetters even for this purpose the press and public discussion, and prohibits meetings, etc., supplying it by a pyramid of official bureaus, controlling each other, or, as the case may be, deceiving each other. This is called bureaucracy.

The centralization of the business in New York, Philadelphia, and similar cities, makes it unwieldly. The citizens of such places are not able to control their officials, being strangers to each other. This applies also to towns and counties. Even in monarchical Europe, where the people are controlled by officials, large cities are not so much centralized in regard to their administration as New York. Paris has at least twelve mayoralities or municipalities; London is divided into some thirty odd wards, with an alderman for each, who together are properly the subordinate governors of their respective wards, under the direction of the lord-mayor, whom they elect. Besides, there is a legislative council, forming a court of two hundred and fifty members. Dresden, of about one hundred thousand inhabitants, is divided into three districts, which possess corporative rights and jurisdiction. Generally, the modern suburbs of old cities are under separate jurisdictions and administrations. Moreover, large places are there guarded by strong garrisons, and often by fortifications and citadels. Centralization has with us become more than a fashion—a mania. Men have a strong desire for forbidden things. Monarchy is a forbidden fruit for us; still, by centralizing towns, by letting towns grow up to states, and states to empires, we follow the monarchical policy. The centralization of the public business, especially the legislature, in a few hands, is the philosophy and substance of monarchy. To keep the business resulting from it in one or a few hands, with the emoluments, patronage, and influence, standing armies are made use of. Still, neither standing armies, nor castes, nor state churches would help make monarchies without the previous centralization of the political business. By devoting, in the outset, a county for a city, as has been done in New York, Philadelphia (?) San Francisco, etc., and making thus a clean sweep with the townships, we graft a monarchical scion upon the liberty tree of a free society.

It is a political error, except we give to the wards a similar organization which properly belongs to the townships, which, of course, would then involve a mere change of names. *All regularly-settled states, counties, and towns, within the size I have indicated, are, so far as I am acquainted with them, well managed, and free of corruption*, which proves the correctness of my position.

Exceptions make mushroom states or territories, as California, Kansas, Utah, forced into existence by extraordinary circumstances. Their failure proves that republics are not the work of miners, projectors, and Sharpe's rifle associations and priestcraft. So we may safely argue that all states, counties, and towns, beyond the indicated size, have outrun their republican career. They may, under favorable circumstances, be for a while well managed; still, this is then more the work of accident than of necessity. Gradually and irresistibly corruption will creep in, and increase in proportion as the mutual control becomes less practicable. This is a most important truth.

You will now see why, especially our large cities, swim in constant trouble, either with their officials or with mobs; because the first can not grasp the business, and if they could, do not serve long enough to become thoroughly acquainted with it, or they may do as they please, being without a practical control of the people; and further, because mobs will invariably rise under such circumstances. We can reform this. According to all we know of the Japanese, they understand very well how to organize large, densely-populated districts, evidently by avoiding the centralization of the public business, and by sustaining independent town organizations, as the following extract from Commodore Perry's report will show. He says, page 437, vol. ii. of Hakodadi :—

" The town contains a thousand houses (probably ten thousand inhabitants), belonging to the imperial fief of Matsmai, and is the largest town on the island of Tesso, with the exception of Matsmai, from which it is distant about thirty miles in an easterly direction. An excellent road connects the two places, and a large trade is carried on between them. This town is regularly built, with streets running at right angles with each other. They are between thirty and forty feet in width, and all carefully macadamized to allow of the proper draining of water. There are open gutters on each side, which receive the drippings of the houses and the washings of the street, and also well-constructed sewers, through which the surplus water and the refuse are poured into the bay. The sidewalks, which are frequently paved, are curbed with stone planted on edge as with us; but as no wheeled carriages are found in the town, the middle of the street is used indiscriminately in dry weather by the pedestrian. Hakodadi, like all the Japanese towns, is remarkably clean, the streets being suitably constructed for draining, and kept, by constant sprinkling and sweeping, in a neat and healthful condition. Wooden picket fences with gates cross the streets at short intervals; these are opened for the passage of the people during the day, but closed at night. The same municipal regulations obtain in Hakodadi as in all the other towns of Japan. The inhabitants of the several streets (blocks, wards) form so many separate communities, as it were, responsible for the conduct of each other, each governed by an official called 'ottona' (alderman), who is also held responsible for the good order of the people under his especial charge, and these ottonas are also made responsible for the conduct of each other. The gates and picket fences would seem to mark out the separate fields of duty of these officials. At one side of the street, among the houses, there is ordinarily a sentry-box for a watchman, whose duty it is to guard the town against disturbance, and give early notice of the occurrence of fire. A general quiet pervades the streets—no turbulent mob disturbs the general peace and tranquillity."

I regret that this voluminous pictorial report is silent about the city government proper, its costs, income, election, appointment, taxes, etc. The administration of the cities in America and Europe is still so imperfect, that such information should have taken the place of the many useless pictures and local descriptions in this work. But this notice, as meagre as it is, is highly significant and instructive. The distribution of the police should be imitated at once. The mutual control and responsibility of the wards and the night police are excellent. By such minute districting large densely built-up towns can be alone made orderly.

Much depends upon the political arithmetic and geometry. Without minding its rules, our society must and will become unruly. Who can, should shun with his family large places with centralized administrations, to be not troubled by mobs, corruption, high exorbitant taxes, public debts, vigilance committees, extras, and other evils incident to such defective political organizations.

There is, also, a certain just measure for private affairs, as for everything, which to transgress is imprudent. Experience proves that over-large farms, manufactures, railroads and similar works, yield less revenue, suffer more from the ever-occurring fluctuations of trade, and are more exposed to losses by fraud than smaller controllable establishments of this kind. In the late crisis, the crash began with the largest business concerns. But private business being foreign to my subject, I must leave it to you to ponder upon that which is "overlarge" in this regard, and add rather a few words about the proportion of a confederation like ours. Upon this subject the political geography has naturally much influence. The introduction of steam and telegraphs, and other mechanical discoveries, facilitate the uniting of numerous small states. If the central government be strictly confined to national business, it may be extended until the political geography advises or forces to stop.

If Congress is to meddle with such business as road-building, sand-banks, snags and flats removing, hospital and harbor building, cotton-seed, plants, Dutch tulips, sugar cane, camels, books and pictorials, and the like, then our confederation is already much too large. Instead of making the seed-man for the farmers, and the livery-stable man for those who cross the Plains, it should first discharge all legitimate claims against its treasury, to give a telling example of Christian righteousness and Washingtonian scrupulous honesty to the people.

Thus we see how important is a correct understanding of what is exactly political business and what not, and where it ought to be performed, and the right size of the public business-districts. System is a natural condition of our mind. Wherever combined labor is required, it is brought into a system, and divided, distributed, and so employed that, with proper supervision, it MUST work well. The necessity of system, order and proportion, is as self-evident in educational, mechanical, manufacturing, mercantile, and agricultural establishments, as in households, towns, counties, states, and confederations of states. A written regulation for any one of these concerns may be as well called a constitution ; but it is usual to give this name only to one for a social political organization. Still its object is the same: regulation of labor, business, or functions. From this plain common-sense view, we comprehend best why political organizations or constitutions ought to be strictly adapted to the actual state of society and business, or, in one word, ought to be practical, and not visionary and utopian. The American ladies are excellent organizers. I hope, then, that my letters will find favor with them, however long and tedious they are, according to the *jejune* nature of their subjects.

The non-political business, if free, is immensely expansive and progressive, like society itself. Sciences, arts, religion, commerce, etc., belong to all, are for all. But the political business is confined to certain districts. Governments are not universal not for all; their business is exclusive, conservative, stable, protective. It is, as I mentioned before, a mistake to call the state institutions progressive. Society alone is progressive under it, and therefore this ought to be stable to prevent confusion. Insular position, like that of Great Britain, or distance from powerful nations, like that of the United States, increases this exclusiveness, and adds to the security and strength of the government. From the exclusive character of the political business, sprung up what is called the *Monroe doctrine*, or the principle that no government has a right to meddle with the affairs of others. This principle applies with as much force to families, towns, and counties, as to states and nations, because each of those concerns is, within its proper sphere, exclusive or independent. This rule may be extended over a continent, viz. over America, in regard to Europe, etc., if all American governments would adopt and execute it. This principle, however, will fall to the ground, if all states aim at nothing but justice, for then there would be no chance for interference or encroachments, or even treaties, at all.

By means of licenses a certain class of public business is committed to the care of private persons, as the establishing and building of ferries, bridges, roads, etc., who derive their rights from the tenor of the license, which they forfeit by violation. Justice towards the public is the true cause of this expedient. Still many governments, also in the United States, have this licensing extended for the purpose of raising revenues, which, of course, is an abusive infringement of free social business, as commerce, trading, industry, etc.

The real humane development and culture depends upon the liberty of industry. In the proportion governments interfere with it, man is enslaved. The lowest degree is absolute serfdom. Then come the Chinese and Japanese systems, which admit a certain degree of internal industrial freedom, but are exclusive in regard to foreigners. The system of classifying the trades, and arming them with monopolistic privileges, still prevalent in many states on the European continent, follows next. Then we meet the different custom systems, which are more or less exclusive, or —Chinese. Even the patent rights must be mentioned here. There has not existed a single government which, in one way or another, even only by raising taxes, has not interfered with the liberty of industry, so that one may come to the conclusion that a full enjoyment of this freedom from all shackles is impracticable, if not impossible. Still, the truth can not be denied that a full expansion of humanity depends upon the full enjoyment of this noble gift of nature.

"The interest of the man must be connected with the constitutional rights of the place," so says Publius (A. Hamilton) in one of his excellent articles on the federal constitution in the *Federalist.* This is perfectly right, because by such a connection these interests are protected. Hence the necessity not to unsettle or disturb these constitutional rights, and my ardent pleading for good stable town and county organizations by the constitution, in order to render the naturally settling down force of business secure.

The same writer and statesman remarks, that a great difficulty of free governments is to create an effective control of them. Now, is not the only practical and effective self-control of a government in a constitution which expressly prohibits to meddle, by special laws, with the constitutional business of towns and counties, and with the free non-political business of society at large, school-books and the bible included?

Men of culture are attached to their business interests like slaves to their masters. It is also well known that the regular occupation of man leaves an indelible impression upon his character and manners. The same is true of the political business. Consolidate the public affairs of the small state-districts, called Cantons in Switzerland, and soon the government of the whole will become monarchical, and the same men who were with soul and body republicans, will become with body and soul monarchical subjects, because their interest, their business, is managed in a monarchical manner.

All the power of the English government is a product of business centralization, eulogized by D'Israeli in his late speech against the Palmerston cabal. Still the "military disasters," the complaints of the clumsy management of the army and the civil service, filling the blue books for years, are the result of this business accumulation in London. Of course, Napoleon III. praised centralization highly in his speech at the occasion of the celebration of the enlargement of the Luxembourg palace.

Let us apply this political business-theory to an important event at home, the abolition of the so-called Missouri compromise. Why is this, I ask, a most judicious statesmanlike political act? Answer: because it removes from Congress the last vestige or precedent of a power to legislate on a local business, bound labor, which does not belong to its constitutional sphere, the direct consequence of which now is, the full liberty to divide overgrown states in the north, without exciting the fear of the southern states about their local domestic affairs, by altering the senatorial representation. You see that by a slight mistake about such a single plain local business—all labor is business—we may risk the stability of our Union, because our southern fellow-citizens will rather secede from the Union than give up the management of their own local interests; and by doing so they are pre-eminently right, and those who interfere with them exceedingly wrong.

It remains for me to answer a single question more, before I conclude this long epistle; that is, what government is the most stable? that which allows the greatest liberty of industry. A government which follows the opposite theory must surround itself by a great number of officials of all sorts, in which regard we have again to mention first the Chinese and Japanese governments as examples. Commodore Perry, in his report, complains often of swarms of officials and spies, commanded to exclude the people from the intercourse with the Americans. The vexatious busybodiness of the mandarins is well known. Then follow Russia, France, Austria, Prussia, etc., with their public, secret, and detective police, gendarmes, custom-line guards, standing armies, etc., etc., contrivances which, in their nature, interfere with industry, are galling to the people, and undermining the stability of governments. People, with a delicate frame of mind, revolt at the idea that a government may fetter the press, confiscate books and papers, or tamper with the spelling and reading-books in schools. The first may cost Napoleon III. his crown, the second will deprive a republican government of its dignity, the crown which adorns it and gives it authority. Also, the business of teaching should enjoy full liberty. Upon the use of school-books the teacher has to decide, and not statesmen.

Suppose there should be a class of the citizens, from theological reasons, opposed to the use of the bible in the public schools, and a political party interested in the *vote* of this class, and the legislature attempted to enforce by law the use of the bible for instruction, then this party would oppose the law, in order to profit by that vote. If now the use of the bible depends upon the law or state interference, and not upon the free agency of teachers and parents, the bible will likely remain excluded from ALL public schools as long as the government is allowed to interfere with such private affairs; while the use of this book would be almost general if it depended, as it ought, wholly upon teachers and parents to decide whether it shall be used or not. But let me conclude this rambling over the immense field of occupation, industry, and business.

LETTER XLI.

Election Impulses. — Social Movements organized in the United States, Health producing. — Social Movements in Europe destructive. — Famine, Gold, Conquest, Religion, Liberty. — Main Social-Impulses. — Liberty-Impulse of the Republican Party. — American Party acting unimpulsive. — Dear Union-Impulse of the Democratic Party.

I ADD an article, for the benefit of party politicians, written on the result of the presidential election in 1856, which may have a bearing upon the election in 1860.

Masses and large assemblages move by impulses, which may be right or wrong, genuine or sham, according to circumstances. Masses do not reason like individuals. Reason is cold, void of caloric, the impulses of society are warm, electric, and powerful, like those which lift the ocean waves from their repose, while those of individuals are like the forces which make a rivulet meandering. Still individuals and society, like rivulets and oceans, require for their health MOTION. In free society like ours the motion of the masses is foreseen, organized, legalized, the individual is master of himself; in subject society, however, like that in Europe, its motion is left to nature, social tempests, called wars, emeutes, revolutions, and the individual is bemastered by restrictions, caste distinctions, and a great many other political and clerical contrivances well known. Social movements in Europe are mostly destructive, while with us they are a necessary part of our social regimen and well-being. As a general thing famine, gold, conquest, religion, and liberty are the main impulses of grand social movements.

The presidential election which just moved the social sea of twenty-six millions can not be understood without an examination of the various impulses at work. The movement of the republicans was propelled by the impulse of liberty (and gold or offices besides), that of the democrats by the impulse of union (with the same indispensable golden appendage); the effort of the Americans did not amount to an impulse. Hunger or famine, conquest or religion, the great social impulses in Europe, Asia, etc., had, of course, nothing to do with the fourth of November, this movement being appointed by law. It is obvious that in free society only that impulse should succeed at national elections which is just required by circumstances. Now, I ask, was the liberty-impulse of the republicans, indeed, a necessity, or merely manufactured for the political trade? My opinion is that it was spurious and mere sham, because in our country the impulse of liberty has been long ago, at the time of the revolution and by the successful establishing of the federal constitution, entirely used up; both events have rendered us sufficiently free, independent, and self-governing. When the republicans cried out on the stump, in the tabernacle, in Wall street, "we strike for liberty," everybody must have been struck by the folly and absurdity of the thing in our absolutely free society.

But there are slaves in the southern states! Well there are. Can they, in our free and well-organized society, be freed by a social movement, or anybody else but their masters? Sane men in Massachusetts have as little to do with this business in Georgia or Kansas, as with the liberation of the subjects in Great Britain and of the serfs in Russia. This sham liberty impulse has been justly rebuked in the city of New York. It failed there in spite of the most tremendous exertion of a host of able editors, powerful speakers, and inspired preachers to the contrary notwithstanding. People here appreciated this charlatan liberty-cry well. But not so in the distance; there people believe in the Metropolitan and Boston liberty stuff, as they are apt to patronize other charlatans from these latitudes. Hence the total failure of the republicans here, and their comparative success in the provinces. Nobody is easier carried away by the liberty impulse than the Europeans, from very natural reasons. The most influential German newspapers joined the republicans.

The Americans have been entirely unsuccessful because they acted unimpulsive from the beginning. A SECRET society for the control of the PUBLIC affairs is not impulsive, but to a great many indeed repulsive, and so it is the disapproving of the abolition of the Missouri line; so it is the prolongation of the Congressional naturalization term of five years, actually disregarded by all state legislatures. Even the sentiment that we shall be ruled by our own laws, can never act as a social impulse, because it is a plain matter-of-course. All this is not moving, not propelling, not warming—it is political, cold water clinic.

Now, was the union-impulse, which moved the democratic masses, the true one in our time? The result of the election says, yes! It was high TIME to settle in the Union by a decisive popular vote the most vexatious business-question: shall the legislation of the late Congress in regard to the equal rights of our citizens in the territories to rule themselves by their own laws, as the rest of us, also in regard to free and bound labor, be conclusive or not? That people in Pennsylvania were not deceived by the liberty agitation, like others, is owing to their steering for this union-result since 1819, by resolves of their legislature and state democratic committee, an important item in the history of this election.

The plain result of this grand election movement is, then, that the union sentiment is a stronger social impulse than abstract liberty, and justly so, because without a firm harmonious union we could not enjoy our liberty at all. May this sentiment predominate for ever.

I mentioned the year 1860. Then returns the presidential election and a new run for the offices and their emoluments. It may be that pretext, liberty of the slave, will then be again made use of to strengthen the party out of office and power. You will know then what it means, and not be deceived.

LETTER XLII.

Declaration of Independence. — Defining of the Position of the Young Nation. — Explanation of the Sentence, "that all men are born equal." — Jefferson's Letter explaining it.

In this letter I devote a few words to the Declaration of Independence, adopted, after an animated debate, on the 4th of July, 1776, by the Congress. Its author, as you know, was Thomas Jefferson, the most illustrious compeer of Washington. The principal object of this celebrated document was: *To define the position of the young nation and its government; to declare why a separation from the government of Great Britain had taken place, and to enlisten the sympathies of the civilized nations and their governments in their favor.* This declaration bears the character of the exciting times; it boldly defies the authority of a proud royal master, who could not listen to humble reiterated petitions for relief and remonstrances against arbitrary legislation in small matters, involving, however, important principles. It was, for the time-being, the platform of the young American nation, upon which the war of the Revolution was fought. You may call it an arraignment, an appeal, a challenge, or the "shriek" of an outraged people; but it is no law. It takes high ground, in powerful words, which, when sharply examined, would not always bear criticism. The sentence, that all men are created equal, is not exactly true, both physically and politically. Not two men, even not two children in the same family, are created alike. The same diversity which distinguishes all created things, animate and inanimate, prevails in our race. Politically men are as different as the *policies* under which they are born. Not two men are politically equal, and never will be. Women and men are never absolutely equal in political regard. There is no absolute equality of civil rights, although every member of society has a right to be treated according to the general principles of justice. Such allocutions to nations, or to masses, meetings, etc., are of a rather poetical nature, calculated to rouse the feelings. Only in this form they answer to their purpose; it is wrong to take them from another view. All platforms, all addresses of generals to their armies on the battle-field, belong to the same class of literary and oratorical products. If this sentence has a political meaning, it is no other than that the authors of this declaration were of the opinion, that privileged classes, as nobles, possessed of exclusive *hereditary* rights, as governing, exemption from taxes, etc., are incompatible with justice. And then it was a seasonable fling at the English king and nobility, who opposed the independence of the thirteen colonies, because *the people there were* BORN SUBJECTS *of the English crown.* This was especially opposed by Jefferson. In a much later letter, dated Monticello, June 24, 1827, upon an invitation to the anniversary of American Independence, the patriot wrote: "May it [our form of government] be to the world what I believe it will be, [to some parts sooner, to others later, but finally to all], the signal of arousing men to burst the chains under which monkish ignorance and superstition had persuaded them to bind themselves, and to assume the blessings and security of self-government. The form which we have substituted restores the free right to the unbounded exercise of reason and freedom of opinion. All eyes are opened or opening to the rights of man. The general spread of the lights of science has already laid open to every view the palpable truth, *that the mass of mankind has not been born with saddles on their backs, nor a favored few, booted and spurred, ready to ride them legitimately, by the grace of God.*"

No better explanation of the true meaning of this much-disputed sentence can be found than that in these lines of the author of the Declaration of Independence. He hated in 1827, as well as in 1776, the men who pretend that they are born expressly to rule mankind. This Jefferson considered wrong, and denied that God ever had created a man for this purpose. So you may never mistake this sentence about the equal creation of men, as so many do, from mere party views, or a too strictly literal interpretation.

DECLARATION OF INDEPENDENCE, JULY 4, 1776.

The unanimous Declaration of the Thirteen United States of America in Congress assembled.

WHEN, in the course of human events, it becomes necessary for one people to dissolve the political bands which have connected them with another, and to assume among the powers of the earth the separate and equal station to which the laws of nature and of nature's God entitled them, a decent respect to the opinions of mankind requires that they should declare the causes which impel them to the separation.

We hold these truths to be self-evident: that all man are created equal; that they are endowed by their Creator with certain unalienable rights; that among these are life, liberty, and the pursuit of happiness; that, to secure these rights, governments are instituted among men, deriving their just powers from the consent of the governed; that, whenever any form of government becomes destructive of these ends, it is the right of the people to alter or to abolish it, and to institute new government, laying its foundation on such principles, and organizing its powers in such form, as to them shall seem most likely to effect their safety and happiness. Prudence, indeed, will dictate that goverments long established should not be changed for light and transient causes; and, accordingly, all experience hath shown that mankind are more disposed to suffer, while evil are sufferable, than to right themselves by abolishing the forms to which they are accustomed. But when a long train of abuses and usurpations, pursuing invariably the same object, evinces a design to reduce them under absolute despotism, it is their right, it is their duty, to throw off such government, and to provide new guards for their future security. Such has been the patient sufferance of these colonies, and such is now the necessity which constrains them to alter their former systems of government. The history of the present king of Great Britain is a history of repeated injuries and usurpations, all having in direct object the establishment of an absolute tyranny over these states. To prove this, let facts be submitted to a candid world:—

He has refused his assent to laws the most wholesome and necessary for the public good. He has forbidden his governors to pass laws of immediate and pressing importance, unless suspended in their operation till his assent should be obtained; and, when so suspended, he has utterly neglected to attend to them. He has refused to pass other laws for the accomodation of large districts of people, unless those people would relinquish the right of representation in the legislature — a right inestimable to them, and formidable to tyrants only. He has called together legislative bodies at places unusual, uncomfortable, and distant from the repository of their public records, for the sole purpose of fatiguing them into compliance with his measures. He has dissolved representative houses repeatedly for opposing with manly firmness his invasions on the rights of the people. He has refused, for a long time after such dissolutions, to cause others to be elected; whereby the legislative powers, incapable of annihilation, have returned to the people at large for their exercise — the state remaining, in the meantime, exposed to all the dangers of invasion from without and convulsions within.

He has endeavored to prevent the population of these states — for that purpose obstructing the laws of naturalization of foreigners, refusing to pass others to encourage their migration hither, and raising the conditions of new appropriation of lands.

He has obstructed the administration of justice, by refusing his assent to laws for establishing judiciary powers.

He has made judges dependent on his will alone for the tenure of their offices and the amount and payment of their salaries.

He has erected a multitude of new offices, and sent hither swarms of officers to harass our people and eat out their substance.

He has kept among us, in times of peace, standing armies, without the consent of our legislatures.

He has affected to render the military independent of, and superior to, the civil power.

He has combined with others to subject us to a jurisdiction foreign to our constitution and unacknowledged by our laws — giving his assent to their acts of pretended legislation.

For quartering large bodies of armed troops among us; for protecting them, by a mock trial, from punishment for any murders which they should commit on the inhabitants of these states; for cutting off our trade with all parts of the world; for imposing taxes on us without our consent; for depriving us, in many cases, of the benefits of trial by jury; for transporting us beyond seas to be tried for pretended offences; for abolishing the free system of English laws in a neighboring province, establishing therein an arbitrary government, and enlarging its boundaries, so as to render it at once an example and fit instrument for introducing the same absolute rule into these colonies; for taking away our charters, abolishing our most valuable laws, and altering, fundamentally, the *forms* of our governments; for suspending our own legislatures, and declaring themselves invested with power to legislate for us in all cases whatsover.

He has abdicated government here by declaring us out of his protection and waging war against us.

He has plundered our seas, ravaged our coasts, burnt our towns, and destroyed the lives of our people.

He is at this time transporting large armies of foreign mercenaries to complete the works of death, desolation, and tyranny, already begun with circumstances of cruelty and perfidy scarcely paralleled in the most barbarous ages, and totally unworthy the head of a civilized nation.

He has constrained our fellow-citizens, taken captive on the high seas, to bear arms against their country, to become the executioners of their friends and brethren, or to fall themselves by their hands.

He has excited domestic insurrections among us, and has endeavored to bring on the inhabitants of our frontiers the merciless Indian savages, whose known rule of warfare is an undistinguished destruction of all ages, sexes, and conditions.

In every stage of these oppressions, we have petitioned for redress in the most humble terms. Our repeated petitions have been answered only by repeated injury. A prince, whose character is thus marked by every act which may define a tyrant, is unfit to be the ruler of a free people.

Nor have we been wanting in attentions to our British brethren. We have warned them, from time to time, of attempts, by their legislature, to extend an unwarrantable jurisdiction over us. We have reminded them of the circumstances of our emigration and settlement here. We have appealed to their native justice and magnanimity, and we have conjured them, by the ties of our common kindred, to disavow these usurpations, which would inevitably interrupt our connections and correspondence. They, too, have been deaf to the voice of justice and of consanguinity. We must, therefore, acquiesce in the necessity which denounces our separation, and hold them, as we hold the rest of mankind, enemies in war, in peace, friends.

We, therefore, the representatives of the United States of America, in general Congress assembled, appealing to the Supreme Judges of the World for the rectitude of our intentions, do, in the name, and by the authority of the good people of these colonies, solemnly publish and declare that these united colonies are, and of right ought to be, free and independent states; that they are absolved from all allegiance to the British crown, and that all political connection between them and the state of Great Britain is, and ought to be, totally dissolved; and that, as free and independent states, they have full power to levy war, conclude peace, contract alliances, establish commerce, and to do all other acts and things which independent states may of right do. And for the support of this declaration, with a firm reliance on the protection of Divine Providence, we mutually pledge to each other our lives, our fortunes, and our sacred honor.

LETTER XLIII.

Federalist. — Hamilton. — Monroe. — Jay. — Washington's Circular Letter to the Governors of the several States. — Articles of Confederation a loose Wickerwork. — Enviable National and Political Condition of the Citizens of America. — Civilization. — A Compact Indissoluble Union, a Sacred Regard to Public Justice, a Proper Peace Establishment, a Good Friendly Mutual Feeling among the People, the Four Essential Things to the Well-Being, Existence, and Independent Power of the United States. — Liberty is the Baisis of the Whole. — Crisis, Political and Monetary.

YOU know from the history of the United States that the first effort to form a government under certain articles of confederation was almost a total failure. To save the country, some distinguished patriots wrote a series of anonymous articles in favor of a better Union, now collected in a book called the Federalist. The authors were Hamilton, Monroe, and Jay. Washington never wrote except in his official duty. But a few productions of his pen may have exercised more sway over the minds of his countrymen than books. They are patterns for official reports, which, in modern times have vastly degenerated. That you may have them at hand I insert here an extract from a circular letter, written by General Washington, as commander-in-chief of the armies of the United States of America, to the governors of the several states, dated, Headquarters, Newburgh, June 18, 1783. In this letter he states, first, that he is preparing to resign and return to that domestic retirement which it is well known he left with the greatest reluctance, and after the great object of his public activity had been accomplished. He further offers, before retiring from public service, his sentiments respecting some important subjects which appeared to him to be intimately connected with the tranquillity of the United States. That he did not give them to the public at large, or to Congress, but laid them before the governors of the young independent states, was a happy hit of that common-sense sagacity of which few men possessed an ampler share than Washington. The people were oppressed by the burdens of the war; the present Union far from being formed; the articles of confederation a loose wickerwork which could be broken down by the defeat of a single state; the citizens were in a state of fermentation, harboring expectations difficult or impossible to realize, and even inclined to revolt. (Shay's revolt). How wise was it, then, under these critical circumstances, to make the governors, instead of a book or newspaper, the depositories of his sentiments! Nothing was better calculated to dispose them favorably for their realization as state measures. The principal subject of this address is in his own words, as follows:—

"The citizens of America, placed in the most enviable condition, as the sole lords and proprietors of a vast tract of continent, comprehending all the various soils and climates of the world and abounding with all the necessaries and conveniences of life, are now, by the late satisfactory pacification, acknowledged to be possessed of absolute freedom and independency; they are from this period to be considered as the actors on a most conspicuous theatre, which seems to be peculiarly designed by Providence for the display of human greatness and felicity. Here they are not only surrounded with everything that can contribute to the completion of private and domestic enjoyment, but Heaven has crowned all its other blessings by giving a surer opportunity for *political happiness* than any other nation has ever been favored with.

"Nothing can illustrate these observations more forcibly than the recollection of the happy conjuncture of the times and circumstances under which our republic assumed its rank among the nations. The foundation of our empire has not been laid in a gloomy age of ignorance and superstition, but at an epoch when the rights of mankind were better understood and more clearly defined than at any former period. *Researches of the human mind after social happiness have been carried to a great extent;* the treasures of knowledge acquired by the labors of philosophers, sages, and legislators, through a long succession of years, are laid open for use; and their collected wisdom may be happily applied in the establishment of our forms of government. The free cultivation of letters, the unbounded extension of commerce, the progressive refinement of manners, the growing liberality of sentiment, and, above all, the pure and benign light of revelation, have had a meliorating influence on mankind and increased the blessings of society. At this auspicious period the United States came into existence as a nation, and if their citizens should not be completely free and happy, the fault will be entirely their own.

"Such is our situation and such are our prospects. But notwithstanding the cup of blessing is thus reached out to us — notwithstanding happiness is ours if we have the disposition to seize the occasion and make it our own, yet it appears to me there is an option still left to the United States of America whether they will be *respectable* and *prosperous* or *contemptible* and *miserable as a nation.* This is the time of their political probation; this is the moment when the eyes of the whole world are upon them; this is the time to establish or ruin their national character for ever; this is the favorable moment to give such a tone to the federal government as will enable it to answer the ends of its institution; or this may be the ill-fated moment for relaxing the powers of the Union, annihilating the cement of the confederation, *and exposing us to become the sport of European politics, which may play one state against another, to prevent their growing importance, and to serve their own interested purposes;* for, according to the system of policy the states shall adopt at this moment, they will stand or fall; and by their confirmation or lapse, it is yet to be decided whether the revolution must ultimately be considered as a blessing or a curse; a blessing or a curse not to the present age alone, *for with our fate will the destiny of unborn millions be involved.*

"With this conviction of the importance of the present crisis, silence in me would be a crime. I will therefore speak to your excellency the language of freedom and sincerity, without disguise. I am aware, however, those who differ from me in political sentiments may perhaps remark I am stepping out of the proper line of my duty; and they may possibly ascribe to arrogance or ostentation what I know is alone the result of the purest intention; but the rectitude of my own heart, which disdains such unworthy motives — the part I have hitherto acted in life, the determination I have formed of not taking any share in public business hereafter, the ardent desire I feel and shall continue to manifest of quietly enjoying in private life, after all the toils of war, the benefits of a wise and liberal government — will, I flatter myself, sooner or later convince my countrymen that I could have no sinister views in delivering with so little reserve the opinions contained in this address.

"There are four things which I humbly conceive are essential to the well-being, I may even venture to say, to the existence of the United States as an independent power:—

"*First.* An indissoluble union of the states under one head;

"*Second.* A sacred regard to public justice;

"*Third.* The adoption of a proper peace establishment; and

"*Fourth.* The prevalence of that pacific and friendly disposition among the people of the United States which will induce them to forget their *local prejudices* and *politics,* to make those mutual concessions which are requisite to the general prosperity, and, in some instances, to sacrifice their individual advantages to the interest of the community.

"These are the pillars on which the glorious fabric of our independence and national character must be supported. *Liberty is the basis, and whoever would dare to sap the foundation or overturn the structure, under whatever specious pretext he may attempt it, will merit the bitterest execration and the severest punishment which can be inflicted by his injured country!*"

This will amply compensate you for all ennui which I may have caused you by these letters. You will, from the tenor of this extract, of which I have put some lines in italics, be aware how clearly the political creation, the present United States of America, was projected or rather cast in the mind of this great master of the political art. This beautiful and dignified address evidently produced the most beneficial effects. The fourth point should be the apostolic rule for all Congress and assemblymen, put into all political platforms, on all party banners, at the head of each issue of a political paper. Dignity, the prominent feature of Washington's character, is the secret of power depending upon public opinion. This secret seems to be lost in Congress and legislatures and our public affairs in general. The political party press has much to answer for it.

When General Washington wrote those lines the nation was in "a portentous crisis," in his own words, owing to the imperfect organization of the national affairs. The different crises the people of the United States have witnessed since, and which have retarded their steady onward progress so much, originated mostly in defective municipal organization and legislation, especially in regard to the monetary affairs. As by the federal constitution all causes for political national crises have been happily removed; it is now with the states to stop their tampering with the currency. which mars the splendid picture drawn by Washington of the future of this nation.

LETTER XLIV.

Defenders of the Country. — Popularity. — Citizen-soldier. — Standing-Army-Soldier. — Washington. — Frederick. — Napoleon. — Conquest. — Vain-glory. — Universal Peace. — Dualistic Nature of Man. — Farewell Orders to the Armies by Washington. — Review of the Past Struggle. — Conduct for the Future.

THOSE who sacrifice their lives for their country, when in danger of war, will always command the esteem of their fellow-citizens, and acquire great popularity, especially if the war be one of defence for the protection of liberty, and required by justice and honor. There is, however, a great difference between a citizen-soldier or general and a hired standing-army-soldier or princely commander. The Americans are so fortunate as to have in Washington a perfect pattern of a citizen-general, while the Europeans are proud of théir great Fredericks and Napoleons. It is of the highest importance that a citizen should never indulge in ambitious ideas of conquest. No general was ever freer from them, and of the pernicious passion of military vain-glory than Washington. Although a republican government, by itself, is not in need of the support of a standing army, like that of a prince, still, as mankind are organized, no commonwealth can exist, as such, without a strong arm for the common defence. Universal peace is an absolute idea, like that of general virtue, goodness, etc. We, as rational beings, can form such ideas; but the absolute universal perfection, which they pre-suppose when realized, mankind never will attain, because it is against our nature. This is of a dualistic kind, as life and death, wisdom and foolery, good and bad, etc., mixed up in such a manner that we are not able to form an idea of good without the help of its opposite, that is, bad. No one would sigh for eternal peace if he was not surrounded by an eternal conflict of antagonistic forces. It is, then, clear that the rights of nations can not be maintained without an adequate extensive establishment for the common defence, as the federal constitution speaks of the military force, just as the rights of individuals would be entirely insecure without the institution of courts, jails, etc.

All I desire from you, my sons, in this regard, is to keep the example of a citizen-soldier, as set up by General Washington, before your eyes, when in times that try men's hearts and courage you are called to arms for the defence of your country. Read the following extract, from his farewell orders to the armies of the United States, dated Rocky Hill, near Princeton, November 2, 1783. I insert them in my letters because they come from the greatest pattern of a citizen-soldier, and they obviously contain sentiments, which have influenced the public men of his time, and especially those who framed the federal constitution. He says:—

"Before the commander-in-chief takes his final leave of those he holds most dear, he wishes to indulge himself a few moments, in calling to mind a slight review of the past: he will, then, take the liberty of exploring with his military friends, their future prospects, of advising the general line of conduct which, in his opinion, ought to be pursued; and he will conclude the address by expressing the obligations he feels himself under for the spirited and able assistance he has experienced from them in the performance of an arduous office.

"A contemplation of the complete attainment (at a period earlier than could have been expected) of the object for which we contended against so formidable a power, can not but inspire us with astonishment and gratitude. The disadvantageous circumstances, on our part, under which the war was undertaken, can never be forgotten."

"In order to remove the prejudices which may have taken possession of the minds of any of the good people of the states, it is earnestly recommended to all the troops, *that with a strong attachment to the Union, they should carry with them into civil society the most conciliating dispositions;* and that they should prove themselves not less virtuous and useful citizens, than they have been persevering and victorious as soldiers. What though there should be some envious individuals who are unwilling to pay the debt the public has contracted, or to yield the tribute due to merit, yet let such unworthy treatment produce no invective, or any instance of intemperate conduct; let it be remembered that the unbiased voice of the free citizens of the United States has promised the just reward, and given the merited applause; let it be known and remembered that the reputation of the federal armies is established beyond the reach of malevolence; and let a consciousness of their achievements and fame still excite the men who composed them, to honorable actions, under the persuasion that the private virtues of economy, prudence and industry, will not be less amiable in civil life than the more splendid qualities of valor, perseverance, and enterprise were in the field. And, although the general has so frequently given it as his opinion, in the most public and explicit manner, *that unless the principles of the federal government were properly supported, and the powers of the Union increased, the honour, dignity, and justice of the nation would be lost for ever*, yet he can not help repeating, on this occasion, so interesting a sentiment, and leaving it as his last injunction to every officer and every soldier who may view the subject in the same serious point of light, to add his best endeavors to those of his worthy fellow-citizens, toward effecting these great and valuable purposes, on which our very existence as a nation so materially depends!"

We learn here again how this eminent man and citizen, and true prototype of a civil and military chief, tried to realize his great idea of a *more perfect union* of the then liberated colonies. How nobly does he speak to his fellow-soldiers and companions! He concludes this address with the following touching words:—

"Being now to conclude these his last public orders, to take ultimate leave, in a short time, of the military character, and to bid a final adieu to the armies he has so long had the honor to command, he can only again offer, in their behalf, his recommendations to their grateful country, and his prayers to the God of armies. May ample justice be done them here, and may the choicest of heaven's favors, both here and hereafter, attend those, who under the divine auspices, *have secured innumerable blessings for others.* With these wishes and his benediction, the commander-in-chief is about to retire from service. The curtain of separation will soon be drawn, and the military scene to him will be closed for ever"

Under such a commander, could the final issue of the war be doubtful? It makes one a better man and citizen to read Washington's public documents. They are monuments more lasting than brass. You must keep them before your mind as perfect patterns of just and noble sentiments, that when comparing them with the products of modern politicians in Congress and legislatures, you may easily separate the wheat from the chaff, and be guided by them through life.

LETTER XLV.

Washington elected President. — Organization of the General Government. — Retires from the Presidency. — His Farewell Address to the People of the United States, Sept. 17, 1796.

Gen. Washington was not permitted to enjoy his rural retirement long, which, like the ancient Roman republicans, he loved so much. The legislature of Virginia chose him a member of the convention which framed the federal constitution; hé was the presiding officer of this most important assemblage, and, by the grateful people, elected as their first president, under the constitution which bears his name, and for which he labored so long. He organized the government, was elected for a second term, and this he closed with an address to the nation, universally known as Washington's Farewell Address, and acknowledged by all thinking men as an eminently clear and true exposition of the common-sense principles of free democratic governments. I have added appropriate heads, and recommend it to your most careful attention. It is the real foundation of our American common law, considering the source from which it comes, of more value than English, Roman, and Greek law-maxims, and precedents. I add it entire as follows:—

Declining a Re-election.

"Friends and Fellow Citizens — The period for a new election of a citizen to administer the executive government of the United States being not far distant, and the time actually arrived when your thoughts must be employed in designating the person who is to be clothed with that important trust, it appears to me proper, especially as it may conduce to a more distinct expression of the public voice, that I should now apprize you of the resolution I have formed, to decline being considered among the number of those out of whom a choice is to be made.

Reasons for Declining.

"I beg you, at the same time, to do me the justice to be assured, that this resolution has not been taken without a strict regard to all the considerations appertaining to the relation which binds a dutiful citizen to his country; and that, in withdrawing the tender of service which silence in my situation might imply, I am influenced by no diminution of zeal for your future interest, no deficiency of grateful respect for your past kindness; but am supported by a full conviction that the step is compatible with both.

State Reasons for serving a Second Time.

"The acceptance of, and continuance hitherto in, the office to which your suffrages have twice called me, have been a uniform sacrifice of inclination to the opinion of duty, and to a deference for what appeared to be your desire. I constantly hoped that it would have been much earlier in my power, consistently with motives which I was not at liberty to disregard, to return to that retirement from which I had been reluctantly drawn. The strength of my inclination to do this, previous to the last election, had even led to the preparation of an address to declare it to you: but mature reflection on the then perplexed and critical posture of our affairs with foreign nations, and the unanimous advice of persons entitled to my confidence, impelled me to abandon the idea.

The State of the Public Affairs favors his Retirement from Office.

"I rejoice that the state of your concerns, external as well as internal, no longer renders the pursuit of inclination incompatible with the sentiment of duty or propriety; and am persuaded, whatever partiality may be retained for my services, that, in the present circumstances of our country, you will not disapprove my determination to retire.

"The impressions with which I first undertook the arduous trust were explained on the proper occasion. In the discharge of this trust, I will only say, that I have with good intentions contributed toward the organization and administration of the government, the best exertions of which a very fallible judgment was capable. Not unconscious, in the outset, of the inferiority of my qualifications, experience in my own eyes, perhaps still more in the eyes of others, has strengthened the motives to diffidence of myself: and every day the increasing weight of years admonishes me more and more, that the shade of retirement is as necessary to me as it will be welcome. Satisfied that if any circumstances have given peculiar value to my services, they were temporary, I have the consolation to believe, that while choice and prudence invite me to quit the political scene, patriotism does not forbid it.

Sentiments of Gratitude for Confidence.

"In looking forward to the moment which is intended to terminate the career of my public life, my feelings do not permit me to suspend the deep acknowledgment of that debt of gratitude which I owe to my beloved country, for the many honors it has conferred upon me; still more for the steadfast confidence with which it has supported me; and for the opportunities I have thence enjoyed of manifesting my inviolable attachment, by services faithful and persevering, though in usefulness unequal to my zeal. If benefits have resulted to our country from these services, let it always be remembered to your praise, and as an instructive example in our annals, that under circumstances in which the passions, agitated in every direction, were liable to mislead—amidst appearances, sometimes dubious—vicissitudes of fortune often discouraging—in situations, in which not unfrequently, want of success has countenanced the spirit of criticism—the constancy of your support was the essential prop of the efforts, and a guaranty of the plans by which they were effected. Profoundly penetrated with this idea, I shall carry it with me to my grave, as a strong incitement to unceasing wishes, that heaven may continue to you the choicest tokens of its beneficence—that your union and brotherly affection may be perpetual—that the free constitution, which is the work of your hands, may be sacredly maintained—that its administration, in every department, may be stamped with wisdom and virtue—that, in fine, the happiness of the people of these states, under the auspices of liberty, may be made complete by so careful a preservation, and so prudent a use of this blessing, as will acquire to them the glory of recommending it to the applause, the affection, and the adoption, of every nation which is yet a stranger to it.

Advice and Warnings of a parting Friend.

"Here, perhaps, I ought to stop. But a solicitude for your welfare, which can not end but with my life, and the apprehension of danger natural to that solicitude, urge me, on an occasion like the present, to offer to your solemn contemplation, and to recommend to your frequent review, some sentiments which are the result of much reflection, of no inconsiderable observation, and which appear to me all-important to the permanency of your felicity as a people. These will be offered to you with the more freedom, as you can only see in them the disinterested warnings of a parting friend, who can possibly have no personal motive to bias his counsel. Nor can I forget, as an encouragement to it, your indulgent reception of my sentiments on a former and not dissimilar occasion.

Of American Liberty, and its main Pillar the Union.

"Interwoven as is the love of liberty with every ligament of your hearts, no recommendation of mine is necessary to fortify or confirm the attachment.

"The unity of government, which constitutes you one people, is also now dear to you. It is justly so; for it is a main pillar in the edifice of your real independence—the support of your tranquillity at home, your peace abroad; of your safety, of your prosperity, of that very liberty which you so highly prize. But, as it is easy to foresee, that from different causes, and from different quarters, much pains will be taken, many artifices employed, to weaken in your minds the conviction of this truth; as this is the point in your political fortress, against which the batteries of internal and external enemies will be most constantly and actively (though often covertly and insiduously) directed, it is of infinite moment that you should properly estimate the immense value of your national Union to your collective and individual happiness; that you should cherish a cordial, habitual, and immovable attachment to it; accustoming yourselves to think and speak of it, as of the palladium of your political safety and prosperity; watching for its preservation with jealous anxiety; discountenancing whatever may suggest even a suspicion that it can, in any event, be abandoned; and indignantly frowning upon the first dawning of every attempt to alienate any portion of our country from the rest, or to enfeeble the sacred ties which now link together the various parts.

The Name of American to be sacredly appreciated by Citizens by Birth or Choice.

"For this you have every inducement of sympathy and interest.

Citizens, by birth or choice, of a common country, that country has a right to concentrate your affections. The name of AMERICAN,* which belongs to you, in your national capacity, must always exalt the just pride of patriotism, more than any appellation derived from local discriminations. With slight shades of difference, you have the same religion, manners, habits, and political principles. You have, in a common cause, fought and triumphed together; the independence and liberty you possess are the work of joint councils, and joint efforts, of common dangers, sufferings, and successes.

Union of Interests. No North, no South, no East, no West, in regard to them.

"But these considerations, however powerfully they address themselves to your sensibility, are greatly outweighed by those which apply more immediately to your interest. Here every portion of our country finds the most commanding motives for carefully guarding and preserving the union of the whole.

"The North, in an unrestrained intercourse with the South, protected by the equal laws of a common government, finds in the productions of the latter great additional resources of maritime and commercial enterprise, and precious materials of manufacturing industry. The South, in the same intercourse, benefiting by the agency of the North, sees its agriculture grow, and its commerce expand. Turning partly into its own channels the seamen of the North, it finds its particular navigation invigorated—and while it contributes, in different ways, to nourish and increase the general mass of the national navigation, it looks forward to the protection of a maritime strength, to which itself is unequally adapted.

"The East, in like intercourse with the West, already finds, and in the progressive improvement of interior communication, by land and water, will more and more find a valuable vent for the commodities which it brings from abroad, or manufactures at home. The West derives from the East supplies requisite to its growth and comfort; and what is, perhaps, of still greater consequence, it must of necessity owe the secure enjoyment of the indispensable outlets, for its own productions, to the weight, influence,

* For Washington's sake this name should never have been degraded to a party cognomen.

and the future maritime strength of the Atlantic side of the Union, directed by an indissoluble community of interest as one nation. Any other tenure by which the West can hold this essential advantage, whether derived from its own separate strength, or from an apostate and unnatural connection with any foreign power, must be intrinsically precarious.

In Union, Security from External Danger and Internal Commotions, without requiring a large Army.

"While then every part of our country thus feels an immediate and particular interest in union, all the parts combined can not fail to find in the united mass of means and efforts, greater strength, greater resource, proportionably greater security, from external danger—a less frequent interruption of their peace by foreign nations—and, what is of inestimable value, they must derive, from union, an exemption from those broils and wars between themselves, which so frequently afflict neighboring countries not tied together by the same government, which their own rivalships alone would be sufficient to produce, but which opposite foreign alliances, attachments, and intrigues, would stimulate and embitter. Hence, likewise, they will avoid the necessity of those overgrown military establishments, which, under any form of government, are inauspicious to liberty, and which are to be regarded as particularly hostile to republican liberty. In this sense it is, that your Union ought to be considered as a main prop of your liberty, and that the love of the one ought to endear to you the preservation of the other.

The Government of the Union will be Efficient, if the whole is properly organized in States, Counties, Towns, (Cities, Villages).

"These considerations speak a persuasive language to every reflecting and virtuous mind, and exhibit the continuance of the Union as a primary object of patriotic desire. Is there a doubt whether a common government can embrace so large a sphere? Let experience solve it. To listen to mere speculation in such a case were criminal. We are authorized to hope that a proper organization of the whole, with the auxiliary agency of governments for the respective sub-divisions, will afford a happy issue to the experiment. It is well worth a fair and full experiment. With such powerful and obvious motives to union, affecting all parts of

our country, while experience shall not have demonstrated its impracticability, there will always be reason to distrust the patriotism of those, who, in any quarter, may endeavor to weaken its bands.

Geographical Parties and their Danger. No Missouri Lines.

"In contemplating the causes which may disturb our Union, it occurs, as a matter of serious concern, that any ground should have been furnished for characterizing parties by geographical discriminations, Northern and Southern, Atlantic and Western—whence designing men may endeavor to excite a belief that there is a real difference of local interest and view. One of the expedients of party to acquire influence within particular districts, is to misrepresent the opinions and aims of other districts. You can not shield yourselves too much against the jealousies and heart-burnings which spring from these misrepresentations; they tend to render alien to each other those who ought to be bound together by fraternal affection. The inhabitants of our western country have lately had a useful lesson on this head: they have seen, in the negotiation, by the executive, and in the unanimous ratification, by the senate, of the treaty with Spain, and in the universal satisfaction at that event throughout the United States, a decisive proof how unfounded were the suspicions propagated among them, of a policy in the general government and in the Atlantic states unfriendly to their interests in regard to the Mississippi: they have been witnesses to the formation of two treaties, that with Great Britain, and that with Spain, which secure to them everything they could desire, in respect to our foreign relations, toward confirming their prosperity. Will it not be their wisdom to rely for the preservation of these advantages on the Union, by which they were procured? Will they not, henceforth, be deaf to those advisers, if such there are, who would sever them from their brethren, and connect them with aliens?

A Common National Government Preferable to State Alliances.

"To the efficacy and permanency of your Union, a government for the whole is indispensable. No alliances, however strict, between the parts, can be an adequate substitute; they must inevitably experience the infractions and interruptions which alliances, in all times, have experienced. Sensible of this momentous truth, you have improved upon your first essay, by the adoption of a constitution of government, better calculated than your former, for an intimate union, and for the efficacious management of your common concerns. This government, the offspring of our own choice, uninfluenced and unawed, adopted upon full investigation and mature deliberation, completely free in its principles, in the distribution of its powers, uniting security with energy, and containing within itself a provision for its own amendment, has a just claim to your confidence and your support. Respect for its authority, compliance with its laws, acquiescence in its measures, are duties enjoined by the fundamental maxims of true liberty. The basis of our political system is the right of the people to make and to alter their constitutions of government. But the constitution which at any time exists, until changed by an explicit and authentic act of the whole people, is sacredly obligatory upon all. The very idea of the power and the right of the people to establish government, pre-supposes the duty of every individual to obey the established government.

Factions Opposing the Government to be Discountenanced.

"All obstructions to the execution of the laws, all combinations and associations, under whatever plausible character, with the real design to direct, control, counteract, or awe, the regular deliberation and action of the constituted authorities, are destructive of this fundamental principle, and of fatal tendency. They serve to organize faction, to give it an artificial and extraordinary force, to put in the place of the delegated will of the nation the will of a party, often a small but artful and enterprising minority of the community; and according to the alternate triumphs of different parties to make the public administration the mirror of the ill-concerted and incongruous projects of faction, rather than the organ of consistent and wholesome plans, digested by common councils and modified by mutual interests.

Warnings against Factions Subverting Constitutions, Franchises, and the Rights of the People.

"However combinations or associations of the above description may now and then answer popular ends, they are likely, in the course of time and things, to become potent engines by which cunning, ambitious, and unprincipled men will be enabled to subvert the power of the people, and to usurp for themselves the reigns of government, destroying afterward the very engines which had lifted them to unjust dominion.

Warnings against Innovations made in the Constitution by unprincipled Men.

"Toward the preservation of your government and the permanency of your present happy state, it is requisite not only that you steadily discountenance irregular oppositions to its acknowledged authority, but also that you resist with care the spirit of innovation upon its principles, however specious the pretexts.

"One method of assault may be, to effect in the forms of the constitution alterations which will impair the energy of the system, and thus undermine what can not be directly overthrown. In all the changes to which you may be invited, remember that time and habit are at least as necessary to fix the true character of governments as of other human institutions; that experience is the surest standard by which to test the real tendency of the existing constitutions of a country; that facility in changes upon the credit of mere hypothesis and opinion exposes to perpetual change, from the endless variety of hypothesis and opinion; and remember, especially, that for the efficient management of your common interests in a country so extensive as ours, a government of as much vigor as is consistent with the perfect security of liberty is indispensable. Liberty itself will find in such a government, with powers properly distributed and adjusted, its surest guardian. It is, indeed, little else than a name, where the government is too feeble to withstand the enterprises of faction, to confine each member of the society within the limits prescribed by the laws, and to maintain all in the secure and tranquil enjoyment of the rights of person and property.

Warnings against Parties; their Violence; Spirit of Revenge leading to Despotism.

"I have already intimated to you the danger of parties in the state, with particular reference to the founding of them upon geographical discriminations. Let me now take a more comprehensive view and warn you in the most solemn manner against the baneful effects of a spirit of party generally.

"This spirit, unfortunately, is inseparable from our nature, having its root in the strongest passions of the human mind. It exists under different shapes in all governments, more or less stifled, controlled, or oppressed; but in those of the popular form it is seen in its greatest rankness and is truly their worst enemy.

"The alternate domination of one faction over another, sharpened by the spirit of revenge natural to party dissension, which in different ages and countries has perpetrated the most horrid enormities, is itself a frightful despotism. But this leads at length to a more formal and permanent despotism. The disorders and miseries which result, gradually incline the minds of men to seek security and repose in the absolute power of an individual; and sooner or later the chief of some prevailing faction, more able or more fortunate than his competitors, turns this disposition to the purposes of his own elevation, on the ruins of the public liberty.

Warnings against Parties who Open the Door to Foreign Influence and Corruption.

"Without looking forward to an extremity of this kind, (which nevertheless ought not to be entirely out of sight), the common and continual mischiefs of the spirit of party are sufficient to make it the interest and duty of a wise people to discourage and restrain it. It serves always to distract the public councils and enfeeble the public administration. It agitates the community with ill-founded jealousies and false alarms; kindles the animosity of one part against another; foments occasionally riot and insurrection. It opens the door to foreign influence and corruption, which find a facilitated access to the government itself through the channels of party passion. Thus the policy and will of one country are subjected to the policy and will of another.

Parties (especially Standing), not to be Encouraged.

"There is an opinion that parties in free countries are useful checks upon the administration of the government, and serve to keep alive the spirit of liberty. This, within certain limits, is probably true, and in governments of a monarchical cast patriotism may look with indulgence, if not with favor, upon the spirit of party. But in those of the popular character, in governments purely elective, it is a spirit not to be encouraged. From their natural tendency it is certain there will always be enough of that spirit for every salutary purpose; and there being constant danger of excess, the effort ought to be, by force of public opinion, to mitigate and assuage it. A fire not to be quenched, it demands a uniform vigilance to prevent its bursting into a flame, lest, instead of warming, it should consume.

Caution in regard to Schemes of Politicians to avoid Encroachments, Consolidations, Centralization, Despotism.

"It is important, likewise, that the habits of thinking in a free country should inspire caution in those intrusted with its administration to confine themselves within their respective constitutional spheres, avoiding in the exercise of the powers of one department to encroach upon another. The spirit of encroachment tends to consolidate the powers of all the departments in one, and thus to create, whatever the form of government, a real despotism. A just estimate of that love of power and proneness to abuse it which predominate in the human heart, is sufficient to satisfy us of the truth of this position. The necessity of reciprocal checks in the exercise of political power, by dividing and distributing it into different depositories,* and constituting each the guardian of the public weal against invasions by the others, has been evinced by experiments ancient and modern; some of them in our country and under our own eyes. To preserve them must be as necessary as to institute them. If, in the opinion of the people, the distribution or modification of the constitutional powers be in any particular wrong, let it be corrected by an amendment, in the way which the constitution designates.

Warnings against Precedents of Usurpation of Power.

"But let there be no change by usurpation; for though this, in one instance, may be the instrument of good, it is the customary weapon by which free governments are destroyed. The precedent must always greatly overbalance in permanent evil any partial or transient benefit which the use can at any time yield.

Religion, Virtue, and Morality, the great Pillars of Human Happiness, and the necessary Springs of Popular Government.

"Of all the dispositions and habits which lead to political prosperity, religion and morality are indispensable supports. In vain would that man claim the tribute of patriotism, who should labor to subvert these great pillars of human happiness, these firmest props of the duties of men and citizens. The mere politician, equally with the pious man, ought to respect and to cherish them.

* Such depositories are towns, counties, states, and in them the legislative, executive, and judiciary.

A volume could not trace all their connections with private and public felicity. Let it be simply asked, where is the security for property, for reputation, for life, if the sense of religious obligation desert the oaths which are the instruments of investigation in courts of justice? And let us with caution indulge the supposition, that morality can be maintained without religion. Whatever may be conceded to the influence of refined education on minds of peculiar structure, reason and experience both forbid us to expect that national morality can prevail in exclusion of religious principle.

"It is substantially true, that virtue and morality are necessary springs of popular government. The rule indeed extends, with more or less force, to every species of free government. Who, that is a sincere friend to it, can look with indifference upon attempts to shake the foundation of the fabric?

Institutions for the general Diffusion of Knowledge.

"Promote, then, as an object of primary importance, institutions for the general diffusion of knowledge. In proportion as the structure of a government gives force to public opinion, it is essential that public opinion should be enlightened.

Preservation of Public Credit; shunning of Public Debts and the Inconvenience of Taxes.

"As a very important source of strength and security, cherish public credit. One method of preserving it is to use it as sparingly as possible; avoiding occasions of expense, by cultivating peace; but remembering also, that timely disbursements to prepare for danger, frequently prevent much greater disbursements to repel it: avoiding likewise the accumulation of debt, not only by shunning occasions of expense, but, by vigorous exertions in time of peace, to discharge the debts which unavoidable wars may have occasioned, not ungenerously throwing upon posterity the burden which we ourselves ought to bear. The executions of these maxims belongs to your representatives; but it is necessary that public opinion should co-operate. To facilitate to them the performance of their duty, it is essential that you should practically bear in mind, that toward the payment of debts there must be revenue —that to have revenue there must be taxes—that no taxes can be devised which are not more or less inconvenient and unpleasant

—that the intrinsic embarrassment, inseparable from the selection of the proper objects (which is always a choice of difficulties), ought to be a decisive motive for a candid construction of the conduct of the government in making it, and for a spirit of acquiescence in the measures for obtaining revenue which the public exigencies may at any time dictate.

Good Faith and Justice toward all, as an Example for all Nations.

"Observe good faith and justice toward all nations—cultivate peace and harmony with all. Religion and morality enjoin this conduct; and can it be, that good policy does not equally enjoin it? It will be worthy of a free, enlightened, and (at no distant period) a great nation, to give to mankind the magnanimous and too novel example of a people always guided by an exalted justice and benevolence. Who can doubt, that in the course of time and things, the fruits of such a plan would richly repay any temporary advantages which might be lost by a steady adherence to it? Can it be, that Providence has not connected the permanent felicity of a nation with its virtues? The experiment, at least, is recommended by every sentiment which ennobles human nature. Alas, it is rendered impossible by its vices?

Avoiding National Antipathies or Passionate Attachments.

"In the execution of a plan, nothing is more essential than that permanent, inveterate antipathies against particular nations, and passionate attachments for others, should be excluded, and that in place of them, just and amicable feelings toward all should be cultivated. The nation which indulges toward another an habitual hatred or an habitual fondness, is in some degree a slave. It is a slave to its animosity or to its affection, either of which is sufficient to lead it astray from its duty or its interest. Antipathy in one nation against another, disposes each more readily to offer insult and injury, to lay hold of slight causes of umbrage, and to be haughty and intractable, when accidental or trifling occasions of dispute occur.

"Hence frequent collisions, obstinate, envenomed, and bloody contests. The nation, prompted by ill-will and resentment, sometimes impels to war the government, contrary to the best calculations of policy. The government sometimes participates in the national propensity, and adopts, through passion, what reason would reject. At other times it makes the animosity of the nation subservient to projects of hostility, instigated by pride, ambition, and other sinister and pernicious motives. The peace often, sometimes perhaps, the liberty of nations has been the victim.

"So likewise, a passionate attachment of one nation for another produces a variety of evils. Sympathy for the favorite nation, facilitating the illusion of an imaginary common interest, in cases where no real common interest exists, and infusing into one the enmities of the other, betrays the former into a participation in the quarrels and the wars of the latter, without adequate inducements or justification. It leads also to concessions to the favorite nation, of privileges denied to others, which is apt doubly to injure the nation making the concessions, by unnecessarily parting with what ought to have been retained, and by exciting jealousy, ill-will, and a disposition to retaliate, in the parties from whom equal privileges are withheld; and it gives to ambitious, corrupted, or deluded citizens (who devote themselves to the favorite nation) facility to betray or sacrifice the interests of their country, without odium, sometimes even with popularity; gilding, with the appearances of a virtuous sense of obligation, a commendable deference for public opinion, or a laudable zeal for public good, the base or foolish compliances of ambition, corruption, or infatuation.

"As avenues to foreign influence in innumerable ways, such attachments are particularly alarming to the truly enlightened and independent patriot. How many opportunities do they afford to tamper with domestic factions, to practise the arts of seduction, to mislead public opinion, to influence or awe the public councils. Such an attachment of a small or weak nation, toward a great and powerful one, dooms the former to be the satellite of the other.

Warnings against Foreign Diplomatic Wiles and Influence.

"Against the insiduous wiles of foreign influence (I conjure you to believe me, fellow-citizens), the jealousy of a free people ought to be constantly awake, since history and experience prove that foreign influence is one of the most baneful foes of republican government. But that jealousy, to be useful, must be impartial, else it becomes the instrument of the very influence to be avoided, instead of a defence against it. Excessive partiality for one foreign nation, and excessive dislike of another, cause those whom they actuate to see danger only on one side, and serve to veil, and even second the arts of influence on the other. Real patriots, who may resist the intrigues of the favorite, are liable to become suspected and odious, while its tools and dupes usurp the applause and confidence of the people to surrender their interests.

Warnings against Political or Diplomatic Connections with Foreign Governments, and European Interests in General.

" The great rule of conduct for us, in regard to foreign nations, is, in extending our commercial relations, to have with them as little political connection as possible. So far as we have already formed engagements, let them be fulfilled with perfect good faith. Here let us stop.

" Europe has a set of primary interests, which to us have none, or a very remote relation. Hence she must be engaged in frequent controversies, the causes of which are essentially foreign to our concerns. Hence, therefore, it must be unwise in us to implicate ourselves by artificial ties in the ordinary vicissitudes of her politics, or the ordinary combinations and collisions of her friendships or enmities.

Assuming an Independent National Attitude.

" Our detached and distant situation invites and enables us to pursue a different course. If we remain one people, under an efficient government, the period is not far off when we may defy material injury from external annoyance ; when we may take such an attitude as will cause the neutrality we may at any time resolve upon, to be scrupulously respected ; when belligerent nations, under the impossibility of making acquisitions upon us, will not lightly hazard the giving us provocation ; when we may choose peace or war, as our interest, guided by justice, shall counsel.

" Why forego the advantages of so peculiar a situation ? Why quit our own to stand on foreign ground ? Why, by interweaving our destiny with that of any part of Europe, entangle our peace and prosperity in the toils of European ambition, rivalship, interest, humor, or caprice ?

No Permanent Alliances. Honesty the best Policy.

"'Tis our true policy to steer clear of permanent alliances with any portion of the foreign world; so far, I mean, as we are now at liberty to do it; for let me not be understood as capable of patronizing infidelity to existing engagements. I hold the maxim no less applicable to public than to private affairs, that honesty is always the best policy. I repeat it, therefore, let those engagements be observed in their genuine sense. But, in my opinion, it is unnecessary, and would be unwise to extend them.

"Taking care always to keep ourselves, by suitable establishments, on a respectable defensive posture, we may safely trust to temporary alliances for extraordinary emergencies.

Liberal, not enforced Commercial Intercourse. Warnings against Courting National Favors.

"Harmony and liberal intercourse with all nations, are recommended by policy, humanity, and interest. But even our commercial policy should hold an equal and impartial hand, neither seeking nor granting exclusive favors or preferences, consulting the natural course of things, diffusing and diversifying, by gentle means, the streams of commerce, but forcing nothing; establishing, with powers so disposed — in order to give to trade a stable course, to define the rights of our merchants, and to enable the government to support them — conventional rules of intercourse, the best that present circumstances and mutual opinion will permit, but temporary, and liable from time to time to be abandoned or varied, as experience and circumstances shall dictate; constantly keeping in view that 'tis folly in one nation to look for disinterested favors from another, that it must pay with a portion of its independence whatever it may accept under that character; that by such acceptance it may place itself in the condition of having given equivalents for nominal favors, and yet of being reproached with ingratitude for not giving more. There can be no greater error than to expect or calculate upon real favors from nation to nation. 'Tis an illusion which experience must cure, which a just pride ought to discard.

Hope that these Counsels will Moderate the Fury of Party Spirit.

"In offering to you, my countrymen, those counsels of an old and affectionate friend, I dare not hope they will make the strong and lasting impression I could wish; that they will control the usual current of the passions, or prevent our nation from running the course, which has hitherto marked the destiny of nations. But if I may even flatter myself that they may be productive of some partial benefit, some occasional good; that they may now and then recur to moderate the fury of party-spirit, to warn against the mischiefs of foreign intrigues, to guard against the impostures of pretended patriotism; this hope will be a full recompense for the solicitude for your welfare, by which they have been dictated.

"How far, in the discharge of my official duties, I have been guided by the principles which have been delineated, the public records and other evidences of my conduct must witness to you and to the world. To myself, the assurance of my conscience is, that I have, at least, believed myself to be guided by them.

Neutral Position in the then Existing War in Europe.

"In relation to the still subsisting war in Europe, my proclamation of the 22d of April, 1793, is the index to my plan. Sanctioned by your approving voice, and by that of your representatives in both houses of Congress, the spirit of that measure has continually governed me, uninfluenced by any attempts to deter or divert me from it.

"After deliberate examination, with the aid of the best lights I could obtain, I was well satisfied that our country, under all the circumstances of the case, had a right to take, and was bound in duty and interest to take, a neutral position. Having taken it, I determined, as far as should depend upon me, to maintain it with moderation, perseverance, and firmness.

"The considerations which respect the right to hold this conduct, it is not necessary on this occasion to detail. I will only observe, that according to my understanding of the matter, that right, so far from being denied by any of the belligerent powers, has been virtually admitted by all.

"The duty of holding a neutral conduct may be inferred, without anything more, from the obligation which justice and humanity impose on every nation, in cases in which it is free to act, to maintain inviolate the relation of peace and amity toward other nations.

"The inducements of interest for observing that conduct will be best referred to your own reflections and experience. With me, a predominent motive has been, to endeavor to gain time to our country to settle and mature its yet recent institutions, and to progress without interruption to that degree of strength and consistency which is necessary to give it, humanly speaking, the command of its own fortunes.

Anticipation of the Sweet Enjoyment of Living in Retirement under a Free Government and Good Laws.

"Though in reviewing the incidents of my administration, I am unconscious of intentional error, I am, nevertheless, too sensible of my defects not to think it probable that I may have committed many errors. Whatever they may be, I fervently beseech the Almighty to avert or mitigate the evils to which they may tend. I shall also carry with me the hope, that my country will never cease to view them with indulgence; and that, after forty-five years of my life, dedicated to its service, with an upright zeal, the faults of incompetent abilities will be consigned to oblivion, as myself must soon be to the mansions of rest.

"Relying on its kindness in this as in other things, and actuated by that fervent love toward it, which is so natural to a man who views in it the native soil of himself and his progenitors for several generations, I anticipate with pleasing expectation, that retreat, in which I promise myself to realize, without alloy, the sweet enjoyment of partaking, in the midst of my fellow-citizens, the benign influence of good laws under a free government—the ever favorite object of my heart, and the happy reward, as I trust, of our mutual cares, labors, and dangers.

"G. WASHINGTON."

No monument of marble or brass can represent this honest and just man better than his public documents, the federal constitution included. It is true, there were brave and good men united with him in the great work of bringing order out of the chaos of the young confederacy; still without the clear mind, and firm hand, of this great citizen, the result would have been different.

Try then, my dear children, for your part, to be faithful to those maxims in public life, which he followed and has embodied in his public documents.

I have tried to explain them in their bearing upon the current business, and hope I have not labored in vain.

LETTER XLVI.

The Prince by Macchiavelli. — Parallel between the Farewell Address and the Prince. — Prof. Lieber. — Anti-Macchiavelli by Frederick the Great. — The Barbarians in Italy. — Difference between the American and European State-systems. — Legitimacy. — Congress of Vienna.

Generally speaking there are only two kinds of governments, republics* and monarchies. The preceding letters have been devoted to the first class, and the forms and principles adopted in the United States.

To interrupt the monotony of my republican discussions, I embody in this letter an abridgement of the celebrated treatise, entitled "The Prince," written by the great "Secretario Fiorentino," Niccolo Macchiavelli, and dedicated to the young duke Lorenzo de Medici, whom he wished to become the deliverer of Italy from the barbarians, (Spaniards, Germans, and French.) (Mazzini attempts to carry out this plan in our days.) Macchiavelli wrote in the beginning of the sixteenth century; he died in 1527. I have made use of a London translation of 1694, the only one I had access to. This book contains much historical research, and naturally bears, as General Washington's farewell address does, the signs of the times. The contrast between both

* Prof. Lieber, in his book on Civil Liberty and Self-government, speaks of an instituted self-government, defining it thus: "Instituted self-government is that popular government which consists in a great organism of institutions, or a union of harmonizing systems of laws instinct with self-government. It is of a co-operative or homocratic character, and, in this respect, the opposite to centralism. It is articulated liberty, inter-guarantying, self-evolving, and generic, the political embodiment of self-reliance and mutual acknowledgment of self-rule—the political realization of equality. It is the only self-government whieh makes it possible to be at once *self*-government and self-*government*." This means nothing but republic.

is striking. Macchiavelli's only hope for Italy was a hereditary prince at the head of a consolidated monarchy. Washington fought, worked, and wrote for the overthrow of a hereditary prince, and the establishment of a federal republic under one elective executive. The first treats more of subjects, and their prudent management; the latter of political business, and its good organization, distribution, and performance. The first advises his prince how to conquer a republic by ruining it, and keep down the influential men; the latter maintains that liberty ought to be the main pillar of the Union. The first suggests that the prince must manage the public affairs, so that in all places, times and occasions, the people may have need of his administration and regimen, or that he has his hands in every thing; Washington sees, in the proper organization and distribution of the public business, the best guaranty for the safety of both the people and the government. According to the first, a prince is to have no other thought or study but war; while Washington believes that by our Union we will avoid the necessity of overgrown military establishments. Frederick the Great, who wrote the anti-Macchiavelli, called that nobleman only a gentleman who served in the army.

Macchiavelli thinks a prince may not shun vices and infamy, if he only can preserve thus his dominion; Washington's guide was the maxim: honesty is the best policy.

A prince ought not to keep his parole when it is to his prejudice, so says Macchiavelli; let all engagements be observed in their genuine sense, and justice, and good faith towards all nations, is the maxim of Washington.

Macchiavelli holds that it is necessary for a prince to have all the good qualities in reality, and to play the hypocrite well; Washington believes that honesty, virtue, and morality, are necessary springs of popular government.

Macchiavelli's prince ought to be terrible at home to his subjects, and abroad to his equals; Washington's ideal is a life under the benign influence of good laws under a free government.

A prince, according to Macchiavelli, must recommend himself to the world by great enterprises and valor (of course expensive things), and monopolize knowledge; Washington is for peace, economy, diffusion of knowledge.

Macchiavelli advises his prince never to league with another more powerful than himself; Washington is against all entangling alliances.

The first warns the prince of the snares of woman; the latter of the wiles of party and faction.

But you may better extend yourselves this parallel at pleasure. The sum is, that Macchiavelli advocates rank king-craft, and Washington undefiled democracy. There are a great many secret and open friends of monarchism in the United States, who attribute the present defective working of our political institutions to intrinsic faults of the republican system. A mere superficial comparison of this treatise, which is still the political bible of absolute and constitutional monarchs, with Washington's address, should undeceive them. Of course, if we manage our republics as princely centralizers, hypocrites, and placemen do their states, they will fare like those in Italy and elsewhere.

Peruse, then, "The Prince" carefully. Its author was one of the best statesmen of the remarkable age in which he lived.

EXTRACTS FROM THE PRINCE OF MACCHIAVELLI.

1. *The several Sorts of Government, and after what Manner they are obtained.*

"There never was, nor is at this day, any government in the world by which one man has rule and dominion over another, but it is either a commonwealth [republic] or a monarchy." (The state of Maryland, however, began with a universal government.)

2. *Of Hereditary Principalities.*

"Hereditary states are preserved with less difficulty than the new, because it is sufficient not to transgress the examples of the predecessors, and next to comply and frame themselves to the accidents that occur; so that if the prince be a person of sufficient activity, he will be sure to keep himself on the throne."

3. *Of Mixed Principalities.*

"Countries that have rebelled, and are conquered the second time, are recovered with more difficulty. Whoever acquires anything, and desires to preserve it, is obliged to have a care of two things: more particularly one is, that the family of the former prince be extinguished; the other, that no new laws or taxes be imposed. But where conquest is made in a country differing in language, customs, and laws, there is the great difficulty that good fortune and great industry are requisite to keep it; and one of the best and most efficacious expedients to do it would be for the usurper to live there himself, as the Grand Turk has done in Greece. Men are either to be flattered and indulged, or utterly destroyed; because for small offences they do usually revenge themselves, but for great ones they can not.

"The conqueror must not omit any pains to gain the inferior nobles in a new province, for they will readily and unanimously fall into one mass with the state that is conquered. He must further take care that they grow not too strong, nor be intrusted with too much authority; and then he can easily with his own forces, and their assistance, keep down the great lords in the vicinity.

"It is no more than natural for princes to desire to extend their dominion, and, when they attempt nothing but what they are able to achieve, they are applauded; in the reverse case they are condemned, and indeed not unworthily.

"Whoever is the occasion of another's advancement, is the cause of his own diminution."

4. *Consummation.*

"An empire like the Turkish, which is governed by the prince and his officers [servants], is harder to be subdued than one with a nobility; but, when once conquered, more easy to be kept."

5. *How Subdued Principalities are to be governed.*

"A commonwealth or republic is to be ruined, in order to keep it as a conquered province; for people, upon all occasions, will endeavor to recover their old privileges." [Hindostan.]

6. *Of Principalities acquired by one's own proper Conduct and Arms.*

"That conqueror who has committed least to fortune, has continued the longest."

7. *Of New Principalities.*

"Conquerors or innovators who stand upon their own feet and arms, succeed better than those who make more use of their rhetoric."

8. *Of Wicked Usurpers.*

"Whoever usurps the government of any state, is to execute and put in practice at once all the cruelties which he thinks material, that he may have no occasion to renew them often; but that by discontinuance he may mollify the people, and by his good deeds bring them over to his side. Such deeds should be distilled by drops, that the relish may be the greater.

"A prince is so to behave himself toward his subjects, that neither good nor bad fortune should be able to alter him; for, being once assaulted with adversity, you have no time to do mischief; and the good which you do, does you no good, being looked upon as forced, and so no thanks are due for it."

9. *Of Civil Principalities.*

"In all cities [states], the meaner and the better sort of citizens are of different humors; and hence it follows that the common people are not willing to be commanded and oppressed by the great ones, and the great ones [aristocrats] are not satisfied without it.

"He who arrives at the sovereignty by the assistance of the aristocrats, preserves it with more difficulty than he who is advanced by the people; because he has about him many of his old associates, who, thinking themselves his equals, are not to be directed and managed as he would have them. Grandees [privileged aristocracy] are hardly to be satisfied without injury to others; while the designs of the people are more reasonable, and they endeavor only to defend and secure themselves. Where the people are adverse, the prince can never be safe, by reason of their numbers.

"These kinds of governments are most tottering and uncertain when the prince strains of a sudden, and passes, as at one leap, from a civil to an absolute power.

"A prince who is provident and wise ought to carry himself so that in all places, times, and occasions, the people may have need of his administration and *regimen*, and ever after they shall be faithful and true."

10. *How the Strength of all Principalities is to be computed.*

"Those princes are capable of ruling [independently] who are able, either by the numbers of their men or the greatness of their wealth, to raise a complete army, and bid defiance to any that shall invade them; and those depend upon others who of themselves dare not meet their enemy in the field, but are forced to keep within their bounds, and defend them as well as they can, especially by fortifying the capital town.

"The nature of man is such, that he takes as much pleasure in having obliged another as in being obliged himself."

11. *Of Ecclesiastical Principalities.*

"The ecclesiastical princes are the only persons who have lands and do not defend them—subjects, and do not govern them; which render those principalities the happiest and most secure."

12. *Of Military Discipline.*

"The principal foundations of all states are good laws and good arms. There can not be good laws where there are not good arms [to execute the laws]."

13. *Of Different Soldiers.*

"The mercenary and auxiliary soldiers are unprofitable and dangerous. A martial commonwealth, that stands upon its own legs, and maintains itself by its own prowess, is not easily usurped, and falls not so readily under the obedience of one of its own citizens, as where all the forces are foreign."

14. *Of the Military Duty of a Prince.*

"A prince is to have no other design, nor thought, nor feeling, but war, and the arts and discipline of it. In time of peace, he should employ his thoughts more studiously therein by bodily exercise, sports, hunting, hawking, and mental occupations, informing himself of the coasts, situation and elevation of mountains, valleys, history, etc., and keep a great pattern before his mind."

15. *Of such Things as render them especially worthy of Blame or Applause.*

"A prince should be so well instructed as to know how to avoid the scandal of vices. He is not to concern himself, if run under the infamy of vices, without which his dominion was not to be preserved; for, if we consider things impartially, we shall find that some things in appearance are virtuous, and yet, if pursued, would bring certain destruction; and others, on the contrary, that are seemingly bad, which, if followed by a prince, procure his peace and security."

16. *Of Liberality and Parsimony.*

"A prince should be liberal; but liberality, so used as not to render him formidable, does but injure him. To keep up the name of liberality among men, it is necessary that no kind of luxury be omitted, which would make him poor and despised. He ought not to dread the imputation of being covetous, for in time he shall be esteemed liberal, when it is discovered that by his parsimony he has increased his revenue to a condition of defending himself against invasion, and to make enterprises upon other people."

17. *Of Cruelty and Clemency.*

"A prince is to desire to be esteemed merciful rather than cruel, but is not to regard the scandal of being cruel, if thereby he keeps his subjects in their allegiance and united; seeing that by a few examples of justice you may be more merciful than they who, by a universal exercise of pity, permit several disorders to follow, which occasion rapine and murder.

"The question, whether it be better to be beloved than feared, or feared than beloved, is answered. Both would be convenient; but, because that it is hard to attain, it is better and more secure, if one must be wanting, to be feared than beloved: for, in general, men are ungrateful, inconstant, hypocritical, fearful of danger, and covetous of gain. To be feared and not hated, is compatible enough. But, before all things, a prince is to have a care of trenching on their patrimony [by high taxes or confiscation]; for men sooner forget the death of their father than the loss of their property.

"As these do love at their own discretion, but fear not their princes, a wise prince is obliged to lay his foundation upon that which is in his own power, not that which depends on other people, but with great caution, that he does not make himself odious."

18. *How far a Prince is responsible for his Promise.*

"There being two ways of contending, by law [or reason] and by force — the first proper to men, the second to beasts — it belongs to a prince to understand both when to make use of the rational and when of the brutal way, in which latter regard he ought to imitate the lion and the fox. A prince, therefore, that is wise and prudent, can not, nor ought not, to keep his parole, when the keeping of it is to his prejudice, and the causes for which he promised are removed. Were men all good, this doctrine were not to be taught; but because they are wicked, and not likely to be punctual with you, you are not obliged to observe any such strictness with them.

"Nor was there ever a prince that wanted lawful pretence to justify his breach of promise. He that best personates the fox, has the best success. Nevertheless, it is of great consequence to disguise your inclination, and to play the hypocrite well; and men are so simple in their temper, and so submissive to their present necessities, that he who is neat and cleanly in his collusions shall never want people to practise them upon. [As Talleyrand, Metternich, Palmerston, and all the genus diplomat and politician.]

"A prince is not obliged to have all the good qualities in reality, but it is necessary to have them in appearance; nay, having them actually, and employing them upon all occasions, they are extremely prejudicial. It is honorable to seem mild, and merciful, and courteous, and religious, and sincere; and, indeed, to be so, provided your mind be so rectified and prepared that you can act quite contrary upon occasions. And this must be premised, that a prince, especially if but lately come to the throne, can not observe all those things exactly which make men to be esteemed virtuous — being oftentimes necessitated, for the preservation of his state, to do things inhuman, uncharitable, and irreligious; and therefore it is important that his mind be at his command, and flexible to all the puffs and variations of his fortune — not forbearing to be good while it is in his choice, but knowing how to be evil when there is a necessity. People are always taken with the appearance and event of things, and the greatest part of the world consists of the people; those few who are wise taking place when the multitude has nothing else to rely upon. There is a prince at this time [king of France] who has nothing in his mouth but fidelity and peace; and yet had he exercised either the one or the other, they had robbed him before this of both his power and reputation." [Napoleon III. declared that "the empire is peace," while he is constantly engaged in war, and organizing France as a conquered country under military rule.]

19. *Moral Policy of Princes.*

"Princes ought to be cautious of becoming either odious or contemptible. As often as they do so, they play their part very well, and will meet with no danger or inconvenience from the rest of their views. Nothing makes a prince so insufferably odious as usurping his subjects' estates and debauching their wives; for while the generality of the people live quietly upon their estates, and unprejudiced in their honor, they live peaceably enough, and all contention is only with the pride and ambition of some few persons who are easily restrained. He has to strive that in all his actions there may appear magnanimity, courage, gravity, and fortitude, and to avoid being accounted effeminate, light, inconstant, pusillanimous, and irresolute. He ought to be terrible in two places — at home to his subjects, and abroad to his equals. One of the best remedies a prince can use against conspiracy is to keep himself from being hated or despised by the multitude; for nobody plots but he expects by the death of the prince to gratify the people; and the thought of offending them will deter him from any such enterprise, because in conspiracies the difficulties are infinite. Many conjurations have been on foot, but few have succeeded, because no man can conspire alone. On the side of the conspirators there is nothing but fear, and jealousy, and apprehension, and punishment; but on the prince's side there is the majesty of the government, the laws, the organized state. When the people are dissatisfied, and have taken a prejudice against the prince, there is nothing, nor any person, which he ought not to fear. It must be his constant care not to reduce the nobility to despair, nor the people to discontent. Princes should leave things of injustice and envy to the ministry and execution of others, but acts of favor and grace are to be performed by themselves.

"It can not be avoided but princes must fall under the hatred of somebody; they ought diligently to contend that it be not of the multitude. If that be not to be obtained, they should not incur the odium of such as are most potent among them."

20. *On Fortifications.*

"A wise prince was never known to disarm his subjects, for, by arming them and inuring them to warlike exercise, those arms are his own; those who are suspicious become faithful, they who are faithful are confirmed, and all the subjects become of his party. To disarm the people is to disgust them. It argues weakness in the prince to encourage dissensions, or parties, or factions, in order to rule people—perhaps newly conquered. Those are to be mollified by degrees.

"Princes, and particularly those who are not of long standing, have often found more fidelity and assistance from those whom they suspected at the beginning of their reign, than from them who at first were their greatest confidents.

"A prince, newly advanced, ought to consider well what it was that disposed some to befriend him; if it be not affection to him, but pique and animosity to the old government, it will cost much trouble and difficulty to keep them his friends, because it will be impossible to satisfy them.

"Fortresses are useful or not useful, according to the difference of time. That prince who is more afraid of his subjects than neighbors, is to suffer them to stand. The fortresses will not protect him if the people have him in detestation, because they shall no sooner take arms but strangers will fall in and sustain them."

21. *How a Prince gains Reputation.*

"Nothing recommends a prince so highly to the world as great enterprises, and noble expressions of his own valor and conduct, either, in war, to allow the people no leisure to be at quiet or to continue any thing against him, or by giving some rare example of his own administration at home, when there is occasion for somebody to perform anything extraordinary in the civil government, whether it be good or bad, and to find out such a way either to reward or punish him as may make him much talked of in the world. A prince is to have a care, in all his actions, to behave himself so as to give himself the reputation of being excellent as well as great. He is likewise much esteemed when he shows himself a sincere friend or a generous enemy—that is, when, without any hesitation, he declares himself in favor of one against another, which, as it is more frank and princely, so it is more profitable than to stand neuter. A conqueror will never understand them to be his friends who would not assist him in his distress; and he that is worsted will not receive you, because you neglected to run his fortune with your arms in your hands.

"A prince is never to league himself with another more powerful than himself in an offensive war, because in that case, if he overcomes, you remain at his mercy; and princes ought to be as cautious as possible of falling under the discretion of other people. If they who contend be of such condition, that they have no occasion to fear let what will overcome, you are in prudence to decline yourself the sooner, because, by assisting the one, you contribute to the ruin of the other, whom, if your confederate had been wise, he ought rather to have preserved, so that the overcoming remains wholly at your discretion, and by your assistance he must of necessity overcome.

"No prince or government, however, should imagine that, in such cases, any certain counsel can be taken, because the affairs of this world are so ordered, that in avoiding one mischief we fall commonly into another. A man's wisdom is most conspicuous where he is able to distinguish between dangers, and make choice of the least.

"A prince, to show himself a virtuoso and honorer of all that is excellent in any art whatever, is to encourage and assure his subjects that they may live quietly in peace, and exercise themselves in their several vocations, whether merchandise, agriculture, or any other employment whatever, to the end that one may not forbear improving or embellishing his estate for fear it should be taken from him, nor another advancing his trade in apprehension of taxes; but the prince is rather to excite them by propositions of reward and immunities to all such as shall any way amplify his territory or powers. He is obliged, likewise, at convenient times in the year, to entertain the people by feastings, and plays, and spectacles of recreation; and, because all cities are divided into companies or wards, he ought to have respect to those societies, be merry with them sometimes, and give them some instance of his humanity and magnificence, but always retaining the majesty of his degree, which is never to be debased in any case whatever."

22. *Of the Secretaries of Princes.*

"The election of his ministers is of no small importance to a prince, for the first judgment that is made of him, or his parts, is from the persons he has about him. Commonly the first error he commits is in the election of his servants.

"In the capacities and parts of men there are three sorts of degrees; one man understands of himself, another understands what is explained, and a third understands neither of himself nor by any explanation. The first is excellent, the second commendable, the third altogether unprofitable.

"But the business is how a prince may understand his minister, and the rule for that is infallible. When you observe your officer more careful of himself than of you, and all his actions and designs pointing at his own interest and advantage, that man will never be a good minister, nor ought you ever to repose any confidence in him."

23. *How Flatterers are to be avoided.*

"Men and princes are generally so fond of their own actions, and so easily mistaken in them, that it is not without difficulty they defend themselves against flatterers, of which kind of cattle all histories are full; and he that goes about to defend himself, runs a great hazard of being despised.

"There is no other remedy against flatterers, than to let everybody understand you are not disobliged by telling the truth. Yet if you suffer every body to tell it, you injure yourself, and lessen your reverence; wherefore a wise prince ought to go a third way, and select out of his state certain discreet men, to whom only he is to commit that liberty of speaking truth, and that of such things as he demands, and nothing else! But, then, he is to inquire of everything, hear their opinions, and resolve afterward as he pleases, and behave himself toward them in such sort, that every one may find with how much the more freedom he speaks, with so much the more kindness he is accepted, that besides them he will hearken to nobody; that he considers well before he resolves; and that his resolutions once taken are never to be altered. A prince, therefore, is always to consult, but at his own, not other people's pleasure, and rather deter people from giving their advice undemanded.

"A prince who has no wisdom of his own can never be well advised, unless by accident he commits all to the government and administration of some honest, discreet man. If a prince, who has no great judgment of his own, consults with more than one, their counsels will never agree, nor he have ever the cunning to unite them; every man will advise according to his own interest or caprice. These will always prove bad, unless by necessity they are compelled to be good. It is clear that good counsels proceed rather from the wisdom of the prince, than the prince's wisdom from the goodness of his counsels.

24. *How Princes lose their Dominions.*

"No defences are good, certain, and lasting, which proceed not from the prince's own courage and virtue, after he has embellished and fortified his principality with good laws, good force, good friends, and good example.

25. *Of Fortune.*

"It is an old opinion, that the affairs of the world are so governed by fortune and divine Providence, that man can not by his wisdom correct them. This may be true of one half of our actions, but fortune leaves the other half, or little less, to be governed by ourselves. It shows its power where there is no predisposed virtue to resist it. A prince who relies wholly upon fortune, being subject to her variations, must of necessity be ruined. That prince will be successful whose manner of proceeding concerts with the times. In things leading to the end of their designs, as riches and honor, we see men have various methods of proceeding, which may possibly all be successful; while two persons, equally cautious, one of them prospers and the other miscarries, so that two persons by different operations do attain the same end, while two others steer the same course, and one of them succeeds and the other is ruined. One, however good, if the face of affairs and the times change, and he changes not with them, will be certainly ruined. There is no man to be found so wise, that knows how to accommodate or frame himself to all vicissitudes and varieties.

"While the obstinacy of princes consists with the motion of fortune, it is possible they may be happy; but when once they disagree, the poor prince comes certainly to the ground. It is better to be hot and audacious, than cautious and apprehensive, for fortune is a woman, and must be *Hectored* to keep her under; and 'tis visible every day she suffers herself to be managed by those who are brisk and audacious, rather than by those who are cold and phlegmatic in their motions, and therefore (like a woman) she is always a friend to those who are young; because being less circumspect, they attack her with more security and boldness."

An exhortation to deliver Italy from the barbarians concludes the work.

These "barbarians" rule still in the best parts of Italy. You will now be able, with the help of the general history of Europe (Asia) and America, to answer easily the question: exactly what difference there is between the European and our own "state-system;" viz., that the first depends upon the principle of self-government applied to public business, the latter upon—*legitimacy.* After the downfall of Napoleon I.'s empire, all the princes of Europe, Turkey included, met in congress at Vienna, and *restored* the European political system *upon the principle of legitimacy,* as they called it, adding the gracious promise of constitutional forms of monarchy. They expressly declared the Napoleonides outside the pale of legitimacy; but one of them has again ascended the throne of France! You see how little faith sensible men should place in such a system, where so much depends upon sheer accident, and the management of the public affairs is made the property-right of a few "legitimate" families, viz. such as believe and pretend to be created by God, to possess and rule the people.

Our system is the product of common sense and plain business necessity, the European that of property-rights in men; ours is made only for the rule of the unruly, the European for the government of men and land; ours is stable for all times to come, provided we keep the several parts of it in strict order with reference to population, state, size, and business; the stability of the European depends upon the frail thread of the life of one or a few persons, and similar accidental circumstances beyond the control of men; ours, finally, depends upon prospective law, the European upon present customs, without the least guaranty for the future. What pity that men abuse also the best things! What would be the United States if their excellent system had been carried out well?

But there is still time enough to do it. We are free yet. Hope then for the best. In this hope let us now part.

PART SECOND.

MUNICIPAL GOVERNMENT.

LETTER I.

Object of a State Constitution.—Introduction to the Constitution of the State of New York.—Preamble.—Union-Slighting.

My intention at first was to limit my political conversation with you to the federal constitution, under which we all live, in whatever state we reside; even when travelling in foreign countries, and sailing on distant seas we depend upon its protection. But after I bade you adieu, and had indulged in a sober, second thought—always a good one—I concluded to place one of our state constitutions in parallel with it, to show better their coördinate working in society, and whether it be harmonious or not. It is the same artistical idea which induced me to place "The Prince" in parallel with Washington.

I have for this purpose selected the constitution of the state of New York, because this is, as the most populous, a kind of leading state, and it is proposed to take the sense of the people at the ensuing election (November, 1858) whether it shall be amended or not. For the latter reason I have also added a few remarks on the state constitution of Maryland. I should, perhaps, have altered the form and addressed these letters to the voters of these states; but as "I speak by permission, and not of commandment, according to my proper gift of God," I will continue in the familiar manner, hoping also to avoid thereby the suspicion of an intention to bias the vote, although I sincerely wish that in my humble efforts I may be able to excite an intense interest on the subject.

The obvious aim of a state constitution, in our Union, must be to prescribe the forms of a government for the realization of justice and order in regard to the municipal political affairs. Accordingly it should be framed, first, from a desire not to interfere with the business province of the federal constitution, as this has been carefully planned from the view not to interfere with the scope of the state constitutions; and secondly, not to meddle with the free social business of which I have spoken in the first part. To this may be added, that in our Union, and free unsubject society, a state is not exactly required for the governing of persons, but only for the management of certain public affairs; because in such society is the real ruler of persons the principle of self-government, which requires every one to control himself well in personal and social regard. This being the most difficult task men—although endowed with reason for this very purpose—have to perform, the state institution is calculated in single instances *to force* them into a proper self-control, in order to preserve justice and prevent injury and anarchy. Without this force a state constitution is nothing to speak of.

If this is well understood, it is not so very difficult to comprehend the real object of a state constitution, especially after the framers of the federal constitution have set up such a master-piece of an organic law for the management of the national affairs.

A political system of this frame, and good execution, should, if this sublinarian world is not a failure withal, impress upon the people living under it a noble character; for as the maternal education moulds the character of an individual, so form the political institutions that of nations. This moral influence of our political system upon our nations and mankind was the beacon-light of hope for those who struggled for years for the deliverance of a proud prince, in order to be free, or the masters of their own destiny. Government can only promote liberty by keeping the lawless and dishonest at bay with the help of an effective judiciary.

Let us, then, examine with diligence the constitution of the state of New York, to ascertain how far it answers to this purpose:—

CONSTITUTION OF THE STATE OF NEW YORK.

"We, the people of the state of New York, grateful to Almighty God for our freedom, in order to secure its blessings, do establish this constitution."

If you will compare this introduction with the preamble of the federal constitution, you will, perhaps, after duly honoring the pious sentiment it expresses, notice that it is vague, and not distinctly pointing out the real object of an American state constitution. To secure the blessings of freedom or absence of subjection, there was not exactly a state constitution required after we got the present federal constitution; because the Union alone can do that, that is, protect us from subjection abroad or at home, and thus alone the independence or blessings of freedom of the people in the states are really and effectively secured. The remaining object of a state constitution, therefore, can only be the political protection of our persons, property, and homes; and this can not be done, as I just remarked, by anything else but a good municipal government, providing justice, which comes home to all, the poor and the rich, the young and old.

But the negative side of this little preamble, or that which is missing in it, is of more consequence. This constitution was written in 1846, of course a considerable time after the enactment of the federal constitution. Without giving more importance to this great compact than is right, I think it would have been but proper, fair, and business-like, to mention in this preamble, that the state in question is one of the United States of America. In the manner this constitution is treating the best and greatest confederation ever made by men, it seems to be but a trifling concern, hardly worth while to be mentioned at all. I think that such a curial or official style is neither right nor prudent. To be a member of this confederation must be our greatest pride, and appear in bold relief upon the escutcheon of every state, and in distinct words in the preamble of every constitution. This Union is our strength, our greatness. The states must acknowledge it before the world, for it is their own work. This may be done in their constitutions, by something like the following words: "We, the people of the state of ———, one of the United States of America, under the constitution of September 7, 1787, bounded as follows: ———, for the purpose of establishing justice and order, and promoting the general welfare, do ordain," etc. This would not be at all an empty phraseology, because by such a preface the political position, relation, and character of the state, and its government, would be at once clear, the guaranty of the constitution by the powerful confederation pointed out, the realization of justice and order made the main purpose of the organic law and state itself; further, all visionary schemes and experiments barred on the outset, and in the course of time wholly excluded from its province. I expressly say in the course of time, because the present bad practice can not be reformed at once, even by the most perfect constitution. Still, we have to begin the reform.

Of these very important points this constitution leaves the reader, and citizens, and the world in darkness. It simply foreshadows that the framers did not start from a distinct principle, like those of the federal constitution. It will not be my fault if I have to point out this difference often. I am sorry for it, because I do not much approve of the criticizing of laws and constitutions, if they are tolerably good. But truth will prevail, whatever my opinion may be about this organic law.

LETTER II.

Bill of Rights. — Peers. — Jury. — Disagreeing. — Acquittals.— Liberty of Conscience and Worship. — Habeas Corpus. — Injunctions. — Bail. — Grand Jury. — Protection of Private Property. — Pauperism. — Charity.

We come now to a subject of which I wrote a few lines in my letters on the federal constitution.

ARTICLE I.

Bill of Rights.

"1. No member of this state shall be disfranchized, or deprived of any of the rights or privileges secured to any citizen thereof, unless by the law of the land, or the judgment of his peers."

A bill of rights is a declaration of certain conditions under which people wish to be governed. When the English people or rather the aristocracy, unmindful of 1 Samuel, chap. viii., choose foreign princes as their kings, they drew up a list of conditions, or rights, or privileges, which they demanded to be respected by the foreign rulers. The thing, therefore, is of a peculiar monarchical origin, and very well for people who make foreign princes their hereditary rulers, but of no use in our republics, provided, that our constitutions distinctly describe the sphere and powers of the officials (an easy task withal), and for which purpose they are, indeed, written down. There is no bill of rights in the federal constitution. Where the object of setting up a state institution or government (legislature, judiciary, executive) is the realization of justice, no man ever will be disfranchized, and if this can not be helped by a constitution, as was the case in the celebrated metropolitan police affair, what difference does it make, whether a person, or city, or county, is disfranchized by law or a judgment of peers?

The proper sense of the phrase, "or the judgment of his peers," is not clear in America, although I can easily perceive its bearing in Great Britain, whose laws are made for a society composed of privileged classes. If there is a duke under judgment, he has probably the privilege to be judged by dukes; a prelate may insist to be judged by peers, viz., prelates; and so on with princes of blood, earls, barons, marquises, counts, freeholders, and tenants, &c., &c. The state of New York, being a republic, does, of course, not recognise any monarchical classification of its citizens; they are before the law equal. If the word peer refers to this state of equality and not, perhaps, to political parties, then the phrase would mean, that we shall be judged by our equals. But this would be self-evident and no privilege, and, therefore, superfluous in a bill of rights.

So we may presume that it has reference to the jury, of which the following clause treats. But in regard to the right of a citizen to be judged by a jury of his equals, special laws have made great inroads upon the bill of rights, by exempting all clergymen, lawyers, teachers, doctors, firemen, militiamen, and those who have formed an opinion on the case under trial, from the jury service, depriving thus all those just-mentioned members of society of the privilege to be judged by their peers. My purpose is to throw the fullest light upon my subject, neither dimmed by the cobweb curtains of law-cant nor by rusty blinds of feudal legislation of bygone times. What is right is a product of common sense and reason, enlightened by culture, expressed by law. Our state constitutions should not be a rehash of unpractical obsolete phrases. How faultless in this regard is our federal constitution!

"2. The trial by jury, in all cases in which it has been heretofore used, shall remain inviolate for ever. But a jury trial may be waived by the parties in all civil cases in the manner to be prescribed by law."

This clause appears not in its proper place, because the jury is a part of the judiciary, and should be provided for under this head. The words "for ever" are exceptionable. We are mortals; our mind follows the clock of time. If the next generation should dislike the jury system, which at present works badly enough, and dispense with it, it would require an alteration of the constitution. This is, as you know, merely a general organizing law, put into operation by special acts. Society is changing and progressing; constitutions, therefore, should be made so that, in substance, they work in consonance with the time. Justice is always the same; but the ways and means to realize it are variable, and, therefore, subject to special laws.

I improve this opportunity to add a few remarks on this branch of the judiciary, which, if well organized, may have still a great influence upon good order in our society; which, however, if destined to be a source of income for mere loungers about the court-houses, deserves to be abolished at once.

Ours is a government of majorities. In all collegiate bodies, in all legislatures, in all boards, in all elections, however important, also in that most decisive event, the ratification of the federal constitution, the law of *majority* is, or has been, recognised as imperative; but the English jury, which is but a judicial board, makes an exception from this rule. Their verdicts require unanimity. The federal constitution, I say again, upon which depended the fate of this nation, went into operation by a majority vote of the thirteen states, while a jury verdict upon a single, perhaps, a very trifling case, shall require unanimity of twelve jurors! The anomaly I speak of is but a caprice, and one of the curiosities of which the English code of procedure, to which this episode refers, abounds. I point out this curiosity here, in order that some one of our legislatures may abolish it.

The majority principle works very well in juries on the continent of Europe. To admit, further, that a judicial board can abandon a case because they do not agree, is tantamount to anarchy and revolution, because a court disables thus the state institution, which, in the main, depends upon its action. Without a judiciary there is no state. We allow our officials, jurors included, too much latitude. I would rather see the whole jury abolished than in a single instance dismissed because they could not agree. There is no better proof of its defective organization, or rather uselessness, than this fact. The sworn duty of the jury is to give a verdict, as that of a court is to give a sentence. What would the public say of a judge who could not agree with himself about a sentence!

As long as the before-mentioned personal exceptions from jury service remains on the statute books, and those who are able to form an opinion on a case under trial may be challenged and rejected, the trial by jury will be offensive to the instinct of justice, and from time to time regulated by Lynch law and vigilance committees, in spite of the constitutional provisions about the eternity of the jury to the contrary.

If a jury acquits a criminal whose guilt is matter of evidence — alas, cases of frequent occurrence — the verdict must be by the agency of a special tribunal, or the governor or the grand jury set aside, and the perfidious jurors at once persecuted for perjury, because such a verdict is legal perjury, and, indeed, treason — nothing else. The autocracy of jury verdicts must cease when their authors use their power to shield criminality, the very evil which to check and eradicate is one of the main objects of the state institution. The home source of the English laws is a dismal swamp of immorality. The profligate personal character of almost all English monarchs, the peculiarly corrupt manner of the composition of the parliament, the notorious sunken morality of the aristocracy and leading men, must necessarily have exercised for centuries a sinister influence upon the laws and the masses. Unprincipled and reckless men never will make good laws, neither in Great Britain nor elsewhere.

"3. The free exercise and enjoyment of religious profession and worship, without discrimination or preference. shall for ever be allowed in this state to all mankind; and no person shall be rendered incompetent to be a witness on account of his opinion on matters of religious belief; but the liberty of conscience hereby secured shall not be so construed as to excuse acts of licentiousness, or justify practices inconsistent with the peace of this state."

I do not think it is necessary to say a word in one of our constitutions about religion, worshipping, speaking, and printing, as little as about teaching, curing diseases, making shoes, etc., because a real free state never interferes with honest industry, never can have anything to do with such private affairs, except they are practised or managed in such a manner that they violate rights and give rise to complaints, when the judiciary will be called upon to look into the matter.

"4. The privilege of the writ of habeas corpus shall not be suspended, unless when, in cases of rebellion or invasion, the public safety may require its suspension."

I have spoken of this so-called privilege in the first part.

A general proviso, forming at the same time a part of the American common law, that no person shall be arrested unless guilty of disobedience when summoned, or of a criminal act (felony) and suspect of flight from justice, *would now* answer better for the real protection against abuse of power than this privilege; because in spite of it, there are constantly persons arrested and set free on bail who should never be molested in this manner.

I refer here only to the injuncture-procedure against the mayor of the city of New York, in the metropolitan police-law controversy, who, in opposing as mayor, this law, became neither a felon nor "suspect" to fly from justice, but was notwithstanding arrested. Secondly, I mention an arrest of the mayor of Brooklyn because some one felt offended by his official acts. For what use is this rigor?

"5. Excessive bail shall not be required, nor excessive fines imposed; nor shall cruel and unusual punishments be inflicted, nor shall witnesses be unreasonably detained."

General phrases of this kind are useless; a witness should never be detained, but instantaneously examined and dismissed.

It should be common law with us, that no person can be forced to bear testimony except before his regular court, to whom, if not the court of litigation or trial, the case, with questions from both parties, may be sent for this purpose. This is the judicial practice, to my knowledge, on the continent of Europe. It works well, is expeditious, and just and humane, while the English custom deserves to be called savage.

"6. No person shall be held to answer for a capital or otherwise infamous crime (except in cases of impeachment, and cases of the militia when in actual service, and the land and naval forces in time of war, or which this state may keep with the consent of Congress in time of peace, and in cases of petit larceny, under the regulation of the legislature), unless on presentment or indictment of a grand jury; and in any trial in any court whatever, the party accused shall be allowed to appear and defend in person and with counsel, as in civil actions. No person shall be subject to be twice put in jeopardy for the same offence; nor shall he be compelled in any criminal case to be a witness against himself, nor be deprived of his life, liberty, or property without due process of law; nor shall private property be taken for public use without just compensation."

The grand jury is also a part of the judicial machinery, at present considered by many of doubtful utility. Its deliberations ought to be *secret*, while in all cases of suspected violent death the coroner's inquest, preceding the action of the grand jury, is *public!* If a person has been acquitted for want of proof, and later clear proof of guilt is found, there is no good reason why the accused should not be tried again. Justice toward society requires, under such circumstances, a new investigation, just as against a condemnatory sentence a new trial is allowed. That an accused may defend himself by counsel is well enough; but it can not be denied that the admittance of counsel from the beginning of the trial is more calculated to defeat the ends of justice than to promote them. The prohibition of confessing a crime or making a clean breast, or as the phrase is, to be witness against one self, is immoral. To deprive one by law of his property, even for the benefit of beggars or paupers, would no doubt be unjust; but it is daily done. All political charity, and all taxes raised by force of law for the support of the poor, are so many violations of this maxim. Therefore no good government should draw *charity* into its sphere. It seems to be done in Great Britain, on account of a general popular custom, expressed by a cant phrase which you may often hear, viz., "the town or county owes me a living." I attribute to it much of our public pauperism. According to the pauper statistics of Brooklyn, N. Y., in 1856–'57 there were relieved, at public expense, by law, 2,295 families, viz., 479 American, 2,519 Irish, 122 English, 15 Canadian, 31 Scotch, 2 Nova Scotians, 1 Welsh, 71 Germans, 183 French, showing an immense preponderance of the English for beggarism, probably because the city owes them a living, a phrase unknown to Germans. There is, if not a larger, an equal proportion of English (Irish included) and German inhabitants in this city. What good have those English beggars done for this city to oblige her to give them a living? I stop for an answer.

Charity, when practised by the state, will be made use of for political capital, and demoralize the indigent, evils easily avoided by prudent private charity. In Europe, many political contrivances, as high taxes, standing armies, frequent wars, interference with industry by laws, produces poverty, which, afterward, political charity tries to mitigate. Our system of government, which leaves every man entirely at liberty to procure by industry his daily bread, is diametrically opposed to such a monarchical policy.

We should, therefore, never have imitated the same. It is a *false* pride to boast of our poor-house palaces. They are giving the lie to the principles of self-government. Both our beautiful rich country and excellent system of governing should have prevented the growth of such foreign social parasitical plants. The *Friends* give the right example in this regard. The ladies should look into this political charity business.

Of the municipal, land, and naval forces of this state, more anon.

LETTER III.

Compensation for Private Property when taken for Public Use.—Roads.—Liberty of the Press.—Libels.—Assembling and Petition Right.—Divorce.—Lottery.—Escheats.—Feudal Tenures.—Allodiums.—Leases of Land.—Fines.—Quarter-Sales.—Indian Land-Sales.—Common Law.—Colonial Law.—Royal British Grants.—Property Laws.—American Common Law.—Rights of Self-Government.—Prohibition of Foreign Laws.—The Church Poor-Laws.—State Scholars.

You will soon perceive that we are in the beehive of society.

"7. When private property shall be taken for any public use, the compensation to be made therefor, when such compensation is not made by the state, shall be ascertained by a jury, or by not less than three commissioners appointed by a court of record, as shall be prescribed by law. Private roads may be opened in the manner to be prescribed by law; but in every case the necessity of the road, and the amount of all damage to be sustained by the opening thereof, shall be first determined by a jury of freeholders, and such amount, together with the expenses of the proceeding, shall be paid by the person to be benefitted."

The proviso that no private property shall be taken for public use without compensation, is perfectly right. Specialities belong to special laws. Even no property of towns or counties shall be taken for the use of the state without compensation. The metropolitan state police-law encroached upon the property-right of towns or cities, by claiming their telegraphs, etc., for state purposes, and was, therefore, unconstitutional.

"8. Every citizen may freely speak, write, and publish his sentiments on all subjects, being responsible for the abuse of that right; and no law shall be passed to restrain or abridge the liberty of speech or of the press. In all criminal prosecutions or indictments for libel, the truth may be given in evidence to the jury; and if it shall appear to the jury that the matter charged as libellous is true, and was published with good motives and for justifiable ends, the party shall be acquitted, and the jury shall have the right to determine the law and the fact."

I refer to my remarks at clause third. It has been a disputed question among jurists, since time immemorial, whether a man who calls his neighbor a thief may be justified by proving that he has

A democratic society can not exist without the right of assembling. Our government officials are our agents; nothing else. That such officials ever should stop peaceable meetings, or refuse to accept petitions, or dare to forbid petitioning, is in our times incredible. Such negative provisoes, quite frequently occurring in the federal constitution, are not subjects for a real bill of rights.

Lotteries are games, and may be allowed to-day and forbidden to-morrow, without mentioning them in a constitution. Divorces are litigious cases belonging by themselves to the tribunals.

"11. The people of this state, in their right of sovereignty, are deemed to possess the original and ultimate property in and to all lands within the jurisdiction of the state; and all lands, the title to which shall fail, from a defect of heirs, shall revert or escheat to the people.

A special escheat law has to settle the rights about property without owner. This may well be left to the towns, a part of the state where it has been presumptively acquired. So the clause will not be missed here if obliterated and transplanted into the statute-book.

"12. All feudal tenures of every description, with all their incidents, are declared to be abolished; saving, however, all rents and services certain which at any time heretofore have been lawfully created or reserved.

"13. All lands within this state are declared to be allodial, so that, subject only to the liability to escheat, the entire and absolute property is vested in the owners according to the nature of their respective estates.

"14. No lease or grant of agricultural land for a longer period than twelve years, hereafter made, in which shall be reserved any rent or service of any kind, shall be valid.

"15. All fines, quarter-sales, or other like restraints upon alienation, reserved, in any grant of land hereafter to be made, shall be void.

"16. No purchase or contract for the sale of lands in this state, made since the fourteenth day of October, one thousand seven hundred and seventy-five, or which may hereafter be made, of, or with the Indians, shall be valid, unless made under the authority and with the consent of the legislature."

There seems to have been no logical connection between those clauses and a real bill of rights. All such things belong to the statute-book.

"17. Such parts of the common law, and of the acts of the legislature of the colony of New York, as together did form the law of the said colony, on the nineteenth day of April, one thousand seven hundred and seventy-five, and the resolutions of the Congress of said colony, and of the Convention of the state of New York, in force on the twentieth day of April, one thousand seven hundred and seventy-seven, which have not since expired, or been repealed or altered; and such acts of the legislature of this state as are now in force shall be and continue the law of this state, subject to such alterations as the legislature shall make concerning the same. But all such parts of the common law, and such of the said acts, or parts thereof, as are repugnant to this constitution, are hereby abrogated, and the legislature at its first session after the adoption of this constitution, shall appoint three commissioners, whose duty it shall be to reduce into a written and systematic code the whole body of the law of this state, or so much and such parts thereof as to the said commissioners shall seem practicable and expedient. And the said commissioners shall specify such alterations and amendments therein as they shall deem proper, and they shall at all times make reports of their proceedings to the legislature when called upon to do so; and the legislature shall pass laws regulating the tenure of office, the filling of vacancies therein, and the compensation of said commissioners; and shall also provide for the publication of the said code prior to its being presented to the legislature for adoption."

All laws enacted by a legislative body of the state of New York, or the colony of New York, must be obeyed until repealed. What laws are valid is the business of the jurists and courts to know. This proviso seems therefore to be superfluous.

"18. All grants of land within this state, made by the king of Great Britain, or persons acting under his authority, after the fourteenth day of October, one thousand seven hundred and seventy-five, shall be null and void; but nothing contained in this constitution shall affect any grants of land within this state, made by the authority of the said king or his predecessors, or shall annul any charters to bodies politic and corporate, by him or them made before that day, or shall affect any such grants or charters since made by this state, or by persons acting under its authority, or shall impair the obligation of any debts contracted by this state, or individuals, or bodies corporate, or any other rights of property, or any suits, actions, rights of action, or other proceedings in courts of justice."

This proviso is in connection with the colonial history. In 1775 the first Congress of the thirteen states assembled at Philadelphia, New York among them. In 1776 appeared the Declaration of Independence. A special act may be useful to guide the courts in regard to the beginning of the political state independence. Constitutions have nothing to decide on private rights. This is the business of the judiciary. All these provisoes from twelve following are in connection with the manor difficulties existing in this state. About the different modes of possessing property, the statute-book must be explicit. A feudal tenure is land, the limited title of which is derived from a feudal lord, or superior proprietor, who retains a superior property right, recognised by tribute, rent, or services. The opposite is allodial property.

We have in a great measure disentangled our state institutions from many features of an English origin, and still have perseveringly to pursue this course of reform to make them American. But before we part from this so-called bill of rights, I should point it out as a sensible trait of this constitution worthy of imitation, that its framers have not inserted the stereotyped phrase generally occurring in other "northern" constitutions, which prohibits involuntary service or bound labor; because it is not only entirely superfluous, this kind of labor being in the north self-prohibitive, but also discourteous toward our southern states, and exceedingly injurious to personal freedom, by frightening away the masters with their bound laborers, from such states, thus depriving the slaves of a chance to become acquainted with society where free labor prevails.

A constitution is a frame, a form, an organic law, and neither a statute, nor a grant or compromise, in the proper sense of these words. The frame must fit society easily; society must not be cramped into the frame.

I take advantage here to add a few remarks on American common law. What bears this name at present is of English origin, and, in regard to general maxims, fair enough, but not better than the Roman law, the main source of all European codes, called, on account of its sound reasoning, written reason. However, the English common law does not exactly answer for our purposes. In order to come to an indigenous common law, our state constitutions should—firstly, prohibit all reference to any foreign law of whatever origin; secondly, it should be a general maxim that the judiciary, if called upon to judge on the constitutionality of laws, shall so construe the constitution as if it never intended to interfere with the rights of self-government, of persons, families, towns, and counties, but that one of their main objects is to protect and guaranty those rights; thirdly, that a rule be laid down for the division of overgrown political districts, and that these districts are prohibited from contracting debts for private or non-political subjects, to avoid all chances for repudiations and similar dishonest acts; fourthly, that towns are made responsible for all damages in persons and property caused by riots of bands; that counties are responsible for the same caused by riots of the people of a whole town, and that they shall be respectively charged and assessed. If persons are killed, the tariff or principles generally followed in railroad and similar accidents may serve as a rule. By-the-by, these railroad indemnifications prove that in law every person, and not a bound laborer only, has a money value.

Those who wish to appreciate the name American, as Washington desired in his farewell address, must long for a common law of our own. We are too much governed by foreign laws antagonistic to our institutions. If I appear as speaking harsh upon such inherited laws, I wish it to be understood that I do not reflect upon men. I recollect to have seen in Sparks's Life of Franklin, an old letter from that true nobleman, Larochefacault, wherein he congratulates the doctor on the federal constitution, adding expressly that it would now become necessary to change our code of laws. I write from memory. If we strip our legislatures of all power to meddle with non-political business, and thus confine their whole attention and time to the better realization of justice, should we not easily and naturally arrive to a more perfect state of public administration and public virtue, too, than the present? Why not make our states in this, their proper sphere, perfect?

My suggestions on the management of our states are at variance with the present practice, and why? because I maintain that only strictly political business should be intrusted to governments, while the usual policy starts from the idea that a state government may do anything it thinks proper for society. The difference, therefore, is in business, not in men. I further maintain that my views are strictly American, and the other European or Asiatic. If our legislatures ordain that the counties shall have power to establish poorhouses, and tax the people to raise the funds for their support, they assume that the supporting of poor men is a political business, while I call it a mere charitable private personal act of brotherly love. The Christian church, from its beginning, took hold of this business, tried to introduce communism on this account, and later, when united with the states, transferred it to them. We have separated the church from the state, and the church has to take back this charity business, if it may not be entirely left with the benevolent, as a mere personal private affair; instead of doing so we have, by bad centralization, made it responsible for the same caused by riots of the people of a whole town, and that they shall be respectively charged and assessed. If persons are killed, the tariff or principles generally followed in railroad and similar accidents may serve as a rule. By-the-by, these railroad indemnifications prove that in law every person, and not a bound laborer only, has a money value.

Those who wish to appreciate the name American, as Washington desired in his farewell address, must long for a common law of our own. We are too much governed by foreign laws antagonistic to our institutions. If I appear as speaking harsh upon such inherited laws, I wish it to be understood that I do not reflect upon men. I recollect to have seen in Sparks's Life of Franklin, an old letter from that true nobleman, Larochefacault, wherein he congratulates the doctor on the federal constitution, adding expressly that it would now become necessary to change our code of laws. I write from memory. If we strip our legislatures of all power to meddle with non-political business, and thus confine their whole attention and time to the better realization of justice, should we not easily and naturally arrive to a more perfect state of public administration and public virtue, too, than the present? Why not make our states in this, their proper sphere, perfect?

My suggestions on the management of our states are at variance with the present practice, and why? because I maintain that only strictly political business should be intrusted to governments, while the usual policy starts from the idea that a state government may do anything it thinks proper for society. The difference, therefore, is in business, not in men. I further maintain that my views are strictly American, and the other European or Asiatic. If our legislatures ordain that the counties shall have power to establish poorhouses, and tax the people to raise the funds for their support, they assume that the supporting of poor men is a political business, while I call it a mere charitable private personal act of brotherly love. The Christian church, from its beginning, took hold of this business, tried to introduce communism on this account, and later, when united with the states, transferred it to them. We have separated the church from the state, and the church has to take back this charity business, if it may not be entirely left with the benevolent, as a mere personal private affair; instead of doing so we have, by bad centralization, made it a county business. The motion made in the legislature of the state of New York of 1857-8, to create a central state-board, for the governing of the poor and almshouse affairs, consisting of a number of commissioners with a salary of four thousand dollars each (I write again from memory), would, if successful, only increase this bad centralization. Still, as gratuitous as this motion appears, it is in fact not worse than the law which creates political county poorhouses.

Another illustration. Sciences and arts are no doubt non-political business. Still at the same legislative session a motion was made to create a state-scholarship. Also this proposition has not been acted upon; but if we have state regents for colleges, etc., why not have state scholars, too? Such things are anti-American, while the Grand Turk and Queen Victoria may create as many state or court histographers, scholars, painters, etc., as they please, and give them salaries, pensions, orders, titles, etc., beside, and Napoleon III. may forbid soldiers to write newspaper articles. Such motions and laws are to be deprecated in our society. They creep into our statutes in spite of our bills of rights, so that they seem not to be set up with an eye to the perfecting of the American system of governing. But this should be the case, if they are for any use at all.

LETTER IV.

Elective Franchise. — Restrictions. — Citizenship. — Ballot. — Family voting right. — Woman. — Connecticut. — Christianity. — Polygamy. — Utah. — Kansas Scandals.

NOTHING has been a greater stumbling-block for legislators, both ancient and modern, than the voting laws, nearly related to the citizenship right. Age, birth, property, taxes, color, religion, and other more or less irrelevant items have been made suffrage conditions, and no two of our states have uniform laws about it. They at least all conflict with those of Congress in regard to the voting of naturalized citizens. Still the suffrage right is the main spring in our political machinery. It brings us good or bad legislators and governors. This constitution has adopted what is called the general suffrage. I have already observed that it is not just, and therefore can not be beneficial for society. On this very ground the representative system has taken the place of the pure democracy in the United States. However, in a republic most important questions, as the adoption or amending of constitutions and charters, must necessarily pass the popular ordeal. The citizens of Brooklyn and Williamsburgh had to vote on consolidation, a purely monarchical measure, in the end detrimental for both cities, each being already too large for a good local administration. They voted affirmatively. No true republican statesman will approve of such a vote. How important, therefore, is this subject for society.

But let us see what our constitution ordains about it.

ARTICLE II.

The Elective Franchise.

"1. Every male citizen of the age of twenty-one years, who shall have been a citizen for ten days, and an inhabitant of this state one year next preceding any election, and for the last four months a resident of the county where he may offer his vote, shall be entitled to vote at such election in the election district of which he shall at the time be a resident, and not elsewhere, for all officers that now are or hereafter may be elected by the people; but such citizen shall have been for thirty days next preceding the election, a resident of the district from which the officer is to be chosen for which he offers his vote. But no man of color, unless he shall have been for three years a citizen of this state, and for one year next preceding any election shall have been seized and possessed of a freehold estate of the value of two hundred and fifty dollars, over and above all debts and encumbrances charged thereon, and shall have been actually rated and paid a tax thereon, shall be entitled to vote at such election. And no person of color shall be subject to direct taxation unless he shall be seized and possessed of such real estate as aforesaid.

Accordingly the right of voting belongs, in this state, exclusively to male persons. This is not right. The political organization is not a personal but a social necessity; not made exclusively for the male persons of age, and, if of color, in the possession of a freehold estate worth two hundred and fifty dollars, but for the people, that is, men, women, children, and all their interests. Human society is not, like armies, clubs, and partnerships, composed of persons, but of *families*. If this is true, and I think it is manifest enough, then to the families, as the constituents of society, belongs exclusively the suffrage right. But this criterion is not all that, in our modern free states, a voting law requires. These are organized by *written* or *printed* constitutions, hence a necessity that the voter, who represents the family, when the family voting-right is legal, should, besides be able to read the language in public use, and to write it too, because he has to vote with the help of printed or written tickets. The working of the machinery of the state depends upon publicity, or upon writing, reading, speaking, and printing. The public business must, in a great measure, remain chaotic for a man who can not read. How will such a man be able to vote with due circumspection? If they were, for the time being, excluded from the polls, it would induce the indolent to learn how to read and write, and have his children instructed, without being forced to it by truant laws and policemen; or by school boards and state laws. Connecticut had the courage to make the knowledge of language a voting law. Give, then, each family a vote, to be cast by its head, retain the term of twenty-one years of age, add the just-mentioned conditions, harmonize the state and Congressional legislation, and you will not only comply with the equitable laws of society, but also reconcile *woman* with the state institutions. They have a greater influence upon their success than is usually believed.

It is an act of sincere chivalry to make woman a silent partner of the citizenship right. The pernicious aberrations about wo man's rights, require, urgently, such a law as a corrective.

"2. Laws may be passed excluding from the right of suffrage all persons who have been, or may be convicted of bribery, larceny, or of any infamous crime, and for depriving every person who shall make, or become directly or indirectly interested in any bet or wager depending upon the result of any election, from the right to vote at such election.

This is matter for a criminal law-code, or statute-book, but generally right. Such men should also be excluded from the jury.

"3. For the purpose of voting, no person shall be deemed to have gained or lost a residence, by reason of his presence or absence, while employed in the service of the United States; nor while engaged in the navigation of the waters of this state, or of the United States, or of the high seas; nor while a student of any seminary of learning, nor while kept at any almshouse, or other asylum, at public expense; nor while confined in any public prison."

Belonging to the statute book.

"4. Laws shall be made for ascertaining by proper proofs the citizens who shall be entitled to the right of suffrage hereby established.

"5. All elections by the citizens shall be by ballot, except for such town officers as may by law be directed to be otherwise chosen."

Partly objects of special laws.

I venture a few lines more upon this subject.

Such a judicious suffrage law as that of families, resting upon a just social basis, must exercise a highly beneficial influence upon the governments, public virtue, and the morals in general.

Christianity has sanctified the family state, the best men of all ages, our Franklin included, have advised its establishment. Why then should the civil law hesitate to support it? By giving to the families exclusively the suffrage right, the state would act in the spirit of Christianity and humanity, and bestow upon woman so much social equality, as naturally belongs to her, while the usual general suffrage law ignores her entirely, and brings men upon the political stage who are not entitled to it. I speak only of the family suffrage right, not of offices, those may be occupied by any qualified person, whether married or not.

There good statesmanship is in request. It should begin with the territories.

It would have prevented polygamy in Utah or elsewhere in the United States, either sanctioned by law, or connived at, especially in large cities; it would prevent Kansas-voting scandal; it would exclude not only the votaries of celibacy from the polls, but also all mobs. It promises better quiet voting than anything which has been devised at present. Why not try it?

What I miss in this article is, that the Congressional legislation on the citizenship rights of emigrants has not been noticed at all, although this constitutes in this regard the supreme law of the land. It would be well to act in such things systematically. The people in New York state must cheerfully respect the laws made by the agency of their own representatives in Congress. By doing so their own proper state laws will be, in turn, more cheerfully respected.

What may we reasonably expect from frequent elections and rotation in office? This is an appropriate question here, which you can only answer if you abstract entirely from persons and parties, and argue merely upon "business, population, and size," as I have often observed. If those three material items are not well adjusted, no election, no change of party, no rotation will improve the public affairs, because no men, however experienced, skillful, and honest, can manage a business well, which, by itself, is unmanageable. A hundred Washingtons can not make of France a good republic, unless the size, population, and public business, are previously republicanized, the standing army disbanded, the state clergy abolished, etc., etc. All our disproportionate cities and states will only, by too much office-rotation and too frequent party shifts, be ruined faster than under a more steady form of government. The history of the last twenty-five years must convince every sensible man that the evil is not personal but material. To have then the least faith in party-shifts is absurd. All parties will make the most of the bad state of things, will with alacrity promise reforms, and the honest men among them will try to the utmost of their abilities to realize them, but not to much real purpose. The mayors of New York since twenty-five years were all able men. In what condition is the city? Every day's paper tells it. I conclude this epistle with a common-sense question: what voyage do you think a first rate sea-captain would make with a vessel whose rudder and sails are not adequate to the size of the craft?

LETTER V.

Legislature. — Senate. — Districts. — Census. — Apportionment. — Assembly Districts. — Compensation. — Civil Appointment. — Congressional Officers. — Election Time. — Quorum. — Journal. — Originating of Bills. — Enacting Clause. — Majority. — Private Bills. — Legislative Powers of the Supervisors. — County Election District. — Family Census. — France. — Connecticut. — Aristotle. — Greeks.

We have now to examine seventeen provisoes on the legislative powers. You will remember that in regard to the national political affairs all legislative powers are committed to the care of one body — the Congress. But a mere glance at a state map or the working of our state institutions, as I have endeavored to describe it in a separate letter in the First Part, will convince you that, in a municipal state, the legislative powers are not so much centralized as in Congress, but divided into three channels or districts, called state, county, and town (cities and villages), an arrangement which is of the highest importance for the good dispatch of the municipal business, and the preservation of order and civil liberty. Interference with the legislative, judicial, and executive rights of these districts are called encroachments or rebellions. Let us see what the constitution contains about the law-making powers of those districts.

ARTICLE III.

"1. The legislative power of this state shall be vested in a senate and assembly."

We meet here the double chamber system again.

"2. The senate shall consist of thirty-two members, and the senators shall be chosen for two years. The assembly shall consist of one hundred and twenty-eight members, who shall be annually elected."

This proviso creates annual sessions, while biennial would promise to prevent too much legislation, a great evil in our times.

"3. The state shall be divided into thirty-two districts, to be called senate districts, each of which shall choose one senator. The districts shall be numbered from one to thirty-two inclusive. District No. 1, shall consist of the counties of Suffolk, Richmond, and Queens. District No. 2 shall consist of the county of Kings. Districts No. 3, 4, 5, and 6 shall consist of the city and county of New York. And the board of supervisors of said city and county shall, on or before the first day of May, 1847, divide the said city and county into the number of senate districts to which it is entitled, as near as may be of an equal number of inhabitants excluding aliens and persons of color not taxed, and consisting of convenient and contiguous territory, and no assembly district shall be divided in the formation of a senate district. The board of supervisors, when they shall have completed such division, shall cause certificates thereof, stating the number and boundaries of each district and the population thereof, to be filed in the office of the secretary of state and of the clerk of the said city and county. District No. 7 shall consist of the counties of Westchester, Putnam, and Rockland. District No. 8 shall consist of the counties of Dutchess and Columbia. District No. 9 shall consist of the counties of Orange and Sullivan. District No. 10 shall consist of the counties of Ulster and Greene. District No. 11 shall consist of the counties of Albany and Schenectady. District No. 12 shall consist of the county of Rensselear. District No. 13 shall consist of the counties of Washington and Saratoga. District No. 14 shall consist of the counties of Warren, Essex, and Clinton. District No. 15 shall consist of the counties of St. Lawrence and Franklin. District No. 16 shall consist of the counties of Herkimer, Hamilton, Fulton, and Montgomery. District No. 17 shall consist of the counties of Schoharie and Delaware. District No. 18 shall consist of the counties of Otsego and Chenango. District No. 19 shall consist of the county of Oneida. District No. 20 shall consist of the counties of Madison and Oswego. District No. 21 shall consist of the counties of Jefferson and Lewis. District No. 22 shall consist of the county of Onondaga. District No. 23 shall consist of the counties of Cortland, Broome, and Tioga. District No. 24 shall consist of the counties of Cayuga and Wayne. District No. 25 shall consist of the counties of Tompkins, Seneca, and Yates. District No. 26 shall consist of the counties of Steuben and Chemung. District No. 27 shall consist of the county of Monroe. District No. 28 shall consist of the counties of Orleans, Genesee, and Niagara. District No. 29 shall consist of the counties of Ontario and Livingston. District No. 30 shall consist of the counties of Allegany and Wyoming. District No. 31 shall consist of the county of Erie. District No. 32 shall consist of the counties of Chautauque and Cattaraugus."

This proviso takes the place of one in the old constitution, which made the county the basis of the senatorial election. It is no improvement — rather the reverse. The counties are the large trunk roots of the state tree — the towns their rootlets. Both are its supporters and feeders. These districts are the schools of citizenship, the nurseries of practical business men, the arenas for the exercise of talent, the receivers of patriotic bounties, the managers of the true political home interests, the fields upon which grow the substantial blessings of liberty, the depositories of the real rights and privileges of freemen. Each may develop a character of its own either good or bad, each is a circle full of attachments, hopes, home-feelings, and recollections, dear even to the rudest. From such a circle we must take our legislators, if we will have trustworthy, self-made, representative men, speaking out the legitimate incorporate voice of the people. There the legislator has his family, his companions, his popular stand and standard; there are his restraints, and there he can and will be held responsible. This proviso now destroys, in a great measure, these guaranties. It transplants him into a district which, being a mere abstraction, cuts him loose from those roots and rootlets of the state tree, throwing him, with body and soul, into the caldron of party, wherein are boiled such laws as the metropolitan police law, and court factions, which create elective judiciaries and similar abortions. A senator from such a paper district represents nothing political — no constitutional interest. This explains why the senate of the state of New York refused to repeal the metropolitan police law, although desired by the four counties in question, with over one million of souls, and voted for by the assembly.

Such a senate knows nothing of counties and their interests, and boldly ignores petitions, however well-founded in right.

Why the state senate shall consist of only thirty-two members and the other house of one hundred and twenty-eight, although both have the same business, even in regard to the state finances, to perform, is, as I observed before, not intelligible, because the main reason of this dualism is to check inconsiderate legislation.

Again, republics must be plainly organized. It must be the tender solicitude of statesmen to make intelligence, patriotism, and all public virtues available for the primitive, indispensable, social working districts, called towns and counties, in order to perfect their constitutional efficacy.

I willingly admit that the districting policy of the constitution may have its origin in the numerical inequality of the counties, and do not believe that it originated exactly in party politics, or a distinct plan to emasculate the counties and towns, or to neutralize their public influence; far from it. Still it does immense harm. Our legislatures or governments rule by the counties and towns; they are their strong hands and arms. To slight them is tantamount to weakening the government. The reverse takes place in monarchies. There the policy is to strip the counties and towns of their rights and independence, and render them subservient to the will of the ruler. If the legislatures keep the counties numerically in order, divide them as often as necessary, they will serve for all election purposes at all times very well.

"4. An enumeration of the inhabitants of the state shall be taken under the direction of the legislature, in the year one thousand eight hundred and fifty-five, and at the end of every ten years thereafter; and the said districts shall be so altered by the legislature, at the first session after the return of every enumeration, that each senate district shall contain, as nearly as may be, an equal number of inhabitants, excluding aliens and persons of color not taxed; and shall remain unaltered until the return of another enumeration, and shall at all times consist of contiguous territory, and no county shall be divided in the formation of a senate district, except such county shall be equitably entitled to two or more senators."

This section is the cause of the state census. It is based upon the inhabitants, and not upon the families. But after a hundred thousand countings of the people in all parts of the world, in ancient and modern times, have elicited the truth, that the number of families, multiplied by five, give as exact a result as the counting of all the inhabitants, in consideration that the constant changes caused by birth and mortality influence minutely the census. Why not, I ask, stick to this truth — which is a law of nature — and repeat that troublesome personal enumeration again and again? We can be with this truth quite as well satisfied as with that that twice two make four. I have written on the family census in other places, and add here, that it not only simplifies the business, but opens also the way to the family suffrage.

We live upon a very much exposed hill; our public affairs are mercilessly scrutinized abroad. A French savant, in favor of republican institutions, some years ago, argued thus: "If those political wiseacres in the United States had long time since adopted the family suffrage, already recommended by Aristotle as the best, we probably would have adopted both, never indulged in the dangerous experiment of the general suffrage — a great insult to woman — excluded thus the vote of the mobs, standing army, and unmarried clergy from the ballot-box, and arrived at other results than we witness now." Why have the most intelligent people of antiquity, the Greeks, not followed the counsel of one of the best philosophers the world has produced? Because they were a branch of the Oriental society, transplanted to Europe, and, therefore, polygamists. The fact that the cunning Napoleons trusted their luck to the general suffrage speaks, no doubt, volumes in favor of the family suffrage. Still it would be impossible to introduce it into France, because Paris and the army and clergy would be against it. But the true friends of social progress will greet it as a great moral and political victory, that Connecticut — just of the right proportion to be a good state, as she really is — has made one step; one more, and all the glory will be with her.

By-the-bye, the items which we collect at the census-taking are, in our eternally-moving society, of a very little worth, and may be as well left with the industry of the friends of statistics, editors, and publishers, to whose business line they belong. A state institution with us is not made to enlighten the people, as I told you before.

"5. The members of assembly shall be apportioned among the several counties of the state, BY THE LEGISLATURE, as nearly as may be, according to the number of their respective inhabitants, excluding aliens and persons of color not taxed, and shall be chosen by single districts."

This clause and the following may lead to a new districting, which can not happen if the counties are organized with due regard to population.

"The several boards of supervisors in such counties of this state, as are now entitled to more than one member of assembly, shall assemble on the first Tuesday of January next, and divide their respective counties into assembly districts equal to the number of members of assembly to which such counties are now severally entitled by law, and shall cause to be filed in the offices of the secretary of state and the clerks of their respective counties a description of such assembly districts, specifying the number of each district and the population thereof, according to the last preceding state enumeration, as near as can be ascertained. Each assembly district shall contain, as nearly as may be, an equal number of inhabitants, excluding aliens and persons of color not taxed, and shall consist of convenient and contiguous territory; but no town shall be divided in the formation of assembly districts.

"The legislature, at its first session after the return of every enumeration, shall re-apportion the members of assembly among the several counties of this state, in manner aforesaid, and the boards of supervisors in such counties as may be entitled, under such re-apportionment, to more than one member, shall assemble at such time as the legislature making such re-apportionment shall prescribe, and divide such counties into assembly districts, in the manner herein directed; and the apportionment and districts so to be made shall remain unaltered until another enumeration shall be taken under the provisions of the preceding section.

"Every county heretofore established and separately organized, except the county of Hamilton, shall always be entitled to one member of the assembly, and no new county shall be hereafter erected, unless its population shall entitle it to a member.

"The county of Hamilton shall elect with the county of Fulton, until the population of the county of Hamilton shall, according to the ratio, be entitled to a member."

I am not called upon to make proposition for a new constitution; but, as an interested looker-on, I take the liberty to suggest: To elect in each county (large cities respectively treated) one senator and one assembly-man, which will make it possible for the people to select able men from the right place and for the right business.

"6. The members of the legislature shall receive for their service a sum not exceeding three dollars a day, from the commencement of the session; but such pay shall not exceed in the aggregate three hundred dollars for per diem allowance, except in the proceedings for impeachment. The limitation as to the aggregate compensation shall not take effect until 1848. When convened in extra session by the governor, they shall receive three dollars per day. They shall also receive the sum of one dollar for every ten miles they shall travel, in going to and returning from their places of meeting on the most usual route. The speaker of the assembly shall, in virtue of his office, receive an additional compensation equal to the one third of his per diem allowance as a member."

This proviso has some excellent features. Its principal purpose is to make legislation respectable, by limiting the time of a session virtually to one hundred days, preventing in this manner speculations with law-making. Still, this bears yet more improving. Suppose the honor to be a legislator of the most enlightened part of society — an American free state deserves this praise without flattering — should be considered by the constitution so highly valuable that no pay would be adequate, and therefore none allowed by the constitution; this would shorten the session still more, curtail superfluous buncomb Kansas speech-making and resolving on heterogeneous things, and oblige the legislators to husband their time. All special (log-rolling) laws would become very scarce, for their objects can be in most instances reached by judiciously-organized counties and towns. It is the price of genuine civilization to be in need of a very little governing. Paul was well aware of this; hence his sound doctrine.

"7. No member of the legislature shall receive any civil appointment within this state, or to the senate of the United States, from the governor, the governor and senate, or from the legislature, during the term for which he shall have been elected; and all such appointments, and all votes given for any such member for any such office or appointment, shall be void.

"8. No person being a member of Congress or holding any judicial or military office under the United States, shall hold a seat in the legislature. And if any person shall, after his election as a member of the legislature, be elected to Congress or appointed to any office, civil or military, under the government of the United States, his acceptance thereof shall vacate his seat.

"9. The elections of senators and members of assembly, pursuant to the provisions of this constitution, shall be held on the Tuesday succeeding the first Monday of November, unless otherwise directed by the legislature.

"10. A majority of each house shall constitute a quorum to do business. Each house shall determine the rules of its own proceedings, and be the judge of the elections, returns, and qualifications of its own members, shall choose its own officers, and the senate shall choose a temporary president, when the lieutenant-governor shall not attend as president, or shall act as governor.

"11. Each house shall keep a journal of its proceedings, and publish the same, except such parts as may require secrecy. The doors of each house shall be kept open, except when the public welfare shall require secrecy.

Neither house shall, without the consent of the other, adjourn for more than two days.

"12. For any speech or debate in either house of the legislature, the members shall not be questioned in any other place.

"13. Any bill may originate in either house of the legislature, and all bills passed by one house may be amended by the other.

"14. The enacting clause of all bills shall be, 'The People of the state of New York, represented in senate and assembly, do enact as follows;' and no law shall be enacted except by bill.

"15. No bill shall be passed unless by the assent of a majority of all the members elected to each branch of the legislature, and the question upon the final passage shall be taken immediately upon its last reading, and the yeas and nays entered on the journal.

"16. No private or local bill which may be passed by the legislature, shall embrace more than one subject, and that shall be expressed in the title.

"17. The legislature may confer upon the boards of supervisors of the several counties of the state, such farther powers, local, legislative, and administrative, as they shall from time to time prescribe."

This is plain. The seventeenth clause contains all the information in the constitution about the local, legislative, and administrative powers vested in the county officials. The names of the counties are also given; but why there are counties, where they are coming from, what difference there is between towns and counties, whether these most important political districts are of Dutch, or English, or American origin, and entirely depending upon the pleasure of the legislature or not, what rights they possess, the constitution does not show. If these political districts are mere accidental, why say a word in the constitution about the canals and canal officers, banks, etc, who, as such, have not the least connection with the state institution proper; or do we require canals or salt springs for the realization of justice? Is there a word in the federal constitution concerning forts, arsenals, and docks, although Congress have built several? The omission of the organic dispositions concerning the towns and counties is, no doubt, a cardinal oversight; for without these districts the state machinery could not work at all; and if they are not organized according to sound, firm, political principles, laid down in the constitution, it will work but badly, while without a line on canals, corporations, education, banks, and the like, this institution would answer to its real purpose very well. These districts are as it were, social breakwaters in regard to the powers of the governing and governed. Without them the government would not take root or be firmly anchored, but drift about at the mercy of the populace, who on the other hand, without them, would be in eternal confusion and commotion. In a word, anarchy would be the rule, and tyranny take the place of civil liberty.

Before I leave this subject, I ask you to imagine what intolerable confusion there would be in a house without division walls and rooms, like a church, occupied by a large number of families to live in. The same confusion would happen in society if it were not divided into convenient business districts, in ancient times known as clans, tribes, etc. Even in absolute monarchies you will therefore find social divisions, answering to our townships and counties. Their importance is my excuse if I am too diffuse.

If you are attentive to the current legislation, you will notice instances of laws failing, because they are declared unconstitutional or repugnant to society. This happens invariably if by such laws the public business is dislocated. As an example, I avert to the state temperance laws. These have everywhere failed, because it is a part of the town government to abate, in conformity with the town (city, village) by-laws, instances of excessive drinking, causing a public nuisance. It is a logical and political necessity to leave the checking of this evil to the town governments, because it is only very relative or personal, and in its nature no subject for a general state-law.

This subject has been misunderstood at all times, otherwise we would not find in Plutarch the following sentence: "Those who carry every trifle (mere local affairs) to the highest magistrate, are the most dangerous enemies of their country."

Very true, especially in republics. My partiality for this beautiful, natural, simple form of government, will excuse this long epistle.

LETTER VI.

Executive. — Governor's Duties. — Legislative Committees. — Lieutenant-Governor. — Eligibility. — Commander-in-Chief. — Messages. — Salary. — Navy. — Army. — Execution of Laws. — President of the Senate. — Reprieves. — Pardon. — Impeachment. — Veto.

THE second department of the government will now occupy our attention.

ARTICLE IV.

Executive.

"1. The executive power shall be vested in a governor, who shall hold his office for two years; a lieutenant-governor shall be chosen at the same time, and for the same term.

"2. No person, except a citizen of the United States, shall be eligible to the office of governor; nor shall any person be eligible to that office, who shall not have attained the age of thirty years, and who shall not have been five years next preceding his election, a resident within this state.

"3. The governor and lieutenant-governor shall be elected at the times and places of choosing members of the Assembly. The persons respectively having the highest number of votes for governor and lieutenant-governor, shall be elected; but in case two or more shall have an equal and the highest number of votes for governor, or for lieutenant-governor, the two houses of the legislature at its next annual session, shall, forthwith, by joint ballot, choose one of the said persons so having an equal and the highest number of votes for governor, or lieutenant-governor.

"4. The governor shall be commander-in-chief of the military and naval forces of the state. He shall have power to convene the legislature (or the senate only) on extraordinary occasions. He shall communicate by message to the legislature at every session, the condition of the state, and recommend such matters to them as he shall judge expedient. He shall transact all necessary business with the officers of government, civil and military. He shall expedite all such measures as may be resolved upon by the legislature, and shall take care that the laws are faithfully executed. He shall, at stated times, receive for his services a compensation to be established by law, which shall neither be increased nor diminished after his election and during his continuance in office."

The first three sections are plain. The fourth seems to be entirely mistaken by the governors themselves, and those who complain that this constitution has stripped the governor of power to such an extent as to discredit the office, because it manifestly makes, in plain words, this officer, by enjoining upon him the duty to take care that the laws are faithfully executed, the *responsible* head of the whole state administration. Accordingly, the governor has the supreme control of all public offices, officers, and affairs, in the several political districts. This is all the constitution can do. The duty of the official, clad with such high power, is now to use it energetically. This requires, of course, courage, a thorough knowledge of the purpose of a state institution, of the proper nature of the political business, to what district it belongs, and of the laws in general. It follows that he has to transact personally, or by writing, all affairs with the officials, who become practical subjects of this control. By pointing out this expressly, the constitution evidently explains the magnitude of the trust.

This control is made with us exceedingly easy by the prevalent general publicity. The press keeps a constant record of all events. Suppose the governor has access to a reading-room containing, at least, one paper from each county, he will be posted of every fact of importance, enabling him to transact the necessary controlling business. Any deviation from official duty, especially if it should originate with the executives of counties and towns (cities, villages), he is obliged to examine and resent, in accordance with the laws. We often notice that state legislatures appoint committees to examine into the local affairs of towns and counties, as poor-houses, prisons, lodging-houses, catholic ladies' seminaries, police (metropolitan or not), etc. Supposing that these affairs are requiring a special examination, is this not, in extraordinary instances, a duty incumbent upon the governor, for which he is paid, and, indeed, an encroachment upon his executive power, when done by legislatures? Legislatures, if they would not degrade purposely the governors to mere showmen, should carefully avoid such steps; and no governor, conscious of his constitutional duty, to see that the laws are faithfully executed, should consent to such erratic legislative measures. They unnecessarily increase the expenses of governing and betray a bad spirit to unsettle the constitution. It is the duty of the legislature to impeach the governor, if neglecting his control duty, but not to step in and to do it itself for extra pay. There is an English circumlocution precedent at the bottom of this objectionable committee system.

I do not claim arbitrary Napoleonic powers for our governors. No, they should only be for the state institution what a sea-captain is for his ship, a husbandman for his farm, a manufacturer for his establishment. In one word, they should take good care that in all parts of the state the laws are faithfully executed, wherefore they are expressly enjoined to transact all necessary business with the officers of the government, and to expedite all measures that may be resolved upon by the legislature, and even convoke the legislature expressly for this purpose. Upon this he is sworn in; he is, therefore, responsible for the good administration of the laws or working of the state institution. Therefore, he is also commander-in-chief of the military and naval forces of the state, although there are some who have doubts about the correctness of this proviso, because, according to the federal constitution, the president shall be the sole commander-in-chief of the army and navy of the United States, and of the militia of the several states, when called into the actual service. There is, indeed, no case imaginable for a state governor to exercise such a function, unless the United States are at war. Moreover, there is no such thing as a navy of the state of New York, or any other state. The Congress is bound to protect the several states against invasion and internal commotions; the federal constitution expressly forbids the states to keep troops, that is, a standing army, or ships-of-war, in time of peace. With all these wise provisoes of the federal constitution, this clause of the state constitution seems to clash. Does not this smack of empire? and why not? this state district comprises at present as many inhabitants as the thirteen colonies when they declared themselves independent! There is something, not exactly curious, but ominous, in such provisoes. There is a tendency to puff our state governments up into the regions of empires and majesties, while we forget to make their organizations complete and perfect downward in regard to the political detail business of home and peaceable daily life. Our states have no military forces at all. State citizens, although drilled, are not troops, soldiers, or military forces, in the proper sense of the word, *unless mustered into service* by the Congress. Before that time they are mere gentleman train-bands.

The fact is, that this gubernatorial control is at present entirely neglected; for I have never seen it working, while every attentive reader of a daily paper may notice frequent instances of the non-execution of the laws, under the very eyes of the governor. I admit that the overlarge size of the state of New York has much to answer for this defective executive surveillance; still it seems as if every man, every newspaper, had more influence upon the execution of the laws than the governor. Lawyers and judges, and other officials, do as they please, and if a criminal escapes, private persons send their ships after him, while the governor sits quietly upon his throne in his mansion, looking at this spectacle, pocketing his salary, without doing anything.

A distinguished New York editor lately honored the European governments with the cognomen of huge impostures. Still, if the governor of California keeps his counsel when the state treasurer is a defaulter, or the common councils of different cities are nothing but swindling concerns, and the magistrates bargain with the criminals about their punishment, until the outraged citizens take the law into their own hands, and then come forward and make a great show of executive power by declaring these citizens to be in a state of rebellion, what appellation deserves such a government? In the constitution of California, art. v., sect. 7, it is expressly ordained: he, the governor, shall see that the laws are faithfully executed! It is, therefore, not the fault of the constitution when the governor does not check the defective execution of the laws, but of the universally prevalent apathy and carelessness in the management of this office. No constitutional prince can ask for more power than that of a general control and veto.

The regular session messages of the governors, together with the reports of the chief administrative officers of the state, spreading information and light over the finances and operations of the administration, are important documents. They form an indispensable basis for legislative action, to bring a system into it and adapt it to the actual wants, as it can not be expected from the members of the legislature, especially of a large state, involved in extensive public works and enterprises, that they may acquire this information at home. If the executive suggestions, in reference to the measures to be acted upon, would be always, without the least delay, and in preference of all others, promptly attended or become incapable of performing the duties of his office, or be absent from the state, the president of the senate shall act as governor, until the vacancy be filled, or the disability shall cease.

"8. The lieutenant-governor shall, while acting as such, receive a compensation which shall be fixed by law, and which shall not be increased or diminished during his continuance in office.

"9 Every bill which shall have passed the senate and assembly, shall, before it becomes a law, be presented to the governor: if he approve, he shall sign it; but if not, he shall return it, with his objections, to that house in which it shall have originated, who shall enter the objections at large on their journal, and proceed to reconsider it. If, after such reconsideration, two thirds of the members present shall agree to pass the bill, it shall be sent, together with the objections, to the other house, by which it shall likewise be reconsidered; and if approved by two thirds of all the members present, it shall become a law, notwithstanding the objections of the governor. But in all such cases, the votes of both houses shall be determined by yeas and nays, and the names of the members voting for and against the bill shall be entered on the journal of each house respectively. If any bill shall not be returned by the governor within ten days (Sundays excepted), after it shall have been presented to him, the same shall be a law, in like manner as if he had signed it, unless the legislature shall, by their adjournment, prevent its return, in which case it shall not be a law."

These three sections are plain. They are partly copied from the federal constitution. The approval of bills must take place during the time of the session. The peremptory term of ten days in the ninth clause is good. Such peremptory terms should be adopted by the Code of Civil Procedure, in all stages of a process, to avoid delays and the starting of new points, too often from mere motives of intrigue and chicanery. The veto of a law should have the effect to transfer the bill to the next following legislature; if this should approve it by a two-third vote, it may become a law, for a vetoed bill, presumptively, is not required by the urgency of circumstances and time, but merely by a party and for party purposes.

The veto power is an important part of the supreme control of the state institution. The state governors, after having taken the oath on the constitutions of the Union and State, are bound to prevent unconstitutional, party, and mere partisan legislation. What is unconstitutional legislation, each governor must make clear to himself before he is sworn in, because, by approving an unconstitutional law, he commits legal perjury. A man who is not able to judge about constitutionality as certain as the court of or become incapable of performing the duties of his office, or be absent from the state, the president of the senate shall act as governor, until the vacancy be filled, or the disability shall cease.

"8. The lieutenant-governor shall, while acting as such, receive a compensation which shall be fixed by law, and which shall not be increased or diminished during his continuance in office.

"9 Every bill which shall have passed the senate and assembly, shall, before it becomes a law, be presented to the governor: if he approve, he shall sign it; but if not, he shall return it, with his objections, to that house in which it shall have originated, who shall enter the objections at large on their journal, and proceed to reconsider it. If, after such reconsideration, two thirds of the members present shall agree to pass the bill, it shall be sent, together with the objections, to the other house, by which it shall likewise be reconsidered; and if approved by two thirds of all the members present, it shall become a law, notwithstanding the objections of the governor. But in all such cases, the votes of both houses shall be determined by yeas and nays, and the names of the members voting for and against the bill shall be entered on the journal of each house respectively. If any bill shall not be returned by the governor within ten days (Sundays excepted), after it shall have been presented to him, the same shall be a law, in like manner as if he had signed it, unless the legislature shall, by their adjournment, prevent its return, in which case it shall not be a law."

These three sections are plain. They are partly copied from the federal constitution. The approval of bills must take place during the time of the session. The peremptory term of ten days in the ninth clause is good. Such peremptory terms should be adopted by the Code of Civil Procedure, in all stages of a process, to avoid delays and the starting of new points, too often from mere motives of intrigue and chicanery. The veto of a law should have the effect to transfer the bill to the next following legislature; if this should approve it by a two-third vote, it may become a law, for a vetoed bill, presumptively, is not required by the urgency of circumstances and time, but merely by a party and for party purposes.

The veto power is an important part of the supreme control of the state institution. The state governors, after having taken the oath on the constitutions of the Union and State, are bound to prevent unconstitutional, party, and mere partisan legislation. What is unconstitutional legislation, each governor must make clear to himself before he is sworn in, because, by approving an unconstitutional law, he commits legal perjury. A man who is not able to judge about constitutionality as certain as the court of appeals, should not be governor. The constitution gives him full power to promote the good of the commonwealth, but he must, of course, understand its laws. It must be a cardinal duty of the governor never to approve any bill, or even resolution, which interferes in the least with the constitutional national business of Congress. All our states, Connecticut included, have been in this regard great sinners, mostly owing to the incapacity of their governors. The powers bestowed in this article upon the executive require special laws to make them operative, to instill more activity into this officer, and terminate the present know-nothing and do-nothing practice, but the constitution is here well enough, the practice in the gubernatorial office, however, deplorable. Most of the public corruption may be traced to the apathy, incapacity, and faithlessness of our state governors. Again, in this constitution nothing is wanting to make the governor of the state of New York an effective officer. And if I claim entire independence for the subdivisions of the state in regard to their own constitutional business sphere, I am far from asking for them an exemption from the supreme executive and state control, plainly defined in this article.

LETTER VII.

Administrative. — Secretary of State. — Comptroller. — Treasurer. — Attorney-General. — Election. — Salary. —English Circumlocution.—Proper Administrators. — American System. — Representative and Non-Representative Officers.— State Engineer.— Surveyor.— Canal Commissioners. — State-Prison Inspectors. — Land Office. — Canal Fund.— Local Inspectors.

YOU are now to become acquainted with the administrative affairs of the state.

ARTICLE V.

Administrative.

"1. The secretary of state, comptroller, treasurer, and attorney-general, shall be chosen at a general election, and hold their offices for two years. Each of the officers in this article named (except the speaker of the assembly), shall at stated times, during his continuance in office, receive for his services a compensation, which shall not be increased or diminished during the term for which he shall have been elected; nor shall he receive, to his use, any fees or perquisites of office, or other compensation."

The first three named officials are subordinate to the governor, the fourth belongs to the state judiciary. But there may be different meanings of the word administration; to avoid misunderstandings, I give you my idea about it. The real administrators of our municipal affairs are only the chief of the state, called governor; the chief of the county, called, in my letters, overseer, and the chief of the town, called mayor, as you will remember from the first part.

The clerical officials and boards, mentioned in this article; are all subordinate to the several governors or administrators, according to the nature and order of the business. I well know that the practice differs from what I say, that there is no head in the county and town administration, that the city mayors have no real central governing power, but this is not right. Farmers will think a mayor in their towns a strange novelty, because there is no such officer in old England; but a sober second thought will convince them, that the government of three selectmen in a town, or of a dozen supervisors in a county, without a responsible head, is one of the causes that villages and cities grow up, requiring charters, and leading to uncontrollable and, therefore, corrupt administrations. In all well-organized communities there ought to be a responsible, leading, and directing executive, similar to the president in the Union. It is so in the best European states, whose administration is praised by our travellers. History tells sad stories of states ruled by several consuls or kings. I would not take the English municipal administration as a pattern. There you find little else than "circumlocution."

These three administrators should be the head-managers of the public affairs in their several districts, and should, therefore, have nothing to do with mere detail office-business. They might serve without a salary; they have to take care that the laws and ordinances are well executed, the business kept in perfect order by the clerks, treasurers, &c., justice well administered, the respective property and interests of their districts faithfully represented, managed, and attended to; in one word, to do all in their power to keep the political organization in those districts in a healthful operation. From such a view has been the national public business placed under one responsible head, the president. I wish to be understood, that all I have said on the better organization of the municipal business, is but abstracted from that system which has been initiated by the federal constitution. If the constitution of the state of New York is to be amended, this article, and one on the local officers, will, probably, receive a different shape, provided the framers of a new constitution will carry out the "American public business system," all that I and, I am sure, the public desire. The subject is full of interest for all thinking citizens. And, happily, we have plenty of such.

Some may object that I carry my veneration for the federal constitution too far, and that, while a secretary of state may be safely trusted to an election, this officer of the federal government should rather be appointed. I admit that these gentlemen have different business spheres, still that is not the reason why the one should be appointed and the other elected; they resemble each other for being mere clerical functionaries and not representatives, and, therefore, to be carefully selected for the function. Whether the framers of the federal constitution acted upon these special grounds, or simply imitated other governments, has no influence upon the merits of their policy.

This policy is a settled fact. People have submitted to it for almost a century, because it is similar to the business order in their households, factories, mercantile establishments, and other well-organized business concerns, and, therefore, plain to their understanding, while the universal elective policy, adopted by this constitution, is a republican extravagancy.

The political offices may be divided into two classes, viz., *representative* and *clerical*. To the first class belong the just-mentioned head-officers, and the aldermen or selectmen, supervisors, and members of legislature. These should be always elected. To the second class belong all clerks, treasurers, inspectors, collectors, surveyors, police, &c., who should all be appointed. I have pointed this out before, as the policy of the federal constitution.

After we have elected our ruling officers, we must allow them to appoint the officers, clerks, or assistants, needed for the business. We may have reason sometimes for grumbling that they did not appoint this or that party-man; still we must, for the time being, submit to that rather than spoil the whole fabric, by reversing the natural order. And if each public district acts in this respect, independently, under the constitution, there never will be more patronage in one hand, than is unavoidably necessary.

"2. The state engineer and surveyor shall be chosen at a general election, and shall hold his office two years, but no person shall be elected to said office who is not a practical engineer."

"3. Three canal commissioners shall be chosen at the general election, which shall be held next after the adoption of this constitution, one of whom shall hold his office for one year, one for two years, and one for three years. [The commissioners of the canal fund shall meet at the capitol on the first Monday of January, next after such election, and determine by lot which of said canal commissioners shall hold his office for one year, which for two, and which for three years;] and there shall be elected annually thereafter, one canal commissioner, who shall hold his office for three years."

All these officers should be appointed. Canals, windmills, and similar works, when drawn into the sphere of political business, should be managed by special acts, and not by the people directly, otherwise they will become political party concerns of the worst kind.

"4. Three inspectors of state-prison shall be elected at the general election, which shall be held next after the adoption of this constitution, one of whom shall hold his office for one year, one for two years, and one for three years. [The governor, secretary of state, and comptroller shall meet at the capitol on the first Monday of January, next succeeding such election, and determine by lot which of said inspectors shall hold his office for one year, which for two, and which for three years;] and there shall be elected annually thereafter one inspector of state-prison, who shall hold his office for three years; said inspectors shall have the charge and superintendence of the state-prisons, and shall appoint all the officers therein. All vacancies in the office of such inspectors shall be filled by the governor, till the next election."

Those officers also should be appointed.

"5. The lieutenant-governor, speaker of the assembly, secretary of state, comptroller, treasurer, attorney-general, and state engineer and surveyor, shall be the commissioners of the land office.

"The lieutenant-governor, speaker of the assembly, secretary of state, comptroller, treasurer, and attorney-general, shall be the commissioners of the canal fund.

"The canal board shall consist of the commissioners of the canal fund, the state engineer and surveyor, and the canal commissioners."

"6. The powers and duties of the respective boards, and of the several officers in this article mentioned, shall be such as now are or hereafter may be prescribed by law."

The provisoes from one to six, contain matter for special laws.

"7. The treasurer may be suspended from office by the governor, during the recess of the legislature, and until thirty days after the commencement of the next session of the legislature, whenever it shall appear to him that such treasurer has, in any particular, violated his duty. The governor shall appoint a competent person to discharge the duties of the office during such suspension of the treasurer."

The suspending and removing power should be alike in regard to all officers.

"8. All officers for the weighing, guaging, measuring, culling, or inspecting any merchandise, produce, manufacture or commodity whatever, are hereby abolished, and no such office shall hereafter be created by law; but nothing in this section contained shall abrogate any office created for the purpose of protecting the public health or the interests of the state, in its property, revenue, tolls or purchases, or of supplying the people with correct standards of weights and measures, or shall prevent the creation of any office for such purposes hereafter."

The offices abolished by this clause are all town (city, village) offices, and should, therefore, depend upon town by-laws. In a good judicial system they are superfluous, because there all fraudulent dealing, which it is the aim to prevent by such officials, will be effectually checked by the judiciary. Honest men are not in need of them. George Washington's brand was considered at home and abroad sufficient guaranty in regard to quality and quantity. But if in a certain town the corruption of the people and remissness of the judiciary should be alarming (which can only happen in over-large, uncontrollable towns or cities), the better class of business men may insist upon the appointment of such officials by the magistrate, to keep up the appearance of honesty. Congress have appointed steam-boiler and drug inspectors. They seem to be also superfluous, provided the judiciary be competent to resent culpable carelessness of captains, engineers, importers, dealers in drugs, &c. It would be as wrong to appoint such local-trade inspectors by the state government, as it would be absurd to appoint judges of the court of appeals or state-prison inspectors by town governments. The correct distribution of the functional affairs of society is a main duty of our law-makers. They must follow their own logic and judgment and not English precedents.

Those have, up to this time, hindered the full development of our simple political business-system. We must try to walk alone, as the federal constitution has made us stand up firmly.

LETTER VIII.

Judiciary. — Impeaching. — Court of Appeals. — Supreme Court. — Judicial Districts. — Salary. — Election. — Testimony. — Removing. — Vacancies. — Modes of appointing Judges.

YOUR attention will now be devoted to the judiciary, the most important part of the state institution.

ARTICLE VI.

The Judiciary.

"1. The assembly shall have the power of impeachment, by the vote of a majority of all the members elected. The court for the trial of impeachments shall be composed of the president of the senate, the senators, or a major part of them, and the judges of the court of appeals, or the major part of them. On the trial of an impeachment against the governor, the lieutenant-governor shall not act as a member of the court. No judicial officer shall exercise his office after he shall have been impeached, until he shall have been acquitted. Before the trial of an impeachment, the members of the court shall take an oath or affirmation, truly and impartially to try the impeachment, according to evidence; and no person shall be convicted, without the concurrence of two thirds of the members present. Judgment in cases of impeachment shall not extend farther than to removal from office, or removal from office and disqualification to hold and enjoy any office of honor, trust, or profit under this state; but the party impeached shall be liable to indictment and punishment according to law."

This is plain.

"2. There shall be a court of appeals, composed of eight judges, of whom four shall be elected by the electors of the state, for eight years, and four selected from the class of justices of the supreme court having the shortest time to serve. Provision shall be made by law, for designating one of the number elected, as chief judge, and for selecting such justices of the supreme court, from time to time, and for so classifying those elected, that one shall be elected every second year.

"3. There shall be a suprema court having general jurisdiction in law and equity."

The judiciary is, as I have observed often, the very offspring and grand purpose of the state organization. We may have plenty of salt springs, roads, canals, telegraphs, railroads, trades, churches, fireworks, illuminations, etc., without a state institution, but no judiciary. It is against the nature of the state to make its child, the judiciary, elective. It is a political monstrosity, especially in a republic, which depends entirely upon the laws and their execution.

"4. The state shall be divided into eight judicial districts, of which the city of New York shall be one; the others to be bounded by county lines, and to be compact and equal in population as nearly as may be. There shall be four justices of the supreme court in each district, and as many more in the district composed of the city of New York as may from time to time be authorized by law, but not to exceed in the whole such number in proportion to its population as shall be in conformity with the number of such judges in the residue of the state, in proportion to its population. They shall be classified so that one of the justices of each district shall go out of office at the end of every two years. After the expiration of their terms under such classification, the term of their office shall be eight years."

Why not give the business, designated for the supreme courts, to the county courts?

"5. The legislature shall have the same powers to alter and regulate the jurisdiction and proceedings in law and equity as they have heretofore possessed."

Is matter-of-course and superfluous.

"6. Provision may be made by law for designating, from time to time, one or more of the said justices, who is not a judge of the court of appeals, to preside at the general terms of the said court to be held in the several districts. Any three or more of the said justices, of whom one of the said justices so designated shall always be one, may hold such general terms. And any one or more of the justices may hold special terms and circuit courts, and any one of them may preside in courts of oyer and terminer in any county."

The words oyer and terminer mean criminal court. And again, why not assign all important civil and criminal business to the county court? The clause, itself, belongs rather to the statute book.

"7. The judges of the court of appeals and justices of the supreme court shall severally receive, at stated times, for their services, a compensation to be established by law, which shall not be increased or diminished during their continuance in office.

"8. They shall not hold any other office or public trust. All votes for either of them, for any elective office (except that of justice of the supreme court, or judge of the court of appeals), given by the legislature or the people, shall be void. They shall not exercise any power of appointment to public office. Any male citizen of the age of twenty-one years, of good moral character, and who possesses the requisite qualifications of learning and ability, shall be entitled to admission to practice in all the courts of this state.

"9. The classification of the justices of the supreme court; the times and place of holding the terms of the court of appeals, and of the general and special terms of the supreme court within the several districts, and the circuit courts and courts of oyer and terminer within the several counties, shall be provided for by law."

Is mostly special-law matter.

"10. The testimony in equity cases shall be taken in like manner as in cases at law."

Special-law and matter of course.

"11. Justices of the supreme court and judges of the court of appeals may be removed by concurrent resolution of both houses of the legislature, if two thirds of the members elected to the assembly, and a majority of all the members elected to the senate concur therein. All judicial officers, except those mentioned in this section, and except justices of the peace, judges and justices of inferior courts not of record, may be removed by the senate, on the recommendation of the governor; but no removal shall be made by virtue of this section, unless the cause thereof be entered on the journals, nor unless the party complained of shall have been served with a copy of the complaint against him, and shall have had an opportunity of being heard in his defence. On the question of removal, the ayes and noes shall be entered on the journals.

"12. The judges of the court of appeals shall be elected by the electors of the state, and the justices of the supreme court by the electors of the several judicial districts, at such times as may be prescribed by law.

"13. In case the office of any judge of the court of appeals, or justice of the supreme court, shall become vacant before the expiration of the regular term for which he was elected, the vacancy may be filled by appointment by the governor, until it shall be supplied at the next general election of judges, when it shall be filled by election for the residue of the unexpired term."

The clauses twelve and thirteen will fall with the present system. If the judges in the several districts are appointed during good behavior, a special law, prescribing the forms of appointing and removing, will be required, wherein should be a clause ordaining that a judge who takes the stump, as the phrase is, at elections, should be removed at once. The honor and impartiality of the office require such a law.

There are two ways of making judges; one by election — of this I have spoken; the other by appointment. And then we may appoint them for a number of years, or during good behavior, as it is called. The federal constitution has adopted the system of appointing the judges during good behavior. This has made the federal judiciary honored and respected. It is the only good system. A judge is but a man. If he occupies his place during good behavior, people may be well assured that he will act his part faithfully, and at a reasonable compensation, too. If elected or appointed for a short tenure, society must be prepared for his making the most out of his term, by unreasonable salary, fees, and other means. In our states, with elective legislatures and executives, with publicity of the court transactions, reporters, free press, etc., there is not the least danger that a judge, even serving for life, will ever assume undue power, because he has no power beyond that of investigating certain cases coming under his cognizance. This system secures, moreover, impartial justice. This we can never expect, in the same measure, from the other modes. It is a strange contradiction in a simple political system like ours, made by the people for the people, to have two kinds of judiciaries. If we wish to be considered as consistent, we should not make an appointed judiciary in the Union and an elective one in the states.

LETTER IX.

County Judge. — Webster. — Surrogate. — Local Officers. — Inferior Courts. — Justices of the Peace. — Clerks. — Files to be sent into the Court of Appeals. — Publication of Statutes. — Code of Procedure. — Tribunals of Conciliation. — Revising Laws. — Systems of Judiciary.

THE following clause contains useful prescriptions, which, however, could be also partly inserted into the statute book: —

"14. There shall be elected in each of the counties of this state, except the city and county of New York, one county judge, who shall hold his office for four years. He shall hold the county court, and perform the duties of the office of surrogate. The county court shall have such jurisdiction in cases arising in justices' courts, and in special cases, as the legislature may prescribe, but shall have no original civil jurisdiction, except in such special cases.

"The county judge, with two justices of the peace, to be designated according to law, may hold courts of sessions with such criminal jurisdiction as the legislature shall prescribe, and perform such other duties as may be required by law.

"The county judge shall receive an annual salary, to be fixed by the board of supervisors, which shall be neither increased nor diminished during his continuance in office. The justices of the peace, for services in courts of sessions, shall be paid a per diem allowance out of the county treasury.

"In counties having a population exceeding forty thousand, the legislature may provide for the election of a separate officer to perform the duties of the office of surrogate.

"The legislature may confer equity jurisdiction in special cases upon the county judge.

"Inferior local courts, of civil and criminal jurisdiction, may be established by the legislature in cities; and such courts, except for the cities of New York and Buffalo, shall have an uniform organization and jurisdiction in such cities."

Accordingly each county, New York county excepted, shall have but one judge. This is an excellent idea, provided this county court is well organized, of which more in the following letter. In like manner, might one justice of the peace, or town judge, be sufficient for all town judicial business. This seems to be answering to the idea of Daniel Webster, that, to get good judges, we should employ them well. The present dilapidation of the judicial business, among a great number of special officials, seems not to agree with this idea. The duty of the legislature should then be to keep the districts in proper size.

'15. The legislature may, on application of the board of supervisors, provide for the election of local officers, not to exceed two in any county, to discharge the duties of county judge and of surrogate in cases of their inability, or of a vacancy, and to exercise such other powers in special cases as may be provided by law."

Rather belongs to a special act. But you read again in these clauses, "en passant," of supervisors. They are at the head of the county government; and, if this district is well organized, among the most important officers, in regard to the judiciary especially, and should therefore derive their power from the constitution.

"16. The legislature may reorganize the judicial districts at the first session, after the return of every enumeration, under this constitution, in the manner provided for in the fourth section of this article, and at no other time; and they may, at such session, increase or diminish the number of districts, but such increase or diminution shall not be more than one district at any one time. Each district shall have four justices of the supreme court; but no diminution of the districts shall have the effect to remove a judge from office.

I do not believe that such districts for supreme courts are, indeed, needed.

"17. The electors of the several towns shall, at their annual town meeting, and in such manner as the legislature may direct, elect justices of the peace, whose term of office shall be four years. In case of an election to fill a vacancy occurring before the expiration of a full term, they shall hold for the residue of the unexpired term. Their number and classification may be regulated by law. Justices of the peace and judges or justices of inferior courts, not of record, and their clerks, may be removed (after due notice and an opportunity of being heard in their defence) by such county, city, or state courts as may be prescribed by law, for causes to be assigned in the order of removal.

"18. All judicial officers of cities and villages, and all such judicial officers as may be created therein by law, shall be elected at such times and in such manner as the legislature may direct."

The justices of the peace are the cause of the word "town" occurring in the constitution. The justices of the peace should be appointed with the greatest care, for they are in importance second to none. The modern police courts seem to supersede them in large cities. The other particulars are special-law matters.

"19. The clerks of the several counties of this state shall be clerks of the supreme court, with such powers and duties as shall be prescribed by law. A clerk for the court of appeals to be *ex-officio* clerk of the supreme court, and to keep his office at the seat of government, shall be chosen by the electors of the state; he shall hold his office for three years, and his compensation shall be fixed by law and paid out of the public treasury.

"20. No judicial officer, except justices of the peace, shall receive to his own use any fees or perquisites of office."

Special-law matter. All such things vary constantly.

"21. The legislature may authorize the judgments, decrees, and decisions of any local inferior court of record of original civil jurisdiction, established in a city, to removed for a review directly into the court of appeals."

Special-law matter. All public papers belonging to the state, counties, towns, cities, and villages, whenever they are officially needed, must be sent without an extra authorization.

"22. The legislature shall provide for the speedy publication of all statute laws, and of such judicial decisions as it may deem expedient. And all laws and judicial decisions shall be free for publication by any person."

Superfluous, being a matter-of-course fact.

"23. Tribunals of conciliation may be established, with such powers and duties as may be prescribed by law; but such tribunals shall have no power to render judgment to be obligatory on the parties, except they voluntarily submit their matters in difference and agree to abide the judgment or assent thereto, in the presence of such tribunal, in such cases as shall be prescribed by law."

Superfluous, for it is the very best part of the office of a justice of the peace to prevent litigation by promoting conciliation, and if there is a special law necessary in this regard, it may be enacted. This may even ordain that no court shall proceed with a lawsuit, unless the case has been before a justice of the peace to promote a conciliation.

"24. The legislature, at its first session after the adoption of this constitution, shall provide for the appointment of three commissioners, whose duty it shall be to revise, reform, simplify, and abridge the rules and practice, pleadings, forms, and proceedings of the courts of record of this state, and to report thereon to the legislature, subject to their adoption and modification from time to time."

This is evidence that there is no code of procedure existing upon which neither courts nor lawyers may have the least influence. We want one containing all the rules invariably to be observed by the bench and bar. The pleasure of the king and *aula regis* must cease. All stages of a law procedure should be prescribed in an explicit, distinct manner, that no stays, or delays, or prevarications can happen, except at the risk of the delaying party. The present procrastination policy should come to an end. We should never read again of conventions of judges talking about the rules of the new term, to suit themselves. Of this trouble they should be relieved by a code of procedure, for all terms to come. The English judiciary is preëminently procrastinating and unreliable, because it is too independent in regard to the forms of the legal procedures. These must be paramount for all concerned. Apropos — the system of court-terms should be abolished; the whole year should be one term, while each cause may have appointed terms. As long as there is business it should be promptly despatched.

"25. The legislature, at its first session after the adoption of this constitution, shall provide for the organization of the court of appeals, and for transferring to it the business pending in the court for the correction of errors, and for the allowance of writs of error and appeals to the court of appeals, from the judgment and decrees of the present court of chancery and supreme court, and of the courts that may be organized under this constitution."

A court for the correction of errors is practically the same as a court of appeals. A court of chancery is set up for the despatch of cases in equity. Both those obsolete institutions are abolished, and very wisely. Oyer and terminer, surrogate, sessions, marine, superior, and supreme courts, with special and general terms, should be abolished too. But more of this in the following letter.

In seventeen states the judiciary is entirely elective by the people, as in New York, Pennsylvania, Maryland, Virginia, Florida, Mississippi, Louisiana, Texas, Tennessee, Kentucky, Ohio, Michigan, Indiana, Illinois, Missouri, Iowa, Wisconsin, and California. These states are of modern origin or have by late amendments adopted the elective system. In Maine, Vermont, and Alabama, the higher courts are appointed, and the lower elective. In eight states, as New Hampshire, Massachusetts, New Jersey, Delaware, North Carolina, South Carolina, Georgia, and Arkansas, the judiciary is appointed by the governor, with the advice of the councils or legislatures, or by the legislatures, during good behavior, or for a certain term of years. Those constitutions which were enacted a short time after the revolution, have followed the system of the federal constitution and created good judiciaries.

The state of New York, by making the judiciary elective, has set the precedent for the remaining states. Those organized since 1847 have followed it. Several states priorly organized have, by amendment, or change of constitution, adopted it; among others, Maryland, of which I shall add a few remarks hereafter.

"The maintenance of the judicial power is essential and indispensable to the very being of this government. The constitution without it would be no constitution; the government no government. The judicial power is the protecting power of the whole government. For the security of the government, the judiciary included, it requires such an extraordinary union of discretion and firmness, of ability and moderation, that nothing in the country is too distinguished for sober sense, or too gifted with powerful talent, to fill the situations belonging to it."

So spoke Daniel Webster in Congress. You will thank me for inserting this sentence.

LETTER X.

Remarks on the Organization of the Judiciary in States, Counties, and Towns in general. — English Judiciary. — Bad Legislation. — Daniel O'Connell. — Aula Regis. — Reform by the Federal Constitution. — District, Circuit, and Supreme Courts. — Municipal Judicial Business, Civil or Criminal. — Its Distribution among Towns, Counties, and States. — Abolition of the present Single Judicial Offices. — Reasons for it. — Webster. — Moses. — Solon. — Justinian. — Napoleon I. — Frederick II. — Joseph II. — Russell. — Thompson. — Brady. — Law.

THE judicial forms or proceedings, to find out what is right or wrong, by means of documents, witnesses, etc., are very simple and but little changing with the culture or moral and intellectual progress of mankind. Colonies generally adopt or rather maintain the laws and judicial forms of the mother-country. This has been the case in the United States. Still the simple form of democratic government required many important alterations in the old complicated English judicial system, which is a venerable relic of the middle age, and at present rather a mere useless antiquarian curiosity. Its foibles have often been exposed on both sides of the Atlantic. The great lawyer, Daniel O'Connell, betrayed a very poor idea of the English law when he said that he could drive through any act of parliament with a coach-and-four. Beautiful sport for rogues! A law-reform movement is just on foot in England: let us not be behind.

A close scrutiny of the present English system of bail, interpretation, and conviction, mostly based upon the testimony of witnesses, must convince an unprejudiced mind that it is generally eminently in favor of villany. I am as jealous of my personal liberty as any person can be, but feel very nervous if this jealousy, which every freeman should possess, is made the pretext of setting murderers, incendiaries, and similar dangerous criminals free on mere straw-bail, because a witness could not be had, or on similar irrelevant grounds. We owe it to this system that it is unsafe to appear unarmed in public, just as if there was no state institution at all. There is still a difference in this regard between cities and country towns, but it grows less very fast.

The political destiny of the United States was brought to a bloody crisis by bad English legislation. This lesson has obviously improved the destiny of our neighbors, the Canadians, but not that of the far-off East Indians; hence the bloody outbreak there, most critical for Great Britain's national career. We are indebted to bad legislation and execution of the laws for all our home troubles. The sensible reader will therefore excuse the outspoken manner in which I write of English law. Through it runs the maxim, like the red thread through the royal navy, that the king is all the judge and court for the whole kingdom. He, like his colleagues in Europe, travelled in the country in old times for this purpose, with some courtiers, barons, judges, etc., and of course he did as he pleased. Soon dukes, barons, bishops, etc., got slices of the royal jurisdiction; substitutes (surrogates) were appointed; and in consequence of the Magna Charta a stable royal court was established in Westminster Hall, called *aula regis*, that is, king's court. Later this court was divided into the courts of exchequer (so called from a checkered table-cloth), common pleas, and king's bench, to which was added the court of chancery and house of lords. Again there happened a split, so that the people got seven courts of exchequer. Following up this manner of patching up a judiciary, there came later, admiralty courts—county, sessions, ecclesiastical, coroners' courts, etc. The common source of this organization was the king and his pleasure. He of course had the original jurisdiction, that is, with full formal trials later prescribed by law, required by the importance of the cases. The court hierarchy went from the throne down to the people. Some of these forms we have retained with the English common law, but much of it has already been discarded. Still our courts wield much of the "pleasure" of the king.

The most important reform in this regard produced the federal constitution, and the judiciary which it created, absorbing a good deal of the common or original English state-judicial business. This organic law made a great division between national and municipal judicial business, never before done in this manner by such a law or a government, and organized for the first time a separate national judiciary, at once breaking up the usual British judicial hierarchy. You will recollect that the third article of the federal constitution contains in a few concise words the dispositions about the national judiciary. The business is at present, if I am not mistaken, distributed among forty-eight districts, ten circuit courts, and one supreme court.

From the constitution of the state of New York you have just learned how the judicial business remaining for the state shall be despatched, viz., by a court of appeals, eight supreme courts, superior courts, surrogates, county courts, justices of the peace, city courts, coroners, police courts, oyer and terminer courts, marine courts, court of sessions, etc. This machinery, according to unmistakable symptoms, has not worked well: and why is this? because our state constitution has not carried out the policy adopted by the framers of the federal constitution, viz: to organize the judiciary and set up the courts strictly according to the natural logical exigency of the remaining municipal judicial business, and not according to dogmatical or historical notions of law and equity cases, original and not original jurisdiction, and other old English customs.

Simply considering the usual judicial business as it is, we have either civil or criminal cases, so that we want civil and criminal courts. The civil cases are more or less important. A subdivision takes place in the criminal judicial business, now generally called police business. To organize this business, the common division of the state into towns and counties seems to answer perfectly well for all practical purposes.

The minor civil and criminal or police cases might be despatched in the towns by a town judge or justice of the peace carefully appointed for each town. In regard to claims, the amount generally serves as a measure, perhaps two hundred dollars. All trials of reconciliation also naturally belong to the town court.

Business not belonging to the town court should be apportioned to the county court, with one judge, as the constitution ordains. All judges appointed now for single business branches should be abolished. The county court might serve as a court of appeals in regard to decisions of the town court. Besides, a state court will be required for appeals from the county courts, and the claims against the state, and on the constitutionality of laws, etc. Some cities will require more than one town court; still not more than one county court. Very large cities will receive exceptional attention. The diverse appointments should, as I have before intimated, originate with the town, county, and state executives and legislative bodies; because they either have the care for the execution of the laws or hold the purse-strings in their hands. Such a simple, logical distribution of the municipal judicial business recommends itself to the general attention—

First. In regard to the *responsibility* of the town and county, which, by their constitutional agents, appoint the judges. They being sworn in to attend to the interests of the town or county, will appreciate the importance of the act the more seriously because it does not often occur. Of such a highly desirable responsibility there is not the least vestige in the elective system. Town and county agents are amenable to law, and not to parties who control the elections.

Second. In regard to the *qualifications* of the judges. A candidate for a county or town judgeship knows that he will occupy the office as long as he fills it ably. He will therefore thoroughly prepare himself for the bench, not even shunning expensive outlays for this purpose.

Third. In regard to the *business.* First it will be managed with ability, talent, and impartiality; second, with honesty and decorum. The proposed combination of the present dilapidated civil, criminal, and police business will keep the judges in their districts well employed, and therefore ripen and sharpen their judgment in deciding causes. Being prohibited from taking a share in other employments, such a judge will be wholly a judge, always a judge, and nothing but a judge, as Webster desired might be the case.

This also applies to the state court. Of course these three courts should all be courts of record, and, in a word, perform all the business at present divided among a swarm of special judicial officials, producing confusion, scandalous feuds among them for business, and a deplorable degradation of this most honorable function. A good impartial judiciary is all the model republic we may boast of. I add that a state of the improper size of New York requires at least four state courts for corresponding districts; while well-proportioned Connecticut requires but one.

History teaches that only those rulers who are distinguished as good legislators and administrators of justice acquire lasting fame and celebrity. To say nothing of Moses, Solon, and Justinian, it is obvious that Napoleon I. has endeared himself to the better class of Frenchmen, not so well by his gained and lost battles, and imperial ambitious schemes, as by his good law-codes and an excellent organization of the judiciary. By similar acts of true statesmanship before him, Frederick II., of Prussia, and Joseph II., of Austria, acquired the appellation of great and good princes. It is their work that these empires still exist and enjoy esteem and credit under most trying vicissitudes. I am sorry that I can not point out a single one of our states which excels in this regard. Still, in our smaller states the administration of justice is better than in the larger. People faithful to an inborn instinct love and honor justice, notwithstanding. They cheerfully erect public halls for her service; they adorn them with statuary and pictures; they fill them with libraries. The goddess of justice, with covered eyes, to prevent biasing by personalities or gold, with the balance, the symbol of equity and righteousness in one hand, and with the sword for the strong arm of the executor in the other, thrones upon our splendid piles and court-halls. Still, what contain the daily reports of the administration of justice beneath their roofs, by their sworn priests? Says Judge Russell in New York, in his address to the grand jury: "It is probable that at this term you will encounter some alleged offences which the law is impotent to reach, and others that, where the law is sufficient by reason of the present practice, motion upon motion and appeal upon appeal may be resorted to, so that the court is rendered impotent to punish. It is the bane of our system, that while the friendless criminals almost step from the stationhouse to the state-prison, others, who have able counsel and friendly bail, may badger justice beyond the power of the most indefatigable district-attorney, or the most industrious judge to prevent." Similar pithy addresses we often notice. I refer to one of Judge Thompson, in Baltimore, and of Mr. Brady, in memory of Justice Duer.

We need a revival in the direction of justice. Let us hope that the proposed revision of the constitution of the leading state will rouse the people and bring out a thorough reform of the judiciary. Then will Maryland and other states follow in the wake.

"We may traverse sea and land on the wings of lightning; we

may cover the globe with a network of railways; our canals may be as the highways of the waters; but without that silent, germinating, sustaining principle, LAW, all our labor, skill, energy, learning, and treasure, will be of little avail, except it be to keep up and adorn the general ruin."

The "amici curial" may then bestir themselves.

LETTER XI.

Finance. — Revenues of the State Canals. — Sinking Fund. — General Fund Debt. — State Stock Loaned to Incorporated Companies. — Selling Canals.

WE now come to the finances.

ARTICLE VII.

Finance.

"1. After paying the expenses of collection, superintendence, and ordinary repairs, there shall be appropriated and set apart in each fiscal year, out of the revenues of the state canals, commencing on the first day of June, 1846, the sum of one million and three hundred thousand dollars, until the first day of June, 1855, and from that time, the sum of one million and seven hundred thousand dollars in each fiscal year, as a sinking fund, to pay the interest and redeem the principal of that part of the state debt called the canal debt, as it existed at the time aforesaid, and including three hundred thousand dollars then to be borrowed until the same shall be wholly paid; and the principal and income of the said sinking fund shall be sacredly applied to that purpose.

This article treats mostly of the income derived from the canals, an object which, originally, has as little connection with the political organization of the society, as the fire police, the regulations of which filled a large chapter of the old constitution, and rests entirely upon special legislation, and private speculation of the government, which, thus far, ceases to be government, and steps down into the arena of private life. If a government sees fit to make money by building canals, manufacturing salt, snuff, china, etc., etc., and is not expressly forbidden to meddle with such business, it should lay down the rules for such things in special laws, just as manufacturers or railroad companies do.

That such special laws of a legislature should be observed sacredly by the legislature itself, is, indeed, very desirable, and a matter of course. But, what shall be done with this proviso and the following, if the canals do not pay, a thing which happens at present?

The federal government spends immense sums annually, has paid up many millions of debts, keeps an army and navy at an expense of some twenty millions of dollars, and does this all in virtue of two very short paragraphs, namely, clause 18, art. I, sect. viii., and clause 7, sect. ix. of the same article. Some such dispositions, inserted into this state constitution, would have answered all reasonable purposes. How shall the officers sacredly manage this fund if the canals bring no revenue? They must borrow, or violate the constitution, of course.

"2. After complying with the provisions of the first section of this article, there shall be appropriated and set apart out of the surplus revenues of the state canals, in each fiscal year, commencing on the first day of June, 1846, the sum of three hundred and fifty thousand dollars, until the time when a sufficient sum shall have been appropriated and set apart, under the said first section, to pay the interest and extinguish the entire principal of the canal debt; and after that period then the sum of one million and five hundred thousand dollars in each fiscal year, as a sinking fund, to pay the interest and redeem the principal of that part of the state debt called the general fund debt, including the debt for loans of the state credit to railroad companies which have failed to pay the interest thereon, and also the contingent debt on state stocks loaned to incorporated companies which have hitherto paid the interest thereon whenever and as far as any part thereof may become a charge on the treasury or general fund, until the same shall be wholly paid; and the principal and income of the said last mentioned sinking fund shall be sacredly applied to the purpose aforesaid; and if the payment of any part of the moneys to the said sinking fund shall at any time be deferred, by reason of the priority recognized in the first section of this article, the sum so deferred, with quarterly interest thereon, at the then current rate, shall be paid to the last-mentioned sinking fund, as soon as it can be done consistently with the just rights of the creditors holding said canal debt.

"3. After paying the said expenses of superintendence and repairs of the canals, and the sum appropriated by the first and second sections of this article, there shall be paid out of the surplus revenues of the canals to the treasury of the state, on or before the thirteenth day of September, in each year, for the use and benefit of the general fund, such sum, not exceeding two hundred thousand dollars, as may be required to defray the necessary expenses of the state; and the remainder of the revenues of the said canals shall, in each fiscal year, be applied, in such manner as the legislature shall direct, to the completion of the Erie canal enlargement, and the Genesee Valley and Black River canals, until the said canals shall be completed.

"If at any time after the period of eight years from the adoption of this constitution, the revenues of the state unappropriated by this article, shall not be sufficient to defray the necessary expenses of the government, without continuing or laying a direct tax, the legislature may, at its discretion, supply the deficiency, in whole or in part, from the surplus revenues of the canals, after complying with the provisions of the first two sections of this article, for paying the interest and extinguishing the principal of the canal and general fund debt; but the sum thus appropriated from the surplus revenues of the canal shall not exceed annually three hundred and fifty thousand dollars, including the sum of two hundred thousand dollars, provided for by this section for the expenses of the government, until the general fund debt shall be extinguished, or until the Erie canal enlargement and Genesee Valley and Black River canals shall be completed, and after that debt shall be paid, or the said canals shall be completed, then the sum of six hundred and seventy-two thousand five hundred dollars, or so much thereof as shall be necessary, may be annually appropriated to defray the expenses of the government."

Those provisoes belong to a statute-book.

"4. The claims of the state against any incorporated company to pay the interest and redeem the principal of the stock of the state loaned or advanced to such company, shall be fairly enforced, and not released or compromised; and the moneys arising from such claims shall be set apart and applied as part of the sinking fund provided in the second section of this article. But the time limited for the fulfilment of any condition of any release or compromise heretofore made or provided for, may be extended by law."

Are officers in New York state in the habit of acting unfairly? The policy of loaning public money or credit to private individuals is bad; it is still worse to put such a proviso in the constitution.

"5. If the sinking funds, or either of them provided in this article, shall prove insufficient to enable the state on the credit of such fund, to procure the means to satisfy the claims of the creditors of the state, as they become payable, the legislature shall, by equitable taxes, so increase the revenues of the said funds as to make them, respectively, sufficient perfectly to preserve the public faith. Every contribution or advance to the canals, or their debt, from any source, other than their direct revenues shall, with quarterly interest, at the rates then current, be repaid into the treasury, for the use of the state, out of the canal revenues, as soon as it can be done consistently with the just rights of the creditors holding the said canal debts."

All special-law business.

"6. The legislature shall not sell, lease, or otherwise dispose of any of the canals of the state; but they shall remain the property of the state and under its management for ever."

This is, indeed, a bold, grasping, disposition, barring the action of statesmen and people for all generations to come. There were railroads in operation when this clause was written and printed! I am far from imputing to its authors any other intention than that to raise money to defray the government's expense with. Still this operation is inseparable from a peculiar party canal-policy, patronage, and sundry items comprised by the word public corruption. The sooner they are sold the better. Canals have had their time, especially when managed by governments. In this respect also, should the federal constitution have served as a pattern.

Arsenals are most certainly establishments closely in connection with the common defence, navy, etc. Still the constitution nowhere says that the arsenals shall remain the property of the Union for ever, and never be sold, etc. In our time Congress disposed of one in Memphis, and may sell them all to-morrow, if not any more needed for the common defences. Or, do the people of the state of New York require canals eternally for the ends of municipal justice, as Congress is in need of arsenals for the navy, a branch of the executive power, inseparable from a national government?

Think of such subjects earnestly, because they are a principal cause of the prevalent public corruption. Demagogues, however, will stick to the present practice of our governments, to meddle with private business, as long as they can, because it is lucrative for them, and strengthens the party ties. There is a thorough reform necessary. May the revision of the constitution bring it.

LETTER XII.

Salt Springs. — Appropriation Laws. — State Credit. — Borrowing Money. — Invasion. — Debt Laws. — Voting upon.

THE following proviso is similar to that concerning canals:—

"7. The legislature shall never sell or dispose of the salt springs belonging to this state. The land contiguous thereto, and which may be necessary and convenient for the use of the salt springs, may be sold by authority of law, and under the direction of the commissioners of the land office, for the purpose of investing the moneys arising therefrom in other lands alike convenient; but by such sale and purchase the aggregate quantity of these lands shall not be diminished."

It is superfluous to tell you my opinion about this clause; it belongs not to the constitution, and is a political error; besides, governments are bad salt manufacturers.

"8. No moneys shall ever be paid out of the treasury of this state, or any of its funds, or any of the funds under its management, except in pursuance of an appropriation by law; nor unless such payment be made within two years next after the passage of such appropriation act; and every such law making a new appropriation, or continuing or reviving an appropriation, shall distinctly specify the sum appropriated, and the object to which it is to be appplied; and it shall not be sufficient for such law to refer to any other law to fix such sum."

There is no better proviso on this subject than that found in the Fed. Const., clause 7, sect. vii., art. I.

"9. The credit of the state shall not, in any manner, be given or loaned to, or in aid of any individual, association, or corporation."

This is very just, and a matter-of-course, because states are no money brokers or bankers.

"10. The state may, to meet casual deficits or failures in revenues, or for expenses not provided for, contract debts, but such debts, direct and contingent, singly or in the aggregate, shall not, at any time, exceed one million of dollars; and the moneys arising from the loans creating such debts, shall be applied to the purpose for which they were obtained, or to repay the debt so contracted, and to no other purpose whatever."

It is utterly impossible that, if our states have nothing to do with speculations and improper business, they will ever be in need of borrowing money, for there can not happen a deficit.

"11. In addition to the above limited power to contract debts, the state may contract debts to repel invasion, suppress insurrection, or defend the state in war; but the money arising from the contracting of such debts shall be applied to the purpose for which it was raised, or to repay such debts, and to no other purpose whatever."

This seems to be superfluous under our federal constitution, because expenses for the mentioned events Congress has to bear.

"12. Except the debts specified in the tenth and eleventh sections of this article, no debt shall hereafter be contracted by or on behalf of this state, unless such debt shall be authorized by a law for some single work or object, to be distinctly specified therein, and such law shall impose and provide for the collection of a direct annual tax to pay, and sufficient to pay the interest on such debt as it falls due, and also to pay and discharge the principal of such debt within eighteen years from the time of the contracting thereof.

"No such law shall take effect until it shall, at a general election, have been submitted to the people, and have received a majority of all the votes cast for and against it at such election.

"On the final passage of such bill in either house of the legislature, the question shall be taken by ayes and noes, to be duly entered on the journals thereof, and shall be: 'Shall this bill pass, and ought the same to receive the sanction of the people?'

"The legislature may at any time, after the approval of such law by the people, if no debt shall have been contracted in pursuance thereof, repeal the same; and may, at any time, by law, forbid the contracting of any farther debt or liability under such law; but the tax imposed by such act, in proportion to the debt and liability which may have been contracted in pursuance of such law, shall remain in force and be irrepealable, and be annually collected until the proceeds thereof shall have made the provision hereinbefore specified to pay and discharge the interest and principal of such debt and liability.

"The money arising from any loan or stock creating such debt or liability shall be applied to the work or object specified in the act authorizing such debt or liability, or for the repayment of such debt or liability, and for no other purpose whatever.

"No such law shall be submitted to be voted on within three months after its passage, or at any general election, when any other law or any bill or any amendment to the constitution shall be submitted to be voted for or against."

There is no "single work or object" imaginable which a real good state government has to undertake besides what belongs to the state establishment itself. Most of the state burdens are borne either by Congress or the towns and counties. The whole clause should not occur in the constitution, because it may induce to all kinds of speculations. Suppose the government would try to make the canals pay, by using the water-power for manufacturing flour, snuff, or paper, with a capital of one million, could people hinder it consistently under this constitution, which makes the government an everlasting canal and salt manufacturing concern. I am not sure that such speculations will not spring up from this article. Selling out is the best policy, if we would have New York salt cheap and plenty. The present is old English royalty policy making a beautiful show in New Caledonia.

LETTER XIII.

Taxes. — Voting on Debt and Tax Laws.

The constitution ordains further:—

"13. Every law which imposes, continues, or revives a tax, shall distinctly state the tax and the object to which it is to be applied, and it shall not be sufficient to refer to any other law to fix such a tax or object."

This seems to be superfluous because self-evident and ministerial.

"14. On the final passage in either house of the legislature, of every act which imposes, continues, or revives a tax, or creates a debt or charge, or makes, continues, or revives any appropriation, of public or trust money or property, or releases, discharges, or commutes any claim or demand of the state, the question shall be taken by yeas and noes, which shall be duly entered on the journals, and three fifths of all the members elected to either house shall, in all such cases, be necessary to constitute a quorum therein."

All this is very well so far as it goes. But a definitive, absolute prohibition of applying public funds for other purposes than those required for the support of the state institution itself, can alone check abuse of state means and power. The financial affairs of an American municipal state, as it ought to be, are exceedingly simple. And of the same character ought to be the constitution itself. The less detail the better. While this young state constitution has been already repeatedly amended, the old federal constitution has stood the fiery ordeal of factions, civil commotions, wars, and other important changes of time, during almost a century, without requiring the least alteration! It is so good that we can still, a long, a very long time, profit by it.

Macchiavelli advises his prince to imitate a great monarch. In making state constitutions we will do well to imitate our federal constitution. No better pattern exists in the world.

LETTER XIV.

Corporations. — General Law. — Banking Corporations. — Suspension of Payment. — Registry of Bills. — Paper Money. — Insolvent Banks. — Boards. — Conflict of State Laws, and the Federal Constitution, respecting Banks of Issue. — Paper and Metallic Money. — Credit System. — Agriculture. — Hunt's Merchants' Magazine.

At the time when this constitution was made there was much popular excitement against incorporated companies, especially bank corporations.

A corporation is, as the name indicates, an association for business purposes, endowed by law, with the rights of a person. A single person may be sued and sue, but a company or partnership, as such, can not, unless it is incorporated, or made a political person. Then the president alone, or with the directors, sue and may be sued on account of the concern and their members, who generally are called stockholders, and may reside where they please. Copartners sue and are sued upon their names. On this subject, and in consequence of those events, the constitution has a separate article, as follows :—

ARTICLE VIII.

Corporations.

"1. Corporations may be formed under general laws; but shall not be created by special act, except for municipal purposes, and in cases, where in the judgment of the legislature, the objects of the corporation can not be attained under general laws. All general laws and special acts passed pursuant to this section, may be altered from time to time or repealed."

This proviso is wise and good, although little regarded by the legislature, when freely chartering all kinds of corporations not belonging to the excepted class, as for turning, pure milk, hospitals, etc. Municipal purposes means, incorporations of counties and towns (cities and villages). I have mentioned elsewhere that the constitution should contain the general provisoes about their organization, because such an organic law is, in fact, nothing but a state, county, and town charter. The expansion of industrial enterprise, or, in other words, large business, requiring more means than a single person usually commands, as the building of canals, railroads, etc., is the cause of this business form or formality. It can be perfectly well arranged, with the help of the county courts or administration, where the business is located, reserving to the state government the supervision; for which purpose the general law on the subject should contain explicit provisions, the principal aim of which should be to prevent and check irresponsible monopolies and too great centralizations by consolidations, etc. The cases mentioned in the proviso where the objects of the corporation can not be attained under general laws, can be, methinks, only such, whose business is not located within the state, as Isthmus transit companies, and the like. But this being no municipal business, it is doubtful whether such concerns should not derive their charters elsewhere. If Rhode Island may charter such a company, why should not all our states have the same right? The restriction from the words, "and in cases," should be expunged, because they unsettle the intention of the main part of the clause.

Governments whose financial powers are little restricted, will always be made use of, by influential parties, for their speculations. The constitution should, therefore, be drawn up with a view to avoid such contacts, ending in special legislation, log-rolling laws, lobby regimen, debts, bankruptcy, repudiation, etc. Whoever is against such governing must restrict the governments to the care of realizing justice. Formalities for legalizing associations, general laws should prescribe for the guidance of the courts and all in concern. The constitution steered that way, but stopped before reaching its end.

"2. Dues from corporations shall be secured by such individual liability of the corporators and other means as may be prescribed by law."

Here the text refers to a special law, to which, rather, the whole clause belongs.

"3. The term corporations, as used in this article, shall be construed to include all associations and joint-stock companies having any of the powers or privileges of corporations not possessed by individuals or partnerships. And all corporations shall have the right to sue and shall be subject to be sued in all courts in like cases as natural persons."

This is doctrinal and not constitutional.

"4. The legislature shall have no power to pass any act granting any special charter for banking purposes; but corporations or associations may be formed for such purposes under general laws."

This is perfectly right, and applicable to all kinds of corporative business. If well carried out, the legislatures remain free to exercise their supervisory power without being in the least concerned or restricted by their own chartering. The legislator should not be complicated with mere ministerial office business.

"5. The legislature shall have no power to pass any law sanctioning in any manner, directly or indirectly, the suspension of specie payments, by any person, association, or corporation, issuing bank-notes of any description."

Perfectly right, nothing would be more unjust, because a political bank promises, upon the faith of the state, to pay cash for its bills of credit when presented. Any deviation from this constitutional policy must impair the credit of both banks and state. Alas! when in 1857, the banks suspended specie payment again, and the governor declined to interfere, the judges of the supreme court stepped in, declaring that this suspension is not exactly a refusal to pay, or an indication of insolvency, and refused, therefore, to proceed against them, as requested. This was generally denounced as an assumption of undue power. The clause obviously wishes to place the political banks and their notes as secure as possible. When the judiciary declares that the refusal of the promised specie is of no consequence, it unsettles the constitution, sports with the credit system, destroys confidence, prostrates the business, and places the banks above the constitution and law, and the confiding public at their mercy. This is more than a dangerous precedent, it is a public calamity. If those judges were appointed during good behavior, they would have been, no doubt, removed, when thus abusing their power. The question remains, whether they would then have acted thus?

The management of our public money affairs reminds one of a farmer, who, having a fine breadth of land, ordered his headman to plant it with wheat. This done, he sent another man out to sow it over with oats. When the harvest arrived the wheat was gone and the oats not worth anything, whereupon came the crisis and bankruptcy of the farmer. A little reflection should teach, that people who establish two antagonistic monetary systems — the one in the states, the other in the Union — both in this regard the same thing, because commerce knows no political boundaries, act very inconsistently. We can not make one and the same business — coining money — at the same time national and municipal, without producing confusion and mischief. Banks, or no banks, make no difference. If such a hermaphrodite monetary system is right, then we may also have state navies, although expressly prohibited, like bills of credit, by chartering companies, as we charter banks, to build them. Good that it would be an unprofitable affair, otherwise we might have plenty of commodore navies, with the help of ingenious interpretation.

"6. The legislature shall provide by law for the registry of all bills or notes, issued or put in circulation as money, and shall require ample security for the redemption of the same in specie."

According to the opinion of Daniel Webster, our most distinguished constitutional expounder, this section is against clause 1, sect. x., art. I., of the federal constitution, for it is the cause of a real state paper-money. If a bank circulates paper-money under its own name, it is private money, if sanctioned by the state it is political or public money. But no state shall circulate money, neither directly nor indirectly, because Congress alone has to provide a circulating medium. This is a conflict which has been, on the ground of a judicial interpretation, waived by Congress up to this time, it must be said, to the great disadvantage of the nation.

"7. The stockholders in every corporation and joint-stock association for banking purposes, issuing bank notes or any kind of paper credits to circulate as money, after the first day of January, 1850, shall be individually responsible to the amount of their respective share or shares of stock in any such corporation or association, for all its debts and liabilities of every kind, contracted after the said first day of January, 1850."

This is plain and just enough, but does not belong to a constitution.

"8. In case of the insolvency of any bank or banking association, the bill-holders thereof shall be entitled to preference in payment, over all other creditors of such bank or association."

Belongs to a bankrupt law.

By allowing banks to circulate paper-money, (about two hundred million dollars in the United States), it is done on the supposition that the public will borrow it. Thus is created what is called a credit system. By this operation the industrious forces are artificially stimulated toward trading, speculating, and, perhaps, manufacturing, to the disadvantage of agriculture. Hence our cities grow fast in population, and the agricultural towns hardly any at all. Immense tracts of land in the vicinity of the greatest thoroughfares and most populous cities in the state of New York remain uncultivated. According to the census of 1850, it appears that Queens county, Long Island, comprises one hundred and twenty-three thousand three hundred and sixty acres of improved, and forty-six thousand two hundred and eighty-six of unimproved land, and Suffolk county one hundred and forty-three thousand six hundred and thirteen acres improved, and two hundred and ten thousand two hundred and ninety-two of unimproved land. This shows that a resistless force draws man from agricultural pursuits even in the vicinity of the best market. This force is the credit system, supported by banks with paper-money circulation; because it induces man to believe that it is the panacea and philosopher's stone which makes him rich without labor. Such stimulation and intoxication, in a free society like ours, must be injurious to the regular course of business and business habits. It creates reckless industrial fillibusters, who never think of the golden rule of the celebrated Virginian, "pay as you go," which may be considered the true panacea of dull times, panics, and crises.

The well-known machinery of modern banks of issue, and of the credit system, is, in the main, the art of making money by debts, on state authority. Some men of property lend money to the state on interest; whereupon they get permission from the state in debt to issue as large an amount in notes as the state has promised to pay them, which they loan to others on interest. Then they take deposits, for which they pay no interest, which, however, they lend again on interest, always taking care that the borrowers get the bank-notes, while the bankers dispose of the metal-money in the market to all who pay the highest price for it.

By thus making money out of money, all depends naturally upon credit, that is, upon the belief of the borrower that the bankers are able to pay his debts to their bill-holders and depositors, and that of the bankers that their debtors are able to pay on demand, *in cash.* But as they seldom or never have any cash, and in the main only promissory notes, it is obvious that this credit is a mere illusion, and must terminate in panics and crises as soon as the real squaring of accounts begins.

The mechanical art which produces a fine durable paper and print, has supported this roundabout debt-making or credit system vastly. It is disgraceful in a society under a government of law, because this is supposed to rest mainly on morals, principles not discernible in this credit system.

"*Debt-money,*" says Hunt's Merchant's Magazine, "is an eternal falsehood, and the New York state-banking system the highest phase and refinement of the falsehood." Such money raises artificially the prices of merchandise, bread, and labor, and lowers the value of gold and silver, which is then bought and exported. It supports the laboring masses in Europe by stimulating importation, to the injury of our home industry.

While this paper-money credit system easily produces on one hand general mercantile derangements, it renders on the other hand a stable financial management of the federal government almost impossible. You know that the main source of the income of Congress is, indirect, from customs. Now who has the power to derange commerce, has the power to cut off the customs and deplete the common treasury. This explains why Congress borrows, at present, in time of peace, millions for the support of the common government, which really means that the whole nation has to fill up the gap caused by the paper-money credit-system crisis. Therefore, as long as the states indulge in such things, a correct estimate of the revenues from the customs, and of the income of the common treasury, is out of the question. And here you see again what an immense difference there is between the words national and municipal. The monetary affairs in regard to coin, standard, and circulation are national, not municipal, as you know from the federal constitution, and no other than a national currency should circulate.

The financial events of 1857, nothing but revivals of prior

commercial revulsions tracing their origin to England, prove again that the framers of the federal constitution understood their task and the true principles of political economy better than their successors, by abstracting from all so-called credit systems and financial commercial experiments, and placing upon the solid basis of liberty and justice, the national industry, commerce included. It is mere infatuation to believe for a single minute that the material progress of our nation rests upon another or better basis. Those who substitute state-bank paper-money do all in their power to counteract the effect of the federal constitution and the blessings of our Union at home and abroad. American investments would be eagerly sought for by intelligent people in all parts of the world, if we had never seen a single dollar of debt-money; for there would be no nation, no state, surpassing ours in solid credit. The state paper-credit system is the greatest enemy of the true progress and substantial wealth and welfare of this nation. It is nonsense to believe that there can be wealth represented by money without labor and industry. Whether industrious people have mines or not, makes no difference; they will always attract and command so much wealth, represented by money, as their industry is really worth, and enjoy a world-wide firm credit; while on the other hand mountains full of gold and silver and Wall-streets full of paper money can not prevent a lazy, indolent, and unpractical people like the Mexicans from sinking into utter ruin and insignificance.

As some of the states have already fairly, as in duty bound, adopted the policy of the federal constitution and prohibited the circulation of bills of credit of state bank-paper money, to their great benefit and honor, it is to be hoped that soon, very soon, the rest will follow and carry out their own supreme law of the land. There is no better credit system in the world, and never will be, than that which is the product of industrial liberty and justice; and this, as I have repeatedly said, has given us this great fundamental law, the patent of our nationality. It has, in this regard, been misunderstood by the judiciary, supporting as it is by a weak amaurotic interpretation or quibble, the state bank-paper money. I write this without the least intention to reflect upon the private business of banking. The fault is not with the banks and bankers, but the politicians, desiring to be teachers of the law, "understanding neither what they say nor whereof they affirm."

LETTER XV.

Cities. — Villages. — History. — Superceded by a Judicious Organization of Towns and Counties. — Saving of Taxes.

LET us read on.

"9. It shall be the duty of the legislature to provide for the organization of cities and incorporated villages, and to restrict their power of taxation, assessment, borrowing money, contracting debts, and loaning their credit, so as to prevent abuses in assessments and in contracting debt by such municipal corporations."

Behind those eight sections on banks, you find this short proviso concerning the organization of cities and villages — mere anomalies — but to the organization of the counties and towns this very verbose and explicit constitution has not devoted two entire lines; just as if banks and similar corporations were more important in political regard, than those political districts in which the public business mostly is performed.

Mutual protection and chance of business induced men, in ancient times, to crowd together in favorable localities. Business is still the mother of cities and villages, but civilization does not require it more for protection. We have no more roving and robbing tribes and barons, the cause which induced people and government to crowd in cities together and make them secure by fortifications. Our policy at present should be to facilitate not at all by *law* the formation of cities and villages, because the latter are but small cities, and the first invariably centers of mischief and mobs, and not always homes of good sciences, wholesome arts, and exemplary morals, and therefore difficult to manage. Civilization is now not local but universal; a free press and liberty of industry in general have set up in every house a college, in every town a Paris, and promoted in every county as much culture as formerly were the boast of capitals, metropolises, and empires. Even business ceases to be building up cities at present, because railroads and steamers facilitate a separation of residence and office in many instances.

When influential speculators and their newspapers insist upon the consolidation of cities, as, Boston, and Charlestown, and Roxbury; or New York and Brooklyn; or Troy and Lansingburgh; and achieve them, as in the case of Brooklyn and Williamsburgh, Philadelphia, etc., they mistake politics and the best interests of society entirely. The legislatures which support and sanction such consolidations purposely demoralize society by increasing artificially, the difficulty of ruling it.

This clause has not exercised any good influence upon the administration of the cities. They are all in difficulties in regard to finances, safety, and order. The defective administration of New York city requires sixteen millions of dollars, all told, while the expenses of the well-governed kingdom of Saxony amounts to only seven millions. But this state of things prevails not alone in New York. Providence, in Rhode Island, with forty thousand inhabitants, increasing in eight years about ten per cent, had, during this time, an increase of expenses at the rate of three hundred per cent, and of debts more than four hundred per cent. For the last two years the excess of expenditures over tax assessed is $518,000. It is obvious, then, that the reform of such evils must begin with the business and business districts. The axiom of one of the best statesman of our age, Jefferson, viz., "that government is the best which governs least," is only applicable to a society whose business districts are of the right size. As those overgrow, the government's business, expenses, taxes, debts, and difficulties will increase proportionately, notwithstanding all constitutions and axioms of the best men to the contrary. Still this clause is laudable because it has been dictated by a sense of economy. The current practice, however, differs from it.

People therefore, when called upon to vote upon consolidations of towns or cities, which are not decreasing in population, should invariably vote against it.

LETTER XVI.

Education. — Funds. — Instruction. — Communes. — Girard. — Peabody. — Cooper. — Popular Education. — Popular Sovereignty.

You may be, perhaps, surprised by the head of the following article, because education proper is a strange subject for a constitution. But let us see.

ARTICLE IX.

Education.

"1. The capital of the common school fund, the capital of the literature fund, and the capital of the U. S. deposit fund shall be respectively preserved inviolate. The revenue of the said common school fund shall be applied to the support of common schools; the revenues of the said literature fund shall be applied to the support of academies, and the sum of $25,000 of the revenues of the U. S. deposit fund shall each year be appropriated to and make a part of the capital of the said common school fund."

Why this article is headed "education," instead of, perhaps, "financial," I can not say. The funds in question have been formed by special laws, which, of course, should never be violated by the legislature, as I remark again, and are to be managed accordingly. Is it sound doctrine to have such funds in our country? The schooling or instruction of the young is not a political, but a simple domestic family affair, either taken care of by nurses, mothers, fathers, guardians, or by others engaged or appointed by them. Town-districts, often also called communes, have been, all over the world, since time immemorial, made use of for the organization of schools; and those, therefore, placed under the surveillance of the town officials, just as everything else of a little common interest, viz., streets, fences, brooks, rivers, commons, pastures, sidewalks, taverns, hotels, etc., and ruled by town resolves, by-laws, customs, etc. Church organizations often helped, also, to foster schools, but the state institution proper had nothing to do with it. Thus the money for schooling went directly from the pockets of the parents into those of the teachers.

Such schools were called commune or common, or town or public schools. These schools can be made very good, without the least interference of the legislature, provided that there are well-organized towns. Of course, the money constituting these funds comes from the people, where, if left, it would produce hundred-fold interest; while, as permanent funds in the hands of state officials, who, according to the constitution, seem to be not always trustworthy, for, otherwise, this law would not so often speak about good faith, or violation of trust, they can not bring more than seven per cent., but never will bring that. Excuse me if I write about such things. I would not do it, if such funds gave no chance for corruption, according to the daily reports. It is natural that all business of this kind, as schools, sciences, literature, arts, etc., if connected with the state, must partake of the predominant political character of the party in power. In a monarchy, all these things will be tinged with the policy of the court; in a republic, every party in power will try to gain influence upon them. Whoever is paid by the state is a state official, and must accordingly rule himself. History proves that, in spite of the Bible and everything sacred about our religion, the clergy depending upon the state are grasping at undue power, and we have, therefore dissolved this connexion. Still we make now the teachers state officials. Are they and clergymen not of the same human kind? In Europe, with a very few exceptions, sciences and arts are under political surveillance. Professors, savans, and writers are, especially when in the pay of the governments, so closely guarded that their products bear the stamp of political partiality, more or less. We should, therefore, never pay much attention to their school, university, and similar expedients to raise subservient scholars. To speak in sober earnest of *education* proper, as a political affair intrusted to politicians, is too curious a thing to dwell upon. There is no better board of education than the family. But the poor! the poor! Well, our present common school system, created by state laws, is positively not calculated to benefit the real poor people, but that class generally well able to pay teachers.

The city of New York pays more than one million dollars for common schools, normal schools, a free academy, etc., and, in 1857, there were 60,000 children not attending any school at all, and of those in the 18th ward alone 2,631, among them 1,340 born Americans. For these children charitable ladies have established schools. The same happens in all towns. The present artificial, expensive system does not work better than the cheap, natural management carried out by families. The public morals now are rather worse than they were in the period before the system was adopted. It, too, interferes with charity and generous liberality. There are a great number of wealthy men among us who seem not to know how to spend their money; or, when arrived at the goal, how to dispose of their earthly treasure. As charity helps the poor children, so would wealthy men, if not interfered with by the state, help the schools in general. The liberal acts of Girard, Peabody, Cooper, and so many others, are proofs of what I am going to say. Also, in this regard, emulation and competition are powerfully at work. Education is the work of families. What errors are committed in families, no school will easily eradicate, no science remedy. Too often rather is a son, well educated by a mother, spoiled in public institutions! Neither schools nor sciences mould the character of men. I think that this article is superfluous in a constitution.

The inventive genius of our politicians enriches, from time to time, our language with new phrases, which serve them in their party warfare as weapons. What all the world, besides ourselves, has called common schools or public instruction, that they call now "popular education." I admit that people have a right to mould their own language, that words become sometimes uncurrent, and that the general use decides upon their value. Still, if phrases are manufactured for party purposes, the opponents must enjoy the privilege to examine them. I deny that there exists such a thing as popular education, in the proper sense of these words. If we have to attribute to families, and especially to the mothers, the care of the education of the young, then each family, each mother will and ought to pursue their own peculiar course or system; a fact which at once excludes the idea of a popular education — that is, an education of the whole people, by the families, according to uniform laws. This is, no doubt, an absurdity. But, if this phrase is tantamount to public or common instruction, then our legislatures, by meddling with it, plainly interfere, as they, alas! so often do, with the very old and good right of towns or communes, to make the needful arrangements for the instruction of children as they please. It is repugnant to the principle of self-government, that a government in free society should be bound to provide funds for common town-schools, or make laws for their organization, school-books, etc. If the teachers and freemen in the towns are not able to do this without state interference, the sooner the republican form of government is abandoned the better. Says a teacher of one of the public schools in New York, Mr. Stewart, in a public meeting of teachers: "Our present school-system was admirable at the time it started, but it is now the contrary. It was based on a pauper system of education (instruction), which is not in any way adapted to the present day. *Our present school-system is miserably detrimental in its effects upon the mental, moral, and physical qualifications of the youth of our city.* Now, at the present time, the school system costs the people of New York considerably over $1,000,000 annually, and it is likely, before long, to cost $1,500,000, or even more." These results are the fruits of state-meddling with town (city, village) business.

Being engaged in discussing political cant-phrases, I add here a few words on that of "popular sovereignty" or "squatter sovereignty," taking, for the sake of convenience, the words popular and squatter for synonyms. I also say, that there exists no such a thing as popular sovereignty in the United States, because it implies *direct* legislation by the people, as in the beginning of Maryland or ancient Greece, but not in vogue at present. People may be independent and free, but, on this account, are not sovereigns in the proper sense of the word, because they are not legislators. The act of voting or electing is not a result of sovereignty, but of organized civil liberty. There is no nation in the world, the Russians and Turks included, without possessing more or less of this liberty, and, consequently, without some voting or electing. They elect not always their governments, as kings, etc., but these rule notwithstanding, with the tacit or presumptive general consent of the people, for, otherwise, they would not be able to maintain themselves at all. In this connection, you will remember that sovereigns, that is those that represent and legislate for society, are either *born* or *elected;* the first happens in monarchies, the latter in republics; but in constitutional monarchies, also, the legislatures are, for the most part, elected, and that all those officers who execute the laws of the state and act in its name, as judges, clerks, military, etc., are *appointed.* I try to be as plain and explicit as possible in this regard, because there are confused ideas afloat about these things, which, if they enter party disputes and constitutions, cause much mischief. Those who make the judiciary and other administrative officials elective labor under such ideas.

LETTER XVII.

Local Officers. — Sheriffs' Clerks. — County, City, Town, and Village Officers. — Their Election. — Vacancies. — Political Year. — Removal. — Vacant Offices. — Metropolitan Police Law.

THE following article, akin of the seventh, seems to contradict, in some measure, what I have said before about the little care bestowed upon the organization of counties and towns by the constitution; but let us see.

ARTICLE X.

Local Officers.

"1. Sheriffs, clerks of counties, including the register and clerk of the city and county of New York, coroners and district attorneys, shall be chosen by the electors of the respective counties, once in every three years, and as often as vacancies shall happen. Sheriffs shall hold no other office, and be ineligible for the next three years after the termination of their offices. They may be required, by law, to renew their security, from time to time; and in default of giving such new security, their offices shall be deemed vacant But the county shall never be made responsible for the acts of the sheriff.

"The governor may remove any officer, in this section mentioned, within the term for which he shall have been elected; giving to such officer a copy of the charges against him, and an opportunity of being heard in his defence."

Here we make the acquaintance of a number of subaltern clerks or officials, originally to be appointed by the courts or boards to whom they belong, or by the respective executive and legislative bodies. The sheriff is the judicial county executive, and should be appointed like the county judiciary. You may compare with it the last sentence in art. II., sect. ii., clause 2, of the federal constitution. Something like that would also answer for a state constitution.

Who are at present the electors?—the citizens who are called so? Not exactly; for, according to the usual party management of elections, the party nominating committees or conventions, which present the candidates to the electors, are the real appointers of the functionaries, and the voting of the electors itself a mere matter of form or ratification. These committees, of course, have their own policies and interests. The more offices there are in the market, the more importance acquire these committees, and, of course, the more bargains will occur. This invariably must terminate in utter corruption. If we now throw out of the elections all clerical offices, as I have suggested repeatedly, a great source of public corruption will be dried up at once, the political machinery simplified, and the pernicious influence of parties checked. We can not be without parties, but should not purposely educate bad parties. This we do by the present elective system.

It seems to be against justice to exempt the counties from responsibily for the acts of their officials. Who else shall be responsible? The subalterns or clerks should be amenable or responsible to those who appoint them. The sheriff should be responsible to the county overseer and supervisors, who should appoint them. If those authorities should neglect their duty, then comes the turn of the governor to see that the laws are executed.

"2. All county officers, whose election or appointment is not provided for by this constitution, shall be elected by the electors of the respective counties, or appointed by the boards of supervisors, or other county authorities, as the legislature shall direct. All city, town, and village officers, whose election or appointment is not provided for by this constitution, shall be elected by the electors of such cities, towns, and villages, or of some division thereof, or appointed by such authorities thereof as the legislature shall designate for that purpose. All officers, whose election or appointment is not provided for by this constitution, and all officers whose offices may hereafter be created by law, shall be elected by the people, or appointed as the legislature may direct."

This seems to be a pretty exclusive proviso, but is vague withal. If the constitution contains the necessary provisoes for the organization and government of counties and towns (cities and villages), and gives them the appointment of the subaltern clerks, all will be clear, and such disputes as that about the right of the legislature to establish a new state police-district for four counties can not happen. The police business is and ever will be *local*, and, of course, belonging to towns. No state, no county, ever can be in need of a policeman or constable if there are towns organized (cities and villages). If a constitution ordains that the towns (cities, villages) shall elect and appoint their town officials, policemen included, it ordains implicitly that nobody else shall do it, neither the county nor state, or an arbitrary paper district of two, three, or four counties. If constitutions are not, by the competent courts, interpreted in this manner, they are positively not to be depended on.

The constitution ordains that there shall be a court of appeals. Well, if now a legislature, in favor of two or a dozen such courts, should create them, because the constitution did not expressly forbid the establishing of more than one, all would at once cry out that this was a wicked quibble—a false interpretation; still the metropolitan police law rests upon no better ground. It is a bold encroachment upon this proviso. Washington utters pithy words on such acts in his Farewell Address.

"3. When the duration of any office is not provided by this constitution, it may be declared by law, and if not so declared, such office shall be held during the pleasure of the authority making the appointment.

"4. The time of electing all officers named in this article shall be prescribed by law."

This is matter of course. A similar proviso like that in sect. iv. is contained in sect. xviii., art. VI.

"5. The legislature shall provide for filling vacancies in office, and in case of elective officers, no person appointed to fill a vacancy shall hold his office by virtue of such appointment longer than the commencement of the political year next succeeding the first annual election after the happening of the vacancy.

"6. The political year and legislative term shall begin on the first day of January, and the legislature shall assemble on the first Tuesday in January, unless a different day may be appointed by law.

"7. Provision shall be made by law for the removal for misconduct or malversation in office of all officers (except judicial) whose powers and duties are not local and legislative, and who shall be elected at general elections, and also for supplying vacancies created by such removals.

"8. The legislature may declare the cases in which any office shall be deemed vacant, where no provision is made for that purpose in this constitution."

All these provisoes do not deserve exactly a place in a constitution. It may suit a later legislature better to begin the political year a couple of weeks before the session, in order to get the message and reports complete in season.

All these details are objects of special legislation or routine.

The head of this article should have taught caution and discretion to the framers of the constitution and the originators of the metropolitan police law; and this case, in particular, should teach how much depends upon a well-informed and honest judiciary in a republic.

LETTER XVIII.

Militia. — Religious Denominations. — Higher Law. — Appointment of officers. — Major-Generals. — Commissary-General. — Commission.

THE god Mars rules not only in Europe supremely, but also in the state of New York.

ARTICLE XI.

Militia.

"1. The militia of this state shall at all times hereafter, be armed and disciplined, and in readiness for service; but all such inhabitants of this state, of any religious denomination whatever, as from scruples of conscience may be averse to bearing arms, shall be excused therefrom, upon such condition as may be prescribed by law."

Compare this article and its six clauses with the few simple lines in the federal constitution, concerning the army and navy and common defense of the United States, and you will judge for yourself that most of it does not belong to the constitution, but in a statute book or one of mere regulations. A simple constitutional proviso, that the militia of the state of New York shall be organized in conformity with the laws of Congress, would be sufficient for all practical purposes. Also the scruples mentioned here should never be made manifest in a constitution. It reflects upon sects and has a smack of higher law reveries and their approval, which is entirely wrong.

"2. Militia officers shall be chosen or appointed as follows: captains, subalterns, and non-commissioned officers shall be chosen by the written votes of members of their respective companies. Field officers of regiments and separate battalions, by the written votes of the commissioned officers of the respective regiments and separate battalions; brigadier-generals and brigadier-inspectors by the field officers of their respective brigades; major-generals, brigadier-generals, and commanding officers of regiments or separate battalions, shall appoint the staff officers to their respective divisions, brigades, regiments, or separate battalions."

From time to time different modes of appointment may be required. But — I ask — why not entrust the election of field officers to the common militiamen, if the same men, as citizen, may be intrusted with the election of county judges, supreme judges, members of court of appeals, comptrollers, engineers, governors, etc.? Is not a judge of the supreme court, as it is at present organized, a much more important and responsible officer, than a harmless, however martial, major of the militia?

"3. The governor shall nominate, and with the consent of the senate, appoint all major-generals, and the commissary-general. The adjutant-general and other chiefs of staff departments; and the aides-de-camp of the commander-in-chief shall be appointed by the governor, and their commissions shall expire with the time for which the governor shall have been elected. The commissary-general shall hold his office for two years. He shall give security for the faithfnl execution of the duties of his office, in such manner and amount as shall be prescribed by law.

This proviso is a very sensible one, because it gives to the governor the appointment of all major-generals, and the powerful commissary-general too. Would it not now be equally sensible, and indeed wise, to let him also appoint all real state officers, viz., those of the court of appeals, and supreme courts, provided the latter are needed? The citizen and militiamen are clubbing and become well acquainted with each other. They may therefore presumptively elect their drill-masters and commanders judiciously enough, and better at present than at the revolutionary war, when Washington complained that they did not always elect gentlemen. But if not trustworthy in this instance, why allow them to elect the highest state judges and other officials? Is there not a good deal of inconsistency and lack of principle in such legislation?

"4. The legislature shall, by law, direct the time and manner of electing militia officers, and of certifying their election to the governor."

Superfluous, because matter-of-course.

"5. The commissioned officers of the militia shall be commissioned by the governor; and no commissioned officer shall be removed from office, unless by the senate on the recommendation of the governor, stating the grounds on which such removal is recommended, or by the decision of a court-martial, pursuant to law. The present officers of the militia shall hold their commissions subject to removal as before provided."

A curious proviso, separating the appointing and removing power there where strict subordination is the first requisite to make the institution effective. Much more regard is paid to the militia than to the judiciary.

"6. In case the mode of election and appointment of militia officers hereby directed, shall not be found conducive to the improvement of the militia, the legislature may abolish the same and provide by law for their appointment and removal, if two thirds of the members present in each house shall concur therein."

This proves that the whole article is superfluous. But it is significant in regard to principles.

LETTER XIX.

Oaths. — Test. — Abuse of Oaths. — Literal Interpretation. — Scandal in Courts.

We come now to some formalities.

ARTICLE XII.

Oaths.

"Members of the legislature, and all officers, executive and judicial, except such inferior officers as may be by law exempted, shall, before they enter on the duties of their respective offices, take and subscribe the following oath or affirmation :—

"'I do solemnly swear (or affirm, as the case may be), that I will support the constitution of the United States, and the constitution of the state of New York, and that I will faithfully discharge the duties of according to the best of my ability.'

"And no other oath, declaration, or test, shall be required as a qualification for any office or public trust."

This is in conformity with the federal constitution, and very well that the state officials shall be bound to support this constitution; but I think the improvement elsewhere proposed upon the preamble of this constitution, will, notwithstanding, find favor with the people at large; because it places the intimate connection between the states created by the federal constitution in the true light. We all love our homes and their constitutional rights and order, but appreciate not less on this account our confederation and its priceless blessings. That improvement binds the whole state, and not some officials only. The last sentence is not so clear as that in the third section of the third article of the federal constitution. Before the word "test" should be found the word "religious." That "no religious test shall ever be required as a qualification to any office or public trust under the United States," in consequence of which all our state constitutions have abolished this test, should have had a radical reforming influence upon the peculiar custom of the English law, which requires a special oath in almost all transactions before the court. The plaintiff complains upon oath, the defendant answers upon oath, and denies, in most cases, upon no other ground than the hope that the plaintiff may not be able to prove the claim, thus committing perjury. We should have been induced by this precedent of the federal constitution to reform this universally-condemned and most immoral feature of the English law-code at once: not so Great Britain, where the religious test is still lawful. Let it be understood that transactions before a court are self-evident. A court sits to elicit the truth in a civil or criminal case, in the name of the state. Whatever the parties called in court affirm or deny, is affirmed or denied before the government represented by the court. The papers delivered by the parties, the records of the court, containing the substance of the transactions, are official public documents and property, and, in virtue of the state authority of the court, perfectly conclusive by themselves. The common custom of asking from a plaintiff an oath about his libel, and one from the defendant about his answer, etc., presupposes that the sitting of the court is not authoritative or official.

As matters are with us, a judge who sits without a religious test, has no right to inquire into the religious tenets of parties or witnesses. A man must be believed in court until the reverse of what he does or says is proved. Should he commit a falsehood, he acts as criminally as if he had acted upon oath; because, by doing so, he violates the truth, the authority of the court, and the state government, which is set up for the purpose of realizing truth and justice. A falsehood committed in court is a kind of treasonable act against the state.

There are more immoral or irrational features in the English jurisprudence, with which it is high time to dispense. One is the prevalent literal interpretation of the law, without a due regard to the rational interpretation, which alone deserves the name of interpretation. The word signifies nothing without regard to its spirit. Suppose the law should dispose that Congress shall meet at the capitol in Washington, on the first Monday of December, and it should happen that the capitol was destroyed by fire before this time, then, according to the literal interpretation in vogue, Congress could not meet at all, there being no capitol; but according to rational interpretation, the meeting of Congress would be considered as the principal object, the house or place of assemblage as secondary, and therefore no obstruction happen, provided a place of meeting was anywhere left for Congress. Another example, founded upon facts. The law ordains that the electors of the President shall meet on a certain day at the state capitals to cast their votes. The electors of the state of Wisconsin, as has been stated, were, in 1856, detained by a violent snow-storm, and did not reach their place of convention on that day; wherefore the vote of that state was considered lost, according to the literal interpretation, while, according to the rational understanding of the law, the casting of the vote, as the principal business, should have proceeded as soon as those electors could surmount the natural obstacles, which was alone necessary to prove or certify at the place of meeting, to make the casting of their votes one or two days after the snow-storm and appointed date perfectly legal; and thus the order and legality of the whole presidential vote would have been saved, while, by the literal interpretation, quite the reverse result might have taken place. Suppose the snow-storm should have visited Pennsylvania, then Mr. Fremont, with the help of a political snow-storm, would have carried the election. Such curiosities may be, and are in fact daily the result of literal interpretation, which, when applied to criminal law, is, in many instances, the shield of evident criminality and the prolific source of savage mobism, roguery, and corruption. This is repugnant to common sense and morality, too.

I mention further that trials of scandalous and obscene cases should not be public, to prevent the courts becoming the advertisers and publishers of scandalous, immoral reports, which, to circulate in book-form, is prohibited by special law. You will excuse these remarks here. but they spring up by the association of ideas. Laws should be strictly logical. common-sense, and moral. Sound public opinion, and absence of licentiousness in the press, will be the result. Thus a good state constitution may have a great influence upon the promotion of morals, and even good taste in general; more, perhaps, than science and art combined.

LETTER XX.

Amendments. — Miscellaneous. — Election Results in Regard to Migration. — Governor Hammond's Speech. — Bound and Free Labor. — Vox Populi — Franklin.

We have arrived at the end of the constitution.

ARTICLE XIII.

Amendments.

"1. Any amendment or amendments to this constitution may be proposed in the senate and assembly; and if the same shall be agreed to by a majority of the members elected to each of the two houses, such proposed amendment or amendments shall be entered on their journals with the yeas and nays taken thereon, and referred to the legislature to be chosen at the next general election of senators, and shall be published, for three months previous to the time of making such choice, and if in the legislature so next chosen, as aforesaid, such proposed amendment or amendments shall be agreed to by a majority of all the members elected to each house, then it shall be the duty of the legislature to submit such proposed amendment or amendments to the people, in such manner and at such time as the legislature shall prescribe; and if the people shall approve and ratify such amendment or amendments, by a majority of the electors qualified to vote for members of legislature, voting thereon, such amendment or amendments shall become part of the constitution."

A similar, but less verbose proviso occurs in the federal constitution.

"2. At the general election to be held in the year eighteen hundred and sixty-six, and in each twentieth year thereafter, and also at such time as the legislature may by law provide, the question, 'Shall there be a convention to revise the constitution and amend the same?' shall be decided by the electors qualified to vote for members of the legislature; and in case a majority of the electors so qualified, voting at such election, shall decide in favor of a convention for such purpose, the legislature at its next session, shall provide by law for the election of delegates to such convention."

A constitution which makes in such a sweeping manner the whole judiciary elective, will ruin the morals of a society in such a large state as New York, which is so much inflated by immigration, in a very short time. Hence the urgent necessity of amending it.

ARTICLE XIV.

Miscellaneous.

"1. The first election of senators and members of assembly, pursuant to the provisions of this constitution, shall be held on the Tuesday succeeding the first Monday of November, one thousand eight hundred and forty-seven.

"The senators and members of assembly who may be in office on the first day of January, one thousand eight hundred and forty-seven, shall hold their offices until and including the thirty-first day of December following and no longer.

"2. The first election of governor and lieutenant-governor under this constitution, shall be held on the Tuesday succeeding the first Monday of November, 1848; and the governor and lieutenant-governor in office when this constitution shall take effect, shall hold their respective offices until and including the 31st day of December of that year.

"3. The secretary of state, comptroller, treasurer, attorney-general, district attorneys, surveyor-general, canal commissioners, and inspectors of state prisons, in office when this constitution shall take effect, shall hold their respective offices until and including the 31st day of December, 1847, and no longer.

"4. The first election of judges and clerk of the court of appeals, justices, of the supreme court and county judges, shall take place at such time between the first Tuesday of April and the second Tuesday of June, 1847, as may be prescribed by law. The said courts shall respectively enter upon their duties, on the first Monday of July, next thereafter, but the term of office of said judges, clerk, and justices, as declared by this constitution, shall be deemed to commence on the first day of January, 1848.

"5. On the first Monday of July, 1847, jurisdiction of all suits and proceedings then pending in the present supreme court and court of chancery, and all suits and proceedings originally commenced and then pending in any court of common pleas (except in the city and county of New York), shall become vested in the supreme court hereby established. Proceedings pending in courts of common pleas and in suits originally commenced in justices' courts shall be transferred to the county courts provided for in this constitution, in such manner and form, and under such regulation as shall be provided by law. The courts of oyer and terminer hereby established, shall, in their respective counties, have jurisdiction, on and after the day last mentioned, of all indictments and proceedings then pending in the present courts of oyer and terminer; and also of all indictments and proceedings then pending in the present courts of general sessions of the peace, except in the city of New York, and except in cases of which the courts of sessions hereby established may lawfully take cognisance; and of such indictments and proceedings the courts of sessions hereby established, shall have jurisdiction on and after the day last mentioned.

"6. The chancellor and the present supreme court shall, respectively, have power to hear and determine any of such suits and proceedings ready on the first Monday of July, 1847, for hearing or decision, and shall, for their services therein, be entitled to their present rates of compensation until the first day of July, 1848, or until all such suits and proceedings shall be sooner heard and determined. Masters in chancery may continue to exercise the functions of their office in the court of chancery, so long as the chancellor shall continue to exercise the functions of his office under the provisions of this constitution.

"And the supreme court hereby established shall also have power to hear and determine such of said suits and proceedings as may be prescribed by law.

"7. In case any vacancy shall occur in the office of chancellor or justice of the present supreme court, previously to the first day of July, 1848, the governor may nominate, and by and with the advice and consent of the senate, appoint a proper person to fill such vacancy. Any judge of the court of appeals or justice of the supreme court, elected under this constitution, may receive and hold such appointment.

"8. The offices of chancellor, justice of the existing supreme court, circuit judge, vice-chancellor, assistant vice-chancellor, judge of the existing county courts of each county, supreme court commissioner, master in chancery, examiner in chancery, and surrogate (except as herein otherwise provided), are abolished from and after the first Monday of July, 1847.

"9. The chancellor, the justices of the present supreme court, and the circuit judges, are hereby declared to be severally eligible to any office at the first election under this constitution.

"10. Sheriffs, clerks of counties (including the register and clerk of the city and county of New York), justices of the peace and coroners, in office when this constitution shall take effect, shall hold their respective offices until the expiration of the term for which they were respectively elected.

"11. Judicial officers in office when this constitution shall take effect may continue to receive such fees and perquisites of office as are now authorized by law, until the first day of July, 1847, notwithstanding the provisions of the twentieth section of the sixteenth article of this constitution.

"12. All local courts established in any city or village, including the superior court, common pleas, sessions, and surrogate's courts of the city and county of New York, shall remain, until otherwise directed by the legislature with their present powers and jurisdiction; and the judges of such courts and any clerks thereof in office on the first day of January, 1847, shall continue in office until the expiration of their terms of office, or until the legislature shall otherwise direct.

"13. This constitution shall be in force from and including the first day of January, 1847, except as is herein otherwise provided."

Clause eight contains valuable reforms, but the judiciary of this state is still in need of more. It is desirable to avoid sweeping changes in our states, and I do not propose one. The adaptation of the districts to the business is an easy thing, and the most important part of the activity of our municipal legislatures. If we prune the towns and counties and plant out new ones at the right season, they will remain healthy and vigorous, and never rot, or become the seat of corruption. Am I then not right, when I say, that not exactly man, but the wrong, careless, political districting of our society is the cause of our troubles, and want of *public* virtue? The prevalent idea that a republic is a land where rogues have fair play, must be destroyed by a good administration of justice.

Some of my letters have been written, and also published, during the late presidential campaign. If those should too much savor of time, I wish you may bear in mind, that there will be more presidential elections, more changes of United States dynasties. With a few modifications, or modulations perhaps, the same issues will be again started in 1860. Parties are, by our exceedingly liberal federal constitution, narrowed down to a very few platform topics for the feuds about the offices or spoils. This force, however, is greater in proportion to the population of a state. This induces me to spend a few lines on the result of this election in the state of New York. I consider, on the whole, the national election excitements as wholesome social movements, because, by extending over an immense area, traversed by telegraphs and steam-engines, they promote, simultaneously, a most variegated general investigation of important principles, and, having more or less reference to the Union, quicken the instinct of patriotism, which so easily dies away in the common business routine of every day life. One of the foremost issues in the canvass of 1856, was the principle of free migration to new territories. With reference to the culture of land, there are two classes of migrators in the United States, one depending upon free, the other upon bound labor. They were represented by political parties. The first pretended that Congress possessed the right to forbid the bound-labor migration to new territories (free soil) ; the latter sided with the present practice of Congress, sanctioned by the Kansas and Nebraska act, mentioned by me before, namely, that Congress has no power to exclude this kind of migration, and that it lodged in the legislatures of the states in concern. This party has been, generally successful in the election of 1856, but not in the state of New York (although in New York city), and this appears as a curious freak of public opinion. It is, under the federal constitution, as we have seen, a matter of course, that the inhabitants of these territories have, *when they form a state*, the right to decide for themselves whether bound labor shall be tolerated therein or not. The result of this policy should now be, that there never will be formed again a state expressly sanctioning bound labor, where free labor is practicable. Free labor being the rule, all unsettled territories, and all slave states, are open to unlimited immigration from all states, and, according to the present practice, from all parts of the world, China included. On the side of free labor we have in the United States seventeen millions, in the Canadas four millions, in Europe about one hundred millions, and in Asia uncounted millions, furnishing immigrants, while on the side of bound labor we have but ten millions, all counted, or more properly, only six millions, after deducting four millions of bound laborors, who can not migrate on their own account, furnishing immigrants. Can there be a chance of a majority in a territory or a new state, fit for white labor, for the immigration from the six millions on the side of slave-labor, against the immigration from the uncounted millions on the side of free labor? I should think not, and so thought Governor Hammond in a late speech. But, as long as the Missouri compromise divided the Union in two parts, people on the southern or bound-labor side had a right to the formation of slave states south, and Congress was bound to support them, if this line drawn by an act of Congress had not been a mere abstraction. But, by the abolition of this line, the greatest liberty is given to migration.

Was it not now, I ask, after this digression, rather singular that the people in the state of New York, through which flows the great mundane stream of eastern migration on rivers and lakes, on state canals and railroads, voted at that time against free migration, which is so highly advantageous for those public and diverse private interests.

The *vox populi*, as Franklin says, never can be the *vox dei*, unless it comes from honest men. It is to be seen at the next national election what will be the pleasure of this vox populi in this leading state.

But, my dear children, I have done now with this great state and its constitution. May my unpretending remarks lead to further investigations and more thorough inquiries into the art of realizing justice, especially at the present time, when soon a popular vote will be cast on the organic law of this commonwealth.

LETTER XXI.

Prisons. — Penal Colonies on the Western Plains, in the Rocky Mountains. — Police. — Prison Associations. — Missionary Societies. — Bible.

THE best laws remain inert if not well executed. The moral tendency of the laws and the aim for which they are made, viz., the protection of life and property, require punishment and restraint of criminal unruly men. It is one of the uncomfortable qualities of republics, that they are rather favorable to the development and accumulation of mischief. Liberty, sweet liberty, will be abused by children and adults. The stream of migration does not alone fertilize our world-wide territory, no, it also deposites, especially in large places where people are fond of congregating, mischievous detritus. Macchiavelli thought of that, and gave his prince the advice to take good care of the amusement and industry of his subjects by shows, *circences*, exhibitions, popular festivals, following an old maxim of mothers who, when teased by mischievous children, try to divert their mind by play or pleasant occupation, well knowing that this is a better method of correcting mischievous habits, than scolding, whipping, or coercing. Mischievous adults should be disciplined in a similar manner.

Instead of confining them in *penitentiaries*, the special object of this letter, and forcing them with the whip to work for the advantage of speculators, and depriving them of the free exercise of their will, the great agent of self-improvement, we should rather try to occupy them on the common land out west with labor for their own exclusive benefit. Instead of forming factory-labor penal-colonies in Sing Sing and Auburn, we should establish agricultural and industrial penal colonies on our great western plains, on the grazing grounds of the buffaloes, in the Rocky mountains, on the Mexican frontiers, for the alarmingly-increasing great number of convicts. This local advantage renders the plan very practicable.

Statesmen or politicians who really wish to manage the state according to St. Paul's sound doctrine, that is, for the true benefit of the fallen man, should take warning from the rapid progress of kindred arts and sciences. The noble medico-surgical art, which aims at the delivery of man from physical sufferings, but half a century ago shed streams of blood to cure fevers, which are in most instances simple curative reactions of the system, now controlled by a few harmless medicaments or water, and crippled thousands by perilous operations, now obviated by simply assisting nature in restoring the injured limb. What immense change has also come over theology, the time-honored art of curing sin? Is there now a single common-sense man in Christendom who thinks or believes that religion without good works is of any use? where are the votaries of idolatry, self-castigation, witchcraft? I dare not describe the stupendous progress of the mechanical arts in all their branches. Where are the caravals, show-coaches, wooden telegraphs, blunderbusses, etc.? Shall then the most noble art of politics, which has to cure lawlessness, dishonesty, aud crime, remain with its penitentiary and workhouse castles, and other clumsy contrivances for ever behind time? It should be the greatest ambition of a free generous people to reform those antiquated things. Neither man, animal, nor plant will ever improve in prison confinement. Liberty is the basis and essence of the development of everything. If the good old book says: "let the captive free," it means, place him there where liberty does not tempt him to do wrong. Congress and states must, in this regard, act in harmony. Both are appointed for the realization of justice. They have nothing else to do.

The acquisition of immense tracts of wild land by Congress, on general grounds of doubtful policy, may become a source of infinite benefit for society, if made use of for penal colonies. Circumstances make the man; alter these and you will alter him, for the worse or better.

None of our constitutions are against the establishment of such settlements. If Congress has a right to bore for water in our western desert and introduce camels there, it can not object to the locating of colonies calculated to make use of that water and the ships of the desert. If the riding on camels shall not remain an amusing occupation of our lieutenants, we must plant our own thriving Arabs in the desert to profit by them.

Our state constitutions in particular are also not against this plan. If they allow to shut men up in castles, and force them to work there against their will and inclination, even interfering thus with the labor of honest business men outside, they can not forbid to place men under the canopy of heaven, on common land, in order to found by labor a new home and better life. There is obviously nothing unconstitutional in the plan.

The actual practice of the governors of New York state is in favor of penal colonies; for they begin to pardon criminals under the condition that they will quit the county or state, as the case may be. This seems to be an imitation of the English circumlocution practice in Australia, where convicts are set at liberty under the condition that they will quit her Majesty's dominions. Still, however this may be, it will terminate in something like a penal colony; for no state will permit such expelled criminals to take up their residence therein. The " Sydney Ducks," as these Australian legal exiles were called in California, were hung by the vigilance committees, after they had played for a while with the courts the game of hide-and-seek. Our politicians have no time to attend to such business as the realization of justice; their office affairs absorb it entirely. People therefore must turn their minds to this subject, if they wish to have their property and lives protected by a good administration of justice.

That part of the judiciary, which has to maintain order in large towns is better known now under the name of police, a force which in large cities is organized, uniformed, drilled, and paraded like standing-army soldiers. Its business is to find out offenders, arrest them, and deliver them to the courts for trial and punishment. Its operation is local, and therefore a part of the local jurisdiction of cities, towns, and villages. As it works at present, its reputation is at stake, unless a regular thinning off of the villains, especially in densely-built towns, shall soon be resorted to by transporting them; for the rogues and police, as matters now stand, play, indeed, a kind of hide-and-seek game, to the apparent satisfaction of all concerned, except the people, who have to pay the police bills. If the rogues are not out on their peculiar nightly business cruises, the police accommodate them also with lodging in the station-houses. The punishment amounts in the main to nothing but the providing of the villains in fine castles with better board and lodging than they enjoy when they are at liberty. When they leave those castles, the hide-and-seek game with the police is generally played over and over again, at the expense of the generous people, who, although grumbling, pay the enormous costs good-humoredly. These remarks apply to all large cities here and in Europe, London and Paris included. They are all wretchedly managed in this respect. We complain that this game is especially enjoyed by immigrants. Well, in the name of common sense, why not at once transport those amateur rogues and voyageur villains to regions where stern necessity will force them to become honest laborers? To give land to those villains whose greatest fault is that they have none and are not honest laborers, is most certainly sounder doctrine than to bestow it on schools or universities. The state institution has to coerce and tame villains, and not to teach good children and educate nice young men. By doing the first, it protects the lives and property of those good men who support the institution; by doing the latter, it unbecomingly tampers with private business. Are not those castles, then, mere monuments of unsound doctrine and political errors? Moreover there is a mass of forces already at work which may easily be turned to very good purposes in this direction.

I mention first the prison associations. It must be clear to them that as long as the usual state-prison system prevails their exertions will turn in an eternal circle. To free a man from prison upon the pledge of reform is very well; but the frequent relapse of the mischievous into their old sins proves that society gains nothing by it.

Another force to be made available here is the missionary societies. No convict likes his prison with all its appendages of chapels, schools, shower-baths, chains, whips, etc. And this is natural. Set him free in a distant settlement, under penalty of death upon leaving it voluntarily, and he will organize schools, build churches, appoint instructors himself, and like them in the bargain. A missionary will be his real comforter. Scoffers, who in their old homes would never listen to a sermon, opened with alacrity, in the California mining ranges, their saloons to the itinerant preachers.

The occasion is proper to speak further that the abolitionists are bound to second this plan. Their professed object is to deliver man from involuntary slavery or bondage. Now there are in our society no greater involuntary slaves than criminals shut up in state-prisons. It is true that our African bound laborer has a limited sphere of action; can not wander, can not use his full time and abilities as he pleases; still, he is reared in this condition; it is his habit, and habit, a kind of bondage, is second nature. He has no higher aspiration, and, as a general thing, is perfectly satisfied with his situation as the slave of labor, so that he even honestly and voluntarily returns to his master, if once decoyed away from him. He obviously is not in need of a liberator, and does not ask for one, and if he wishes to be free he can become so by his own exertion. But compare with him the slave of crime — the convict. He is brought up in liberty; perhaps the spoiled son of wealth, and, if the child of poverty and vice, has tasted the sweets of freedom, although perhaps consisting only in grog-shop revelry and gratuitous harangues of demagogues. What a hell must be for him a penitentiary, established by law by the same men with whom he used to associate on equal terms! With what infinite pleasure would such a man, if there is but a spark of humanity in his heart, bear all deprivations in the loneness of God's wild nature, if he only can thus escape from the drear cell-existence in a watch-surrounded state-prison! No man need be a slave of crime; but no man can help being more or less a slave of labor. The Bible teaches this.

All agree that our criminal-law system and its working is radically wrong. It is nowhere much better in view of the reform of the villains. But it must be admitted that colonizing has always produced the best results. Siberia becomes thus an inhabited and even civilized country. Criminals have made Australia inhabitable. How much of our far west has been cultivated by outcasts is difficult to prove, but easily imagined. Our great west is a fit home for used-up men to recruit morally and financially. The greatest and most efficient lever of our culture is honest labor. In dense society the chances of it for a criminal are but few; but in the mentioned regions, most abundant and brilliant. If this well-tried and very practical plan is carried out with circumspection and energy, the telegraphs and railroads which must soon span those regions will find much support by it.

This may suffice for my purpose.

LETTER XXII.

Large Cities. — Baltimore, Maryland. — Political History. — The People One Assembly. — First Constitution, 1650. — Extract. — Voting. — Slavery. — Abolition. — Divided Legislature. — Trouble. — Revolution. — Constitution of 1776. — Amended. — Judiciary Appointed. — Constitution of 1851. — Elective Judiciary. — Executive elected by Districts. — City and Country Jealousy. — Cities Republics of the Middle Age. — Feuds with the Country Nobility. — Free Cities of Germany. — Switzerland. — Large American Cities. — Their Separation from the Country. — More such Separations. — Apathy and Disgust with the City Affairs. — New Orleans. — Baltimore Vote on the Amending the Constitution. — Hanse Towns. — Crimes of English Law. — Macaulay. — Atlantic Telegraph States.

FROM a paternal desire to make my politico-constitutional explorations as complete and instructive as possible, I beg your attention a little longer for a few stray remarks on large cities. These are not only the hiding places of rogues, but also the centres of enterprise, arts, sciences, munificence, and, moreover, the germs of young states and empires.

Who would forget what Boston, with her Hancocks, has done for this great republic? Alas! for human inconsistency! The same city is now the nucleus of an implacable faction against this Union! Of New York, state and city, I have written enough. Turn now your eyes to Maryland, with Baltimore as a centre, even more overtowering the little Oyster-bay state than stately New York city the Empire state. It is in the same labor-pains as New York, in regard to the regeneration of its constitution, while I am writing. Its legislative history is interesting. In consequence of the very liberal charter to the "proprietor," the Marylanders were permitted to make their own laws, and. being all freemen of the same stamp, religion, competency, and aspirations, made every one of them an assemblyman. This is the only specimen of *popular sovereignty* which I have met with in history. But, as it was to be expected, this state, formed by sovereigns, caused nothing but trouble, lasted only a very short time. As early as 1639, a representative house of assembly was elected, and, in 1650, the first written constitution enacted, by which the legislature was divided between the people and the proprietors! The result of this double-headed organization was constant discord, until the Revolution made an end of it, and was followed by the constitution of 1776, which ordained in the main:—

That the legislature shall consist of a senate and house of delegates, under the name of General Assembly of Maryland, meeting annually, to be elected "by the qualified freemen." (That is all the suffrage law we find in this constitution.)

That a person of wisdom, experience, and virtue shall be chosen as governor, by the joint ballot of both houses, for three years.

That five of the most sensible, discreet, and experienced men shall be elected by the senators and delegates, to be the council to the governor, of whom the first shall be acting governor during vacancy.

That the governor, with the advice of the council, shall *appoint* the judiciary—as the chancellor, all judges and justices, attorney-general, officers in the regular land and sea service, officers of the militia, registers of land office, surveyors, and all other civil officers, (assessors, constables—police, overseers of the roads, sheriffs excepted,) and suspend, and remove any civil officer, who has not a commission, during good behavior.

There is no mention at all made of slavery, which proves that people wisely considered it not as a political thing, but as a mere matter of domestic life, which, without laborers, bond or free, can not exist.

This is a significant fact. It shows the Africans were in America as in Africa not slaves by law, but by usage. And I am satisfied that, in our days, very few of them care little about the laws and constitutions, being entirely satisfied with this usage or custom. This is wholesome second nature. Those bound laborers, hired out in cities, perhaps, excepted, none would leave their masters, if servitude could be abolished by the stroke of the pen, without the previous consent of both masters and slaves. Has the law more influence upon free labor?

This constitution has been often amended. In regard to the judiciary, the state was, in 1803, divided into six districts, for each of which were appointed a chief-judge and two associates, who composed the county-courts in each respective district. In 1805, a court of appeals was created, whose members were to be appointed by the governor and council. In 1810 it was enacted, that the rights of voting shall belong to every white (mark the word!) male citizen of above twenty-one years of age, having resided twelve months within the state and six months in the county. In 1837, the article of the constitution was abolished which prohibited the members of the general assembly to hold any office of profit, as also the council, and the senate were created advisers to the governor. At that time it was also ordained, that the relation between a master and slave shall not be abolished, except under certain forms and for compensation. This shows the effect of a *political* opposition to this domestic affair.

In 1851, the present constitution was established, and the principal difference from the prior one is, that it makes, in imitation of New York, the judiciary and principal administrative officers *elective*, and creates a kind of triangular state for the election of the governor, by providing that it shall be divided into three districts, from one of which he is to be elected every four years. This is a peculiar feature, not occurring in any one of the several states of the Union, to my knowledge.

This proviso, by obviously instituting a clannish executive, more for a part than the whole state, must have been suggested by the old antagonism or jealousy hovering between country and city,*

* Traces of this jealousy appear on the surface of the New York harbor quarantine difficulty, the remote cause of which, however, is the misplacement of the whole business. This is neither a county, city, or state, but a national or congressional business. Taking first our own ships, those, from the time of their clearance until they are discharged again, sail under congressional papers, authority, and protection. When they arrive at quaran-

which, in the middle age, was the cause of that brilliant galaxy of spirited, enterprising, intellectual city republics, the remnants of whom are the present free cities of Germany. Switzerland is indebted to them for its independence. They lived in endless feuds with the country nobility and their retainers. They became, when victorious, proud and oppressive, and, especially in Italy, the theatres of internal commotions, and then an easy prey of mighty princes and their intrigues. This is natural. The democratic form of government can not alter human nature. Business interests will separate the cities still from the country, and produce mischievous antagonism, which, in the length, can not be overcome but by a divorce. Manhattan Island, with over 600,000 inhabitants, mostly city people, is overripe for a state, requiring a careful, very active political management. Philadelphia, covering an area of 129½ square miles, with a circumference of 74½ miles, and more than 400,000 inhabitants is for all practical purposes also a state. Brooklyn, with Long Island, is ripe for state organization. Baltimore, and other great marts must follow in the same wake. And, discerning statesmen will admit the necessity of dissections of this kind for the counties east of the Mohawk river, Western Virginia with Wheeling, Southern Ohio with Cincinnati, etc. I can not forego here the remark that time and mutual advantage required similar divorces between Holland and Belgium, Greece and Turkey, and they can not be, in the length, avoided in the Danubian provinces, Austria, Russia, England, France, and other overgrown states. The monarchs will oppose it, still justice and civilization require such dividing to reform the corruption inseparable from over-large centralized governments. It is a law of nature, and not a mere axiom, that only small states preserve their manners well. Our practical federal constitution has wisely foreseen those changes. It remains, then, only for the practical people, and their statesmen, to come at the right time to an understanding about that which is "overgrown,"

tine, they alter not their character, especially not when the quarantine should be established by state or city laws and officials. It is mere circumlocution to allow state quarantine in *ocean* harbors, of which alone I speak. In regard to foreign vessels, those know nothing at all about ocean state laws and government. Congress can enforce by soldiers and vessels of war quarantine laws, but not the state or a city, because both have no such forces.

and act accordingly. A certain symptom of this political disease, "overgrown," is the *apathy* of the better class of the inhabitants of overgrown cities in regard to their administration, and the spasmodic efforts to shake off the incubus under which they suffer. They are disgusted with their unwieldly administration, and their tampering with it by the legislatures, composed of men who do not appreciate their state-like city interests, or, if they do, consider and treat them as fat party spoils. The question is, then, how can this apathy and disgust be cured?

If the legislatures can not help that, and do not understand the importance of the local municipal interests of such large places, how will their citizens alter that? Simply by a timely divorce, just as grown-up children separate from the paternal stock and try their hand in self-management. A town which has absorbed a county and acquired the corpulence of a state, ought to be organized as a state. Nothing short of that will cure that incubus-like apathy and disgust of the citizens. The best and wisest of the parents lose their hold on out-grown children. And such a separation will at once shiver that pestilential intrigue to atoms, which in the far-off capitals nestles and manages those large cities to the disgust of their inhabitants. They never will get rid of it otherwise. This also will restore the authority of the judiciary in such places. You may then understand the vote of the citizens in Baltimore in May, 1858, FOR the amending of the constitution of 1851, with an elective judiciary, and that of the country people AGAINST it.

You may think that a dividing of those large cities into separate municipalities, or independent business districts, would better answer for a local reform than a state organization. It would, no doubt, improve their administration, provided the legislatures alter entirely their policy of intermeddling, which virtually would amount to a divorce. Still, that a political party should do this I have great doubts. I cheerfully admit that all legislatures are not incompetent, all cities are not treated like New York or Baltimore, still every one of them (even in puritan New England), containing upward of forty thousand inhabitants, is suffering from public corruption, debts, high taxes, etc., as I mentioned before.

It should then be obvious to every person, that in the right proportion of population, state (county, town), size and business is the arcanum of *good* government, especially in republics. Being common law with us that the people, and not Congress, make states, it is a plain duty of the people to make them and their subdivisions adequate to this proportion. Our present states, in regard to size, are either the product of mere accident, that is, of charters given by far-off monarchs who did not know the country, or of congressional arrangements for momentary territorial purposes. Of course, Nebraska, Kansas, and California, as large as continental Europe without Russia, are not destined to be but three states for all time to come! Let us then adjust our political districts right for the business in order to have this well done. A good system in business is the first thing needful, then comes the appointing of the right kind of business-men and their control. Those never work well without the first. Whoever has been once in the office of one of our city mayors, that of New York especially, and noticed with what mere clerical trash of every-day routine business, belonging to regular courts and clerks, they are burdened, will easily understand why they have no time for a careful surveillance over all branches of the city administration, and the respective clerks and subalterns. The usual system is English—circumlocution. There, the lord-mayor must positively tie the sacred knot, do the business of a justice of the peace or police court. Our own old articles of confederation were strictly English, that is, circumlocution. A little attention to the present state of the public affairs in England, and the parliamentary proceedings, blue books, reform propositions, debates, and special committee reports on military and civil service, will convince that a great change is going on there.

It is habit, wholesome second nature, which helps the English subject to bear the "crimes of English law," as Lord Macaulay has it. But the citizens of the United States have done with that.

By-the-by, I never heard of vigilance committees and election riots, *a la* Baltimore, Washington, New Orleans, etc., in the little German Hanse republics. They behave well, and are doing well at home and abroad. Even when Europe is in a blaze, kindled in France or elsewhere, they are quiet. They have, as you know, the largest merchant fleet in Europe after the English, but, keeping no navy, they can not afford to luxuriate in opium, calico, civilization wars, negro blockades, and visiting of other peoples' ships in the Gulf of Mexico or elsewhere. Their seamen protect themselves by good habits, and are, therefore, not unlike ladies, everywhere respected. Their history is, indeed, a beautiful little chapter in the book of civil liberty. But this picture would fade like flowers when touched by winter frost, if they should lose their sweet liberty by annexation or subjection. Their blessed neutrality induces to the hope, that the towns where the Atlantic telegraph taps the land, may be, in the course of time, declared neutral, and become something like Hanse towns.

It is good that there are some republics left in Europe, to serve as precedents.

LETTER XXIII.

Morals. — Virtues and Vices. — Material of History, Arts, Novels, Dramas, Tragedies. — Washington. — Citizen Government. — Military Government. — Priest Government. — Mexico. — The Canadas. — British Northwest Territory. — The Lord's Prayer. — Conclusion.

I AM afraid I have often dwelled too long in the preceding letters upon the social moral influence of state institutions, and, indeed, all my aim has been to induce people and their public men to realize by them exclusively, justice, the first of all virtues; but left it to you and my readers to find out exactly what it is. Every unselfish, sensible man may learn this first by his own experience, reason, and conscience; and secondly, from the precepts of religion, the narratives of history, and the example and history of good and bad men. What is right the law tells. Being but men, and not angels, we are not destined to absolute moral perception; and to this state it must be attributed that in conformity with a dualism pervading the whole known creation, two kinds of forces are eternally at work in our life, which influence our actions and mould our destiny. To facilitate the memory of them I have put them down in parallel. Those of a more plastic nature have been beautifully personified by the ancients. It is perhaps superfluous to add that the virtues are promotive of content and happiness, and the vices, of disappointment and misery in individuals and states. This is our inexorable fate. Good and bad deeds are recorded in the book of time with indelible ink. From the judgment of conscience there is no appeal, no pardon. The remorse of a bad deed remains for ever. Read then :—

MORAL FORCES.

VIRTUES.	VICES.
Justice,	Injustice.
Self-control, Attention.	Carelessness, Recklessness.
Honesty.	Faithlessness, Dishonesty.
Veracity, Truth.	Falsehood, Calumny, Intrigue, Slander, Hypocrisy.
Prudence, Politeness.	Imprudence, Inurbanity.
Piety, Charity.	Profanity, Inhumanity, Avarice.
Modesty, Simplicity.	Impudence, Extravagance.
Economy.	Prodigality.
Patience.	Passion.
Sobriety.	Intemperance.
Pudicity.	Lewdness, Free Love.
Industry.	Laziness, Loaferism.
Conscientiousness.	Treachery, Perfidy.
Fortitude, Glory, Patriotism.	Cowardice, Bombast, Treason.
Righteousness.	Villany, Corruption.
Love.	Hatred, Vengeance.
Humanity.	Cruelty, Barbarism.
EFFECT.	
Order, Peace, Happiness.	*Anarchy, War, Misery.*

This is life's material. Justice crowns the column of virtues. The just man combines within himself all virtues. He, according to St. Paul,* needs no law, no state. Such a man was George Washington. He was just to mankind and to himself. He thought that in our age society may derive from the citizen government what neither military nor priest government have brought, viz., justice. He had a firm faith in his cause and a just God.

Let me now conclude these letters. If they should only convince those who take a sincere interest in our public affairs, that in our time the good management of the municipal affairs is infinitely more important for the true welfare of society than diplomacy, with her eternal wily intrigues for power and conquest, I should feel satisfied.

* The passage in question reads thus : "But we know that the law [state] is good, if a man use it lawfully; knowing this that the law [state] is not made for a righteous man, but for the lawless and disobedient, for the ungodly and for the sinners, for unholy and profane, for murderers of fathers and murderers of mothers, for manslayers, for whoremongers, for those that defile themselves with mankind, for menstealers, for liars, for perjured persons, and if there be any other thing that is contrary to sound doctrine."

Reform of public corruption must begin near home. Great events are ripening before our doors. Mexico is fast collapsing. The Canadas and British Northwest provinces are daily gaining in importance. They will form free states, either separate or united with us. But will they desire a union under present aspects? Time will answer this question, not I.

"It is righteousness which exalteth a nation." We are free to choose the roads to order, peace, and happiness, or to anarchy, war, and misery.

Before you lay the book aside, please peruse once more its preface. I there maintain that a state institution is either the most powerful agent to promote the sense of honesty and justice, the mother of public virtue, or the most effective machinery to sow the seeds of vice, from which public corruption springs up, broadcast over the land. I have tried in this book to show how the latter may be prevented, that this institution may not be furthermore abused anywhere for fraud, peculation, and corrupting contrivances of all kinds, counteracting and neutralizing the influence of the church, school, and home education.

I must confess that one of my leading ideas was derived from a petition in the Lord's prayer, "Lead us not into temptation," applied to statesmen, politicians, and their parties generally. People nowhere should tempt them with other business than the realization of justice; because this, and nothing else, will prevent public corruption, as much as it can be done. *Sapienti sat.*

Contribute, then, your mite to the honor of our great and beautiful country. ADIEU.

www.ingramcontent.com/pod-product-compliance
Lightning Source LLC
LaVergne TN
LVHW020238110826
845151LV00003B/960